A Song for Bohemia

ANNE MARIE
KENNY

A
Song
for
Bohemia

FOREWORD BY MARTIN PALOUŠ

*Dedicated to the life and legacy of Václav Havel
and the people of my ancestral homeland.*

CONTENTS

AUTHOR'S NOTE

M*y mother's grandparents immigrated* in the late nineteenth century
to the United States from Moravia, which at that time was part of the
Austro-Hungarian Empire. Yet my mother always told her children that
we were Bohemian, with never a mention of Moravia. That may be because,
during historic time periods, geographic regions often changed names.
Case in point: during my ten years living in Prague, the country that was
Czechoslovakia changed names at least three times. Therefore, with poetic
license, I may use the word "Czech" to refer to the place, people, and language of the Bohemian lands, which today is called the Czech Republic or
Czechia, comprising the regions of Bohemia, Moravia, and part of Silesia.

The names of people in this book are real. In a few instances, only
their first names appear to protect their privacy. I reconstructed dialogue,
not word-for-word, but in the truest possible meaning and intent. Yet,
some poignant conversations flowed easily, as their precise utterance,
look, and emotion have remained ever-present in my mind.

This is memoir, the perspective of one. I was fortunate to have kept
my personal calendars and diaries, and to have had long interviews with
many people featured in this book. They unreservedly—some for the first
time—shared their experiences and confirmed or corrected mine. Even
so, there will be unintentional mistakes, for which I am solely responsible.

FOREWORD

by Martin Palouš

A *Song for Bohemia* is not only a unique personal reflection on the American experience of the Czech transition to democracy and the profound transformation of the Czech economy that started after the Velvet Revolution—but also a fascinating piece of literature. One can hear the tunes, the rhythms, and the melodies in Anne Marie Kenny's lyrical style, not only when she speaks about her career as a singer in France, but behind all the deeper messages as she winds her way to becoming a businessperson in Prague.

For me, her story is a great demonstration of what human memory is and does. Or at least what it can be, if used wisely, creatively, and with imagination. In my view, the principle message of *A Song for Bohemia* is freedom—whether political or internal—and it comes from reconciling with what it means to be human in an imperfect world.

The virtue of being human is to know we are never perfect. That there is virtue in humility, moderation, and awareness of our own fragility and limitations. At the same time, by possessing the power to forgive and to change our hearts, we thus open new opportunities for ourselves and others.

Anne Marie's story, and that of the Czech lands, are narratives worth remembering because they give us a glimpse of the triumph of humanity. In the words of Václav Havel: "The salvation of this human world lies nowhere else than in the human heart, in the human power to reflect, in human modesty, and in human responsibility."

I believe that this historical memoir beautifully describes the heartfelt journey to freedom. Let us read it attentively, with an open mind, and accept Anne Marie's invitation to accompany her in her recollections of a most incredible celebration of freedom regained miraculously after a long period of oppression. May it open new opportunities and inspiration in partnership with our fellow humans, for each of us, and for the world we all call home.

~ Martin Palouš

PROLOGUE

R*iding on the wings of a song*, I landed in an extraordinary place and time—Prague in the nineties. I was a woman from the American heartland in my late thirties, a professional singer living in France with a gallant older husband, when a sweep of world events gathered me into its fold.

It began in November 1989, when demonstrations erupted in Eastern Europe and the rest of the world witnessed history-in-the-making from their television sets. More than a thousand kilometers from Prague in my apartment in Nice, I found myself rising to the occasion as the groundswell of liberation surged on Wenceslas Square. My Bohemian roots pulled me into this collective momentum and toward a personal hour of reckoning.

I had to respond, and what I did changed my life.

My husband John and I cheered and downed champagne when the East German dissidents tore down the Berlin Wall. Then came the wild cascade of uprisings across the region. Totalitarian governments in one country after the other succumbed to the cries of freedom from people protesting and partying in streets and town squares. I waited in anticipation for the land of my mother's forebears to take its turn. Indeed, Czechoslovakia stood out with distinction. It was the darling in the eyes of the world because of its charismatic leader and graceful manner in conducting an overthrow. Its new president, Václav Havel, was already esteemed internationally for his plays, essays, dissident activities, and imprisonments. The country's nonviolent uprising was dubbed the Velvet Revolution, a metaphor I never equated with softness or cowardice. Their radical revolution had been long in the dreaming, clever in the making, and mightily hard-won. Furthermore, we understood that some credit had to be given to the communist authorities for their renunciation of force, or else the velvet fabric of Czechoslovakia's garment could have been seriously ruffled and torn.

To our horror, barbarism in Romania played out, with the show trial and execution by firing squad of president Nicolae Ceauşescu and his wife Elena. No doubt some Czechs were also tempted to exact revenge on their Soviet oppressors. But Havel quelled his compatriots' anger with noble persuasion: "Those who have for many years engaged in a violent and bloody vengefulness against their opponents are now afraid of us. They should rest easy. We are not like them."

The performing artist in me was dazzled by the dramatic staging of Czechoslovakia's mutinous gatherings, like a theatrical production with sound and light, rock bands, opera singers, and the voice of Marta Kubišová singing her prayer for the country. Speeches were delivered by the greatest symbols of hope—famous literary orators, dissident heroes, and even a banned Catholic priest. It was orchestrated from a third-story balcony in the middle of Wenceslas Square with top-quality technical equipment brought in from local theaters and broadcast to the world. The ecstatic crowds rattled their keys held high as an emblem of solidarity. Something about the joy on their faces and ringing sound of liberty struck a chord in me. Unconsciously, their unbridled humanity gave me hope. Could their emancipation be mine? Could it release my inner turmoil?

I internalized their mix of elation and caution at the chance for self-rule after decades of authoritarian control. Questions of identity and future place in history must have been on their minds as they stepped into the euphoric air and onto a platform of freedom.

It was at this point in the country's narrative that I met the Czech people on their turf. Prior to then, John and I had traveled around Western Europe from our home base in France, yet we hadn't ventured behind the Iron Curtain. In spite of the fact that in the late-nineteenth century my mother's family, the Jandas and Tomans, emigrated from Moravia, the cumbersome bureaucracy for obtaining tourist visas had detracted us from visiting. Moreover, the thought of being a capitalist vacationer among people living under an oppressive regime didn't sit right with me. Little did I know that a few months after watching that allegorical curtain lift, I would be in Prague, at first to give a concert, and shortly after, to make it my home.

It's been thirty years since I was thrust into this scene, or more precisely, onto the stage of Prague's legendary Reduta Theatre at the invitation of the country's newly elected president. With each passing year, the longing to describe this unimaginable experience has quietly welled within me to the point of overflow. I faced a choice, to shut off the tap or let each droplet flow word by word. The moment I chose the latter, and made room for reflection, memories sailed in on currents, some loving souvenirs like the trickling of soft streams, others lamentable escapades battered by stormy seas. And although the raw reality of those heady and bold times grabs me as viscerally today as it did then, I have a loftier motive for sharing what happened.

I'm afraid that people are forgetting, or maybe never knew, that the 1989 revolutions in Europe drastically reshaped the world, freed the lives of millions, offered luminous examples of the role art can play in political change, and demonstrated the importance of the individual in history. One example was Václav Havel, a literary artist and reluctant politician. He espoused personal accountability and responsibility in civil society. He believed that the qualities of love, compassion, humility, and forgiveness are necessary parts of our moral and spiritual potential in becoming a humane world. He warned that "the enforced mask of apathy" and the cynicism that was the norm during the communist regime must never become the norm again.

Havel's timeless vision is all the more relevant today as totalitarian regimes, autocratic leadership, and audacious invasions threaten democracy and human rights. We who heard his message are a living repository of the spirit of the times, and have a duty to share our perspectives of the past and lessons learned.

My life during this astounding era was woven in the rich history of my Czechoslovak roots and threaded by the resilient and gracious people whom I came to deeply admire. I lived and worked alongside them and witnessed their struggles and joys during the transition from communism to democracy, from a centralized economy to a free-market system. The experience changed me, but not without personal anguish and loss.

Anchored deep in my adopted country, those post-revolutionary years resounded much like Leoš Janáček's *Sinfonietta* in which he used brass, kettle drums, and cymbals to celebrate his newly liberated Czechoslovakia from the shadowed suppression of the Austro-Hungarian Empire that dissolved in 1918. The composer Janáček, a native of Moravia, dedicated his work "to honor contemporary free man, his spiritual beauty and joy, his strength, courage, and determination to fight for victory." Now, seventy-one years later, another fight for victory had been won. The triumphant cymbals of freedom struck once again, and I, too, fell into the step of its robust march.

Propelled by hopeful jubilation and unending possibilities, I joined the post-communist boom that shaped the country's future. My company helped tens of thousands of people enter the international marketplace. And though I never in my life worked so hard as during my years in Prague, I owe my business success to the Czech people.

As I sit in my cushioned writing chair, my coveted literary perch near a large window with wooden crisscrossed panes, I look out onto a soothing Nebraska landscape. Outside this old brick house is a vast urban green space surrounded by deep rows of evergreen trees. The thicket of woods and native organic pasture remind me of the Bohemian forests and how much the Czechs love the natural world, their country cottages, mushroom hunting, and gardening. My here and now is saturated with warm kinship connections to my past life in the heart of Europe, and I am devoted to writing about it.

My story needs no embellishment, as a singer is wont to decorate baroque arias with riffs and runs. I hope that the plain telling of my journey—a girl raised by a Czech-American widow in a small U.S. city, who sang in the streets of Paris and later at the Ritz, and became part of the Czech transition to democracy—will proffer its own enlightenment and enjoyment.

What led me to Prague, the invitation itself, was most remarkable. It had nothing to do with my heritage or the company I later founded. It was all on account of a song.

1

THE REDUTA

O*pening night. The house was full.* I peeked through the curtain from backstage. Wafts of cigarette smoke swirled amid stage lights, clouding my search for the only faces in the audience I might recognize: the director of Pragokoncert, my cousin Peggy who lived in Frankfurt, and my husband John. All other audience members were strangers. Familiar strangers, like well-wishing relatives. In the few days I'd been in the country, the people I encountered had features akin to my cousins, aunts, uncles, and grandparents on my mother's side. It was clear that we came from the same hearty stock.

I barely squeezed through the crowd to make my entrance, but I was determined to follow the direction of dancer-choreographer Andy de Groat. Months before, when my song list had been decided, I took the train from Nice to Paris to work with Andy. He staged every number, loosely for some, tightly for others—when to stand, where to sit, how to move, ways to dance, step, and turn so effortlessly that no one would know it was rehearsed. He taught me how to slither up the grand piano, recline comfortably on the contoured lid while I sang my heart out, then slide off and land without a thud.

As a girl who had always been self-conscious of her body—who regretted never having dance lessons, who carried extra weight in adolescence, who crash-dieted to be a certain size—I had overcome the worst of these tendencies, but vestiges of self-doubt about my appearance and my ability to move gracefully remained. Andy set me free. Without words, he dispelled the notion of shame, which I came to realize was anathema to truth and freedom.

When I heard that the surrealist French poet Louis Aragon had reviewed one of Andy's theater pieces, I was in awe. Aragon wrote, "If ever the world changes and men become like the dancer I spoke of, free, free, free . . . it's through freedom man will have changed." The dancer he referred to was Andy de Groat.

Andy would say, "Anne Marie, you're a natural and instinctual mover. Keep that. Trust it." He spoke of "the motion experience" and asked me to "hear with my entire body, allow the sound vibrations to aid in the minutest articulation of movement." Or, simply stand still and let the lyric deliver itself.

Vitally important to any performance, Andy insisted, is the entrance. He assumed (correctly) that the Reduta stage had side wings where the artists entered. When we were announced, Andy wanted only my pianist, Bob McCoy, to make a traditional appearance from the wings to the grand piano and begin his prolonged introduction to our first number, "Sophisticated Lady." His notes were my cue to make an unexpected entrance from the back of the room and walk slowly to the stage.

During our practice run in Paris, Andy and I hadn't predicted the reality I encountered at the Reduta—an overly crowded club with an irregular seating arrangement. There were no rows and aisles, only clusters of rounded velvet banquettes and loose chairs dispersed here and there. As more and more people flowed in, the staff added chairs, filling any empty areas.

Showtime. We were announced. Bob walked on stage and started his formidable intro. I was in place, standing an inch from the back wall, every pore of my being pulsating. It wasn't nervousness; it was feeling fully alive. My sixteen memorized songs and lines of patter were not swirling frantically in my head. Not at all. They held still in my heart, waiting for their moment to pour themselves out, sequentially, passionately.

When audience suspense stirred, I began my approach through the tight space. To my relief and elation, the crowd parted in utter silence (other than soft *oohs* and *aahs*) as I curved through the room toward the stage.

My floor-length emerald-green taffeta gown billowed at the sleeves, cinched my waist, hugged my hips and thighs, and flounced from my knees to the floor, making its own fluid statement. My rounded figure filled it to capacity, much like the room bursting at its seams. I followed Andy's theatrical design exactly as we'd practiced. Leading with my right arm extended toward the path I charted, my body gently angled with the left arm lithely stretched behind. Secured between the index and middle fingers of my left hand was a long amber cigarette holder clutching a lighted Petra that drifted smoke in my trail.

Our opener was intended to mix melodrama with levity, and we pulled it off. My stepping onto the platform cued Bob to vamp the final bars of the intro as I glided to center stage, faced the audience, took a drag from the cigarette, and slowly blew smoke rings in an upward stream.

"They say, into your early life romance came . . ." my voice crooned without a quiver, "and in this heart of yours burned a flame . . ." I continued fully aware that I was in Prague presenting my greatest gift, and in this particular song, telling partial truths about my own life. At the end of, "a flame that flickered one day, and died away . . ." I snuffed the cigarette into an ashtray while proceeding to the next lyrical line. Had a pin dropped, it would have thundered. My voice was at its optimum. The sound system was pure. Bob played exquisitely. I was in my element.

The cigarette gimmick notwithstanding, I felt obliged to have the manager make an announcement before the next night's show asking the audience to refrain from smoking during my sets. The air was so thick on Friday, I thought I might choke during a deep breath.

Singers are advised against starting a program with a slow ballad, but it worked. The famous Duke Ellington song, florid with chromatic slides and unusual intervals, was attention-getting and short. Before the audience knew it was over, we segued seamlessly to Cy Coleman's rhythmically fetching "Witchcraft," after which the audience had their first chance to react. The synergy between performers and audience was codified by a resounding roar of applause.

It was my first chance to speak to the audience. I can still say my opening lines by heart:

Dobrý večer. Jsem ráda, že jsem tady v Praze poprvé. Rodina mojí maminky přijela do Ameriky z Čech a Moravy před několika generacemi. Blahopřeji Vám, československým lidem, k sametové revoluci. My, vaši zahraniční příbuzní, jsme hrdi.

"Good evening. I'm delighted to be here in Prague for the first time. My mother's family came to America from Bohemia and Moravia several generations ago. Congratulations, people of Czechoslovakia, for your Velvet Revolution. We, your kinfolk abroad, are proud."

The mood was palpably happy. From that moment to the final bow, we fell into a surreal flow. Sometimes performing can be deliciously interesting work, but still and all, work. Other times, the performance transcends into a creative process no longer in the artist's conscious control. Together, Bob and I reveled in the latter phenomenon.

Between each song, over-practiced Czech patter rolled off my tongue. We crowned the program with the song I wrote for the country's president and its people, "When We Only Have Love" ("Jen láska stačí nám"). Mr. Havel did not hear it that night. It made no difference. He had read it, and opened his country to me. I was concerned that the lyrics to this song would label me as an idealist, a spoiled American with empty superlatives and pithy clichés. Then I asked myself, when John Lennon wrote "Imagine," was he concerned whether his ode to humanism and peace resonated with the cynics? If the audience rejected my song, they could take it up with their president.

My concerns were unfounded. The warm response from the Reduta crowd mirrored the gracious hospitality I'd encountered during my entire maiden voyage to the City of a Hundred Spires. It was hard to believe that exactly one year before, October 1989, the Czechoslovak people existed inside a restrictive environment, forbidden to enjoy Western art, music, literature. Since then, society and the arts had begun to open up, yet cultural events from abroad were still rare. And here I was performing in this ancient cultural city to a packed house.

After the first show on Friday, I made new friends when local musicians, theater people, and journalists came backstage to thank Bob and me. Some returned for the second night and brought others. Word was out. Reviews were in. A newspaper article said my appearance provided a triple allure—American singer, resident of France, and most endearing, my Czech heritage and willingness to communicate in their language.

The spirit of the Czechs I met through my concerts and post-show parties exuded excitement, bouyancy, and great expectation for the future. I was beguiled by their cultured and polite manner. Mixed with their formal quality was a sweet sort of self-effacement. Their kindness was clearly genuine. Even so, during conversations, I whiffed a distant air of *je ne sais quoi* emanating from my interlocutors, like a quelled shiver or a dissonant arpeggio. I silently strove to tap into their frame of mind. Perhaps it was mistrust of foreigners . . . embarrassment of their past . . . resentment for people who grew up in freedom . . . fear the revolution would only be temporary. I could only guess.

My incomprehension of life behind the Iron Curtain caused me to tiptoe around the subject. Besides, people were looking ahead, not behind. The Czechs I conversed with skipped over any mention of the past, and I lacked the knowledge and diplomacy to pose sensitive questions. So I observed. I saw a people who had lost forty years—fifty plus, if the count begins with the Nazi occupation. The general fashion on the street, in streetcars and shops, did not escape my notice: outmoded clothes, patched winter coats, resoled cracked-leather shoes. The way ordinary people behaved in public was decidedly inconspicuous, with downward-cast eyes that sometimes glanced furtively left or right. People seemed . . . not unfriendly . . . but apprehensive, cautious, suspicious.

I mingled with people who had spent their lives, except for the last eleven months, inside a totalitarian state. The trauma was deep and unspoken. When tongues were loosed after downing shots of Becherovka, their formal reserve became silly, flirtatious, and funny. My newfound friends talked about a hopeful future, but stayed tight-lipped about the past.

I, too, held secret the intimate details of my life and didn't divulge my fear about my husband's infirmity, my binge drinking, or that John and I needed to make a new start for financial reasons. In Czechoslovakia, every single person was making a new start—into a democratic society, a free market economy, a world of fresh opportunities, and a new society motivated by Havel's revolutionary slogan, "Truth and love must prevail over lies and hatred."

When I offered my ballad of love and hope to the people who inspired me to write it, they responded with open arms. Their embrace, magnified by the beauty of the city, the spirit of awakening, and the moral leadership of a poetic president, exhilarated me. I wanted to stay, remain wrapped in the energy, and be part of the great change. I knew that the enormity of work that lay ahead for the Czechoslovaks was far from idyllic. The road to democracy would be a long haul. And though I felt that by answering Havel's invitation, I had made a small contribution, I wanted to do more. To belong. Maybe if I softened as they strengthened, we could walk together the road of new beginnings.

As my Prague debut ended, I thought back on the things that drew me to the Old World in the first place—my love for foreign languages, culture, and music. I thought about that young woman making her way in the world. So much had changed in twenty years. So much was changing now.

2

PASSAGES

I *was eighteen when my mother sent me* to Germany to visit my sister
for the holidays. It was 1970. I had graduated from high school the previous year and was working as a receptionist at an employment agency.
Funnily enough, that one-year experience running the front desk of a
small family-owned staffing firm in Omaha was the precursor, and only
tutorial, to starting my own staffing company years later in Prague. The
owners wouldn't give me two weeks off for the trip abroad, so I quit.
Mother mustered up the plane fare, and I pitched in some of my modest
savings. My sister Mary Lou was living with her husband, George, in
Berstadt, a village forty minutes north of Frankfurt am Main. George
was stationed at the U.S. Army base Gibbs Kaserne located inside
Frankfurt's city proper. When President Richard Nixon had ordered a
random selection lottery system for drafting men to serve in the Vietnam
War, George had enlisted. His voluntary enrollment and marital status
were the likely reasons he was sent to Europe rather than to the conflict
in Southeast Asia.

George had joined two hundred fifteen thousand American troops
in West Germany who were engaged in a different kind of conflict: the

Cold War. They were defending Western Europe from the large Soviet armies in East Germany and elsewhere in Eastern Europe. What I did know was that shortly after World War II, Germany had unconditionally surrendered in 1945, its *Wehrmacht* forces were permanently dismantled, and the Union of Soviet Socialist Republics (USSR or Soviet Union) was no longer an ally of England, France, and the United States.

As a teenager on my first trip overseas, I lacked the curiosity to see or connect the dots that linked World War II, the Cold War, and the Vietnam War.

By 1949, a new country, the Federal Republic of Germany, known as West Germany, was founded with the stipulation it would remain demilitarized. By the mid-fifties, in order to become part of the NATO alliance, it was allowed to establish a modest military. During this post-war period, West Germany became ardently pro-democracy and anti-communist. It longed to be reunified with East Germany, which had become a socialist republic under the grip of the Soviets and officially named the German Democratic Republic (GDR). By 1961, Soviet-controlled East Berlin was so alarmed by the border-crossings of East and West Germans, the GDR built the Berlin Wall, mainly to keep their citizens from fleeing. Hence, these rising tensions on the front line of the Cold War in Europe were the reasons my brother-in-law was there.

George was lucky to be in Germany and not the deadly war in Vietnam that had been raging since 1955. At the time, I didn't know that the conflict may well have remained a localized, anti-colonial struggle in French Indochina had the United States, Soviet Union, and China not intervened in this proxy war. Also in 1955, the Warsaw Pact defense treaty was signed in Poland by the Soviet Union and seven of its satellite states: Albania, Bulgaria, Czechoslovakia, East Germany, Hungary, Poland, and Romania. The animosities and ideologies of the Cold War powers were responsible not only for the Vietnam War, but for other major conflicts, such as the crushing of the 1956 Hungarian revolution by the Soviets, the 1962 Cuban Missile Crisis, and the 1968

Warsaw Pact invasion of Czechoslovakia which squelched the Prague Spring reform movement.

Maybe I would have paid more attention to the region's history had I prophesized that one day I would reside in Western Europe and witness the revolutions that ended the Cold War, and then make my home in liberated Czechoslovakia.

Stepping off the Lufthansa jet and into Frankfurt's international airport in 1970, I encountered a manner of dressing, moving, and interacting that was utterly chic and sophisticated. In pseudo-hippie attire with unruly long red hair, I felt like a hayseed sprouted in a flower garden. Up to that point, my only travels outside of Nebraska had been to visit relatives in the neighboring states of Colorado, Kansas, Iowa, and Minnesota.

Every turn of my visit was awe-striking. We toured Frankfurt, formerly one of the greatest medieval city centers of Europe with its unique Gothic timber-framed architecture. Although history cannot be erased, its edifices can. Of the estimated fifteen thousand historical wooden buildings, only a few remained standing after Frankfurt was destroyed in 1944 by Allied forces. This explained the smattering of high-rise buildings amidst the ancient architectural structures that had either survived or been rebuilt. The Römer Old Town Square had a cluster of ornate medieval-era buildings that were reconstructed in the mid-fifties using authentic blueprint specifications to replicate the originals. We wandered the legendary Christmas markets, sipped hot mulled wine, and rode the underground U-Bahn that had been completed two years earlier. Underneath the ringing holiday sounds, my heart sensed a lamenting dirge still reverberating from the atrocities of the war, the destruction of sacred ground, the millions who lost their lives, and those who brutally took them.

During this bitterly cold winter, my sister and brother-in-law treated me to a road trip to Amsterdam in their old Volkswagen Beetle with a broken heater. Shivering to the bones wasn't as uncomfortable as trying to make conversation with George's loquacious military pal who they towed along, tacitly invited as my companion. I would have preferred to see Paris, but Amsterdam was closer and less expensive. We had two rooms—girls in one, boys in the other—in a quaint hotel in Holland's capital city.

After a day under the stifling guardianship of my brother-in-law, I set out the following morning for a stroll. Heading for the famous Dam Square, I casually met two local young men about my age. We sat near one of the canals, smoked marijuana, and talked for hours. They took me on a walking tour and showed me the highlights of Amsterdam—the Rijks and Van Gogh museums, the Royal Palace, and the house where Anne Frank hid with her family for two years during the Nazi occupation. Born and raised in the Holland province, the young Dutchmen knew the names of all the canals, islands, and bridges. They spoke proudly of their heritage and history. They asked about my country, my life, my opinion about culture and history, and from where my ancestors had emigrated—topics I'd never before been asked about. The boys spoke excellent English with charming accents. To my amazement, they were also fluent in Dutch, German, and French.

When dusk came, we bade farewell, and I was on top of the world. Waltzing back into the hotel that evening, a royal scolding awaited me, which was a small price to pay for a perfect afternoon. I made a secret vow to myself: *I will return and visit Paris.*

Promise kept. Within three years, I moved to France on my own. It was October 1973 and I was twenty-one. This time, I sailed the seas on an Italian ocean liner, the SS *Raffaello*, one of the last ships designed for passenger service across the North Atlantic. My youth allowed me to take advantage of a rock-bottom student rate. The rooms were divided into three classes: first, cabin, and tourist. Once aboard, I upgraded to a private room in cabin class with a twenty-dollar tip—given to the right person, in the right way—a stratagem gleaned from two savvy globetrotters who had traveled on every major passenger liner and who I had encountered at Mr. Toad's Pub in Omaha's Old Market.

For fear I'd be talked out of it, I had discussed with very few people my plans to sell all my worldly possessions and move to Europe, but it felt safe to confide in these sharp-witted strangers from out of town. It was they who suggested taking a ship rather than flying and who outlined specifics on how to go about it, how to obtain a cheap student rate, and how to upgrade onboard. The gentlemen were delighted to expound on shipboard protocol with a soon-to-be fellow world traveler. Procuring real-life information from real-deal people was equivalent to, and more valuable than, the internet searches of today.

My higher education began on the crossing, starting with "Geopolitics and Oil Embargoes 101." The timing of the voyage coincided with the start of a major oil crisis when members of the Organization of Petroleum Exporting Countries (OPEC) proclaimed an oil embargo. The talk at the dinner table apprised me of OPEC countries using the embargo as a strategic move to retaliate against the nations that supported Israel during the Yom Kippur War and to gain leverage in the post-war peace plans.

The oil crisis intentionally created far-reaching and dire consequences. The price of oil doubled, then quadrupled, which imposed unbearable cost increases on consumers and rocked the stability of national economies. Less dramatically, it caused minor inconveniences, such as its effects on me and the other passengers. We boarded the *Raffaello* with the expectation of a nine-day crossing. After pushing out, the captain announced that speed would be reduced to save fuel, adding two days to the schedule.

Eleven days and nights on a luxury liner was hardly an imposition for someone with a blank itinerary. From the onboard daily bulletins and discussions with my dinner companions, I learned that a ship's fuel consumption is measured in tons per diem. The quantity of fuel is calculated on a formula that depends on the vessel's size, the wind direction, and the cruising speed in knots (nautical miles). Ships the size of the

Raffaello might consume three hundred tons of fuel each day, and the price per ton had just increased 400 percent.

As well as becoming edified about world politics, Middle East conflicts, and energy resources, I became enlightened about shipboard hierarchy, social protocols, and upgrades from steerage to coach. I also discovered that a third-class passenger can dine in first class at no extra cost, in-kind or otherwise, if invited. This is not to say that the German gentleman who asked me to accompany him at the splendiferous top-tier dining room didn't, at some point, make a proposition of an intimate nature. I was pleased that he still sought my company after I respectfully declined. Behind my demurral was not so much virtue as a lack of chemistry. To my later undoing, I did find one of the young Italian deck porters irresistibly captivating and allowed him to visit me one evening. For that I had regrets. Not only was the encounter woefully unsatisfactory, but for the remainder of the trip I had to endure puckish glances from the other porters.

Afterwards, I would blame this humiliating incident on an alcohol-related judgment lapse, but I'm not certain that's all there was to it. My drinking was out of control on the ship. That was certain. At the end of five-course *alta cucina* dinners, during which Italian reserve wines flowed, I should have called it a night. Yet the pulsating music in the adjacent ballroom beckoned. I danced with abandon and drank to oblivion. The music stopped and the room kept spinning. When each morning rudely nudged, I reproached myself—the person that I knew could do better, should know better—like a babysitter to an uncontrollable child, "You will only have three drinks tonight. Period." The child paid no heed. By day eleven, I wanted off the ship. I wanted to start over.

Passengers could choose their port of disembarkation on the French or Italian Riviera. Mine was the first port of call, Marseilles. Each step down the gangway had the promise of new beginnings, each breath of warm Mediterranean air infused me with surety, and every sound fell on my ears as a harmonious response to an inner call to adventure.

Leaving home was a tangible enactment of the mythical journey I'd read about in books by the writer and mythologist, Joseph Campbell. He said to "follow your bliss"—not just any whim or passing fancy, but to find your true passion and let it lead you. In one of Campbell's last interviews, when Bill Moyers asked if he ever had the sense of being helped by hidden hands, he responded:

> All the time. It is miraculous. I even have a superstition that has grown on me as a result of invisible hands coming all the time—namely, that if you do follow your bliss you put yourself on a kind of track that has been there all the while, waiting for you, and the life that you ought to be living is the one you are living. When you can see that, you begin to meet people who are in your field of bliss, and they open doors to you. I say, follow your bliss, don't be afraid, and doors will open where you didn't know they were going to be.

Doors were about to open for me. I was a young woman with two suitcases and exactly twenty one-hundred-dollar bills rolled tightly into a handkerchief pinned inside her bra. No credit card. Cellphones did not exist. Suitcases had no wheels; they had handles and were carried.

From my first night in New York where the ship embarked, I had been inching toward my destination for nearly two weeks. The thirteenth night of my journey was on French soil at a spartan, bordering on shabby, hotel within walking distance of the port. Primitive communal shower and toilet facilities were located at the back of the outside courtyard. I went to a nearby brasserie and had a luscious *salade niçoise*, to the chagrin of my waiter who vigorously promoted the *bouillabaisse*, a flavorful seafood stew for which the city is known. The next morning I used the communal lavatory to hastily freshen up, paid the bill, and found a train to the capital city. There was no *train à grande vitesse*

(TGV) as there is today that bullets from Marseilles to Paris in three hours. The ride was twice as long and to my liking. A refined Parisienne *d'un certain age* sat next to me. She asked what I hoped to see during my vacation in Paris.

"Oh, Madame, this is no vacation," I said, putting my high school French into practice, "I am going to Paris to live."

"Isn't that interesting," she replied with a bemused yet affable tone, and after a moment, added, "What do you plan to do there?"

"I am moving to Paris to sing," I said out loud for the first time, and to a stranger.

Her face lit up, which I interpreted as validation, and she smiled. "*Bon courage, Mademoiselle.*"

When the train pulled into the Gare d'Austerlitz, my long-dreamt destination lay at my feet. Paris was no longer Hemingway's *Moveable Feast*, nor Puccini's *Bohème*, nor Gershwin's *American in Paris*—it was my story, my song now. Weighted with suitcases, I stopped in the first halfway-decent hotel on a nearby boulevard where I negotiated a discount for *séjours longue durée*. This would be my home until, heaven forbid, my money ran out, or I found a job.

I fell head over heels in love with France, several Frenchmen, the music, and the language. Nothing I experienced during my year abroad could have happened in my hometown, where I had been trapped inside a box marked "limitation" with only a tiny peephole to view the outside world. *Get me out of here,* my soul wailed. I followed that voice to the depths of its cry, recalling the budding young lady who'd shared an inimitable moment with two free spirits on the banks of Amsterdam. Since then, my heart had stayed in the Old World, and I was about to rejoin it. France spoke a language that I wanted for my own, had songs I yearned to sing, wine I thirsted to drink, and fashions I dreamed of wearing. I couldn't afford the high-end of any of these desires, except perhaps the songs. As it happened, it was music that provided my stay with subsistence, relative longevity, and happiness.

Seeking an *au pair* position was never a consideration. Stepping onto the Parisian scene in a role of live-in babysitter did not fit my mind's image of a *chanteuse*. Nevertheless, after a few days assessing the situation—a foreigner with no work permit—the *au pair* scenario seemed worth trying. Surveying the plentiful newspaper ads, I zeroed in on arrondissements within the city center. Fortune smiled on my first interview. I met with a female medical doctor at her office on the boulevard Saint-Michel directly across from the Luxembourg Gardens. *Madame la doctoresse* Boucheron was attractive, classically bourgeoise, and very pleasant. She explained that her medical practice demanded her attention six days a week, morning to evening, during which time the *au pair* would care for her three young children. She could assure me of one, and occasionally two, free weekends a month when the children went to stay with their father.

Madame added that she was impressed with me, my polite and alert manner, cheerfulness, and that I sat up straight. I wondered what she had encountered in other interviews. After asking a few questions about my background, she offered to hire me on the spot, and in addition to room and board, she would augment the weekly stipend to compensate for the long hours. I politely explained that, while I was flattered and grateful for the generous offer, I was in Paris to experience the culture and explore music, and accepting this position would leave me little time. She understood. She walked me to the door, then hesitated and asked if I'd step back in. She wrote a name and phone number on an engraved calling card and handed it to me. She said this person needed an *au pair* for fewer hours.

I walked back to my hotel posthaste and made the call to a certain Monsieur Marc Guillaume. He answered and said that the doctor had already phoned him to recommend me, and we agreed on a time to meet. The interview locale was a recently renovated, two-story flat with contemporary furnishings on a quiet street off the boulevard Raspail which would become my Parisian residence. A slight-to-medium-framed gentleman with fine features and sparkling eyes met me at the elevator and escorted me into the flat. His demeanor was formal but friendly. His high-placed vocal timbre had a melodic inflection, and his manner of speaking was kind and intelligent. I felt comfortable in the warm setting and the cushioned chair he offered me. To my surprise, he disclosed that the doctor was his ex-wife, and he required occasional help when his three children visited every second or third weekend. I would have a bedroom and bathroom of my own on the lower level, could use the kitchen and other parts of the house when he was away, and the pay would be comparable to what the children's mother offered. *D'accord!*

Monsieur Guillaume worked long hours and traveled often. I had ample time to get to know Paris, pursue music, and sometimes just relax at home. The children were cute, bright, and quite sassy. In his early thirties, Marc was already a well-known economist and author. He was a professor and the recently appointed Vice President at the University of Paris-Dauphine, the only institution in France to be both a *grande école* and a university. Marc's first book, *Anti-économique,* had just been published. Co-authored with his friend and colleague, Jacques Attali, this ground-breaking success was a shrill critique of traditional economic methods. It was the first of his countless books, articles, and essays on the subjects of economics, sociology, culture, ecology, *altérité* (otherness), friendship, and intimacy. His writings continue to elucidate his belief that economics and humanities are inseparable.

My friendship with Marc had an empowering effect on my life. Our conversations were enriching, playful, and profound. On the evenings we were both home, I cooked dinner and we talked into the night. Our discussions took off like rockets heading to new spheres. Marc could condense leading world questions into their essence, point to the heart of the issue, explain why it mattered, and most important to him, show how it affected humanity. His genuine interest in my opinion concerning complex topics was highly complimentary, but I was too captivated to be flattered. When it came to the subject of music, he was moved by my love for French *chansons et poésie*. My artistry struck a chord in Marc, an amateur oil painter himself, whose finished canvases were scattered about, either on walls or sitting upright on the floor.

"*Chante pour moi, Anne-Marie*," he'd gently ask.

"*Oh! je voudrais tant que tu te souviennes . . .*" was one amiable, a cappella response. This line is the first stanza of a poem by the beloved French poet Jacques Prévert and set to music by the legendary Hungarian-French composer Joseph Kosma. A simple translation might be:

> *Oh, I so want for you to remember*
> *those happy days when we were friends.*
> *In those times, life was more beautiful*
> *and the sun more brilliant than today.*
> *The dying leaves are now gathering.*
> *You see, I've not forgotten.*
> *The dying leaves are gathering*
> *memories, and regrets, too.*
> *You see, I've not forgotten*
> *the song that you sang for me.*

The verse flowed into the song's refrain which became known to American audiences as "Autumn Leaves." For me, it would become an evocative reminder of my friendship with Marc.

I loved him, and all that I learned from him. In school, I was taught that socialism was nearly the same as communism and both were evil. I grew up in an America that, spurred on by the Second World War, hailed nationalism and feared socialism and communism to the point of paranoia, as evidenced by McCarthyism, a repressive era that blacklisted left-leaning people because of mostly unsubstantiated charges.

Marc was a member of the French Socialist Party. I discovered that the basic tenets of social democracy aligned with the core values of my Catholic education—human rights, social justice, equality for all—and how they can thrive within a democratically elected government that protects public and private interests. In the spring, a major national event occurred in France that caused Marc to enter the political arena, and he got me involved.

In April 1974, President Georges Pompidou, the protégé and successor of Charles de Gaulle, died in the fifth year of his seven-year term. Because no vice president exists in France, when the presidency is unexpectedly vacated, the Speaker of the Senate becomes interim president, and elections must take place within twenty to thirty-five days. A dozen or so political parties scrambled to put forward their candidates. Marc assisted in advancing the leader of the Socialist Party, François Mitterrand. When the race went to the second round, the top two candidates, Mitterrand and the center-right Valéry Giscard d'Estaing, squared off.

At this juncture, Marc became one of Mitterrand's top economic advisors, in company with Jacques Attali, Michel Rocard, and Édith Cresson. Marc worked day and night and solicited my help to do office work for the campaign. I cheerfully accepted. I boasted about my 60-words-per-minute typing skills. Marc introduced me to the staff at the Mitterrand campaign headquarters located at the Tour Montparnasse, the only skyscraper in the city. I was given letters and lists to type, but quickly discovered that French typewriters had a different keyboard layout, drastically reducing my speed to a hunt-and-peck pace. I was then relegated to errand girl. As I ran sandwiches to workers and delivered envelopes to and fro, I felt exhilarated to be lending a hand in the national election process of my adopted country. It was sadly ironic that, concurrently, my home country was immersed in the Watergate scandal and deeply demoralized. Three months after the May elections in France, President Richard Nixon resigned from office.

The big payoff for volunteering for the Mitterrand campaign took the form of an invitation to the election night reception, a grand party at the Ciel de Paris, the panoramic restaurant and terrace located on the fifty-sixth floor of the Tour Montparnasse. Outwardly cool and collected, but inwardly flabbergasted, I mingled among hundreds of Socialist Party elites dressed in Parisian couture who sipped champagne and nibbled hors d'oeuvres as we waited for the results to come in. No big-screen televisions. It was microphones, podiums, and announcements. Giscard d'Estaing ultimately won, but Mitterrand obtained 49.2 percent of the votes. Marc said the close call was a success for the Socialist Party and would lead to more representation in the next legislative elections. Indeed, Mitterrand won the presidency seven years later.

All this time, I focused on my goal to make music. I lived a stone's throw from the American Center for Students and Artists on the boulevard Raspail, one of several institutions started by the powerful American community in Paris from the 1890s onward. In its lobby was a large bulletin board that young people could reference when seeking jobs, flats, or long-lost friends. I pinned an ad: "American singer looking for musicians," after which I listed my flat's phone number. In a few short days, the phone rang. A hushed basso profundo voice asked to speak with the American singer. The rich-toned inquirer was an Argentine guitarist named Carlos Hergott. After vetting his musicianship and sincerity, I invited him to my place for an interview.

A six-foot-four, soft-featured, bearded, noisette-skinned man in his mid-twenties came through the door with guitar case in hand. We exchanged the requisite niceties and informational coordinates before I asked if he'd kindly play something on his guitar. It became apparent that Carlos could play anything, in any key, with polished musicianship and contagious rhythm. I started singing. We hit it off—in every way.

After a few weeks of rehearsals, we had an eclectic list of songs performance-ready, from bossa nova to American jazz standards to French chansons. He convinced me, after some persuasion, to sing on the streets for tips.

My Parisian debut was on the broad sidewalks of the avenue des Champs-Élysées. It was November 1973, the month I turned twenty-two. We drew large crowds, and the tips were generous. The applause, the smiles, and the verbal accolades from passersby who stopped to listen were wonderfully surprising. On one of our busking nights, I was approached by a producer from the Office de radiodiffusion-télévision française (ORTF), France's national public radio and television. He was rapt by our music and invited us to audition for *Mireille et le Petit Conservatoire*, a popular program in France devoted to upcoming young musicians. We became regulars on the weekly radio and monthly television broadcasts hosted by the mononymous celebrity, Mireille (Hartuch), a beloved songwriter, singer, and teacher. Not only were these paying gigs, they also brought us national exposure and music industry connections.

One such connection became my agent, Bernard Droguet, who collaborated with Mireille as a songwriter and talent scout. Bernard asked to represent me on the condition that I ditch Carlos and work with other musicians. I agreed, despite Carlos's ire.

Bernard and I had a casual affair, but nothing romantic. He was terribly handsome. He booked me in clubs and concert halls and introduced me to French composers. One afternoon, after a particularly long lull between bookings, Bernard phoned and asked me to perform the very next day with a well-known orchestra in place of a singer who was sick. He expected me to jump at the chance, and I should have. Instead, I offered a feeble excuse. In reality, I'd been on a drinking spree, and knew I couldn't rally within twenty-four hours.

As he begged me, his voice elevated from disappointment to anger, saying his reputation was on the line. I brittlely stood my shaky ground, *"Non, Bernard, je suis désolée."* A pattern was emerging in the idle space between intermittent work, especially when Marc was away. Unrestrainedly, I washed away loneliness and insecurity with copious amounts of vin rouge. It frightened me. After this remorseful incident, Bernard's offers dried up, as did Mireille's.

Soon after that, my pleasant situation at Marc's spacious flat changed when his lady friend moved in. She wasn't keen on another woman living under the same roof. Marc was too kind to ask me to move out, so

I told him I'd be leaving and how grateful I was for his hospitality and friendship, a friendship that lasted long into the future.

Through my American dancer friend Shelley Bance, I found a garret room (more like a closet) near the Panthéon on la place Sainte-Geneviève with a tiny window overlooking l'église Saint-Étienne-du-Mont. Plunking down two months' rent gave me a temporary sense of security, although it nearly depleted my resources.

Sometimes when I passed by the church, I'd enter through its ornate purple doors to sit in the cold nave surrounded by gothic architecture. There in the quiet, a loving inner voice spoke truth to me—*You're fighting too hard.*

The nurturing voice narrated the accomplishments, complexities, and contradictions of my past year in the City of Light. I had discovered success in music and felt the power of touching people's hearts with song. I learned that cultivated men and women found me winsome and interesting. I had fallen hopelessly in love with Paris and it requited my love with its beauty, language, and music.

Yet, for reasons beyond my comprehension, I was unable to cope with greater success, at least not right then. My efforts to maintain a music career began to lag after dawdling too long with self-doubt and unwitting addiction. I didn't need to fully understand my predicament to know that I was overwhelmed and off track. The voice was gentle. Like a soft Gregorian chant, it sang—*Go back home. Paris, and all you've attained, will go with you.*

I called Carlos. We started performing in the small restaurants near place de la Contrescarpe for tips. I was heartened by the diners' absorbed attention, verbal praise, and monetary rewards. Music surrounded me once more with a healing aura. But I knew it wasn't enough, and my mind was made up. I quickly earned the means for a ticket home. With fingers crossed, I headed back to Omaha, planning for a temporary change of scene to get my act together, hone my singing skills, and eventually return to Europe.

Although leaving Paris felt like a surrender, my pivotal year in France opened new worlds and affirmed my artistic expression. I'd stepped outside a restrictive box with only my talent to offer, knowing the creative force that pulled me out wouldn't let me down.

3

FOLLOW THE MUSIC

P*aris to Omaha. A tough transition.* I was a lost soul in my hometown again. My mother was relieved that I was back, but she had a rule for all her children: once you leave home, you're on your own. She made an exception and allowed me to stay with her, but only until I found a job and an apartment. She did the same with my oldest sister Susan who entered the convent at age seventeen, then left her religious order after eight years and asked to come home for a while. Mother said she could live there briefly, on the condition she pay room and board and be in by ten o'clock every night. Needless to say, Susan declined the offer, and I didn't stay for long.

My mother, Veronica Janda Kenny, modeled values of self-sufficiency and hard work that stemmed from the frugal mentality of her Bohemian upbringing and from being widowed at age thirty-three. My father, Daniel L. Kenny, was thirty-four when he drowned on a fishing trip. He was a robust young Irish-American attorney and a devoted family man. Dad was getting started professionally with his own law practice after five years overseas in World War II, followed by law school at Creighton University on the GI Bill. He and five of his buddies went fishing in the cold boundary waters between Canada and the United States when their boats capsized in a current of rapids. The others swam to shore. My father was an experienced swimmer, and had been a lifeguard in his youth, but he went under and didn't come up. The men frantically swam back out and searched until dark. Days later, after dredging the lake, the authorities found his body with a gash to his scalp, indicating that the motor had hit his head when he was thrown overboard. We children—Susan, Nancy, Mary Lou, me, and Joe—were ages seven, five, four, two, and six months. Our family would have lived much differently had it not been for this tragedy. Each of us was uniquely marked by it; all of us are stronger because of it.

Mother went to work and accounted for every penny. She put us through parochial schools and piano lessons, sewed our clothes, baked homemade bread, rolls, or strudel on weekends, and went to daily Mass at six-thirty in the morning before getting us off to school and heading to her secretarial job at my dad's former law office. When she needed extra income, she worked evenings as a cashier for the Kraft brothers, who had a retail shop downtown and had been on that fateful fishing trip. Mother found time to volunteer at Saint James Orphanage every few weeks and often took some of us with her. We sat and watched the circle of women chatting away as they patched children's clothing and darned socks. Mom held to the virtues of faith, hope, and charity, and deemed charity in the highest order. She couldn't donate money but she gave of herself. She brought baked goods and offered rides to shut-ins, the bereaved, and the sick.

An accomplished seamstress, Mother sewed tailored suits, dresses, pajamas—even our dolls' clothes—and she was always dressed fashionably, color-coordinated from head to toe. She had a bright and caring personality and an abundance of friends who would describe her as "the salt of the earth." Mom had a social life with her bridge club and parish events, and she came alive hosting dinner parties with elaborate table settings, home cooking, and live entertainment. It was mandatory for

Veronica Janda, before her marriage, (c. 1945). On the back of this photo, in Mother's handwriting, is written: "I made this blouse with parachute material (white silk) brought back by my brother Matt after World War II."

the Kenny children to play and sing for Mom's guests, either performing a solo piano piece or a four-part harmony routine.

My siblings and I were no strangers to work. On Saturdays, the house was cleaned top to bottom through a division of labor. In summer, we woke up to a list on the kitchen table delineating tasks to be completed before Mother got home. Or else. When each of us reached the age of thirteen or fourteen, Mother took us to City Hall to obtain a Social Security card and special work permit from the Nebraska Department of Labor so we could start earning money. Apart from babysitting, my first real jobs were feeding babies and changing diapers in the nursery at Saint James Orphanage, serving meals at Creighton University cafeteria, working as the front desk clerk at a dry cleaners, waitressing at a nearby restaurant, and so on.

Mother drilled us on interviewing skills: what to wear, how to present ourselves with good posture and a sincere smile, and most importantly, never fail to say, "My mother is a widow with five children, and I need to earn money to help with the home expenses." I always got the job.

Decades later at my Prague employment agency, when I taught interviewing skills to Czechoslovak applicants keen to work for the high-paying international companies flooding the market, I often cited my mother's practical wisdom and personal approach that had always produced favorable results. Besides, disclosing my story of personal hardship endeared me to my clients. I wasn't seeking their admiration, but rather their understanding. Recently liberated from behind the Iron Curtain, the Czechoslovak people were inclined to think that Westerners from the free world led charmed lives.

At home and in public, Mother was adamant about exhibiting polite manners and being well-spoken. Improper grammar was met with immediate correction, and curse words with soap in the mouth. She was a detailed organizer, a piano player of waltzes, and an old-fashioned homemaker. Working outside the home hadn't been in the plan, until her world turned upside down. The shock of being suddenly widowed with a slew of kids might have driven anyone to drink, but alcoholism was prevalent in Dad's family, not Mom's. Her outlet for emotional exasperation or physical exhaustion was to yell or cry; while there was plenty of that, her tenderness, smiles, and laughter also poured forth in no small measure. I can still hear her humming melodies while doing chores. Mom's singing and speaking voice were lovely and distinctively resonant. Veronica was beautiful, valiant, sacrificing, and extraordinary.

Cosmopolitan, she was not. That quality belonged to my father, who showered me with paternal love for the first thirty months of my life. It was he who named me Anne Marie because of his years in France and his love for the country and culture. Dad spoke French and Italian fluently and could rattle off enough Czech phrases to delight my mother's family, who grew up "talking Bohemian" at home. *Dej mi hubička, hezká holko!* "Give me a kiss, pretty girl," was his greeting, followed by a sweet peck on the cheek. Of my two parents, Dad was the fun-loving adventurer type. Mom endearingly described her brief and happy life with him as sometimes raising a sixth child. My father surely would have embraced me as an artistic seeker. I would have given anything to feel his arm around me and hear his voice tell me that, but I felt his affirmation in my heart all the same. To Mother, who had her mind set on my becoming a secretary, I was her wayward prodigal daughter.

"I hope you've gotten all this travel out of your system now," was her sincere plea when I came home from my year abroad. I didn't have the heart to respond.

She thought Nebraska, where our ancestors had lived for three generations and where our roots were established, was where I belonged. My home state is part of the Great Plains that run a wide swath down the middle of the country. Once covered in treeless prairie and grasslands, the Plains extend from the Missouri River in the east to the Rocky Mountains in the west, and from Canada in the north down to the panhandle of Texas in the south. On these grounds my ancestors settled—the Jandas and Tomans from Moravia, and the Kennys and Connors from Ireland.

My return from France to Nebraska in 1974 coincided with the homecoming and reintegration of troops from Vietnam, as that war was ending. My first real boyfriend from Omaha, a genuine sweetheart, had gone to war. When he left for overseas, we were no longer dating, but still friends. This bright young man came home an addict, using psychedelics, amphetamines, and heroin. He was not alone. Substance abuse in Vietnam was rampant on the bases, in the field, and on the streets. Some of it was prescribed by commanding officers to improve performance. My friends coming home had been traumatized by combat day after day. I found out that the average World War II infantryman in the South Pacific saw 40 days of combat in *four years*, and the average infantryman in Vietnam saw 240 days of combat in *one year*, because of the mobility of the helicopter. Reintegration back into their hometowns was uniquely difficult for Vietnam soldiers because of the sustained horrors they had witnessed and the disrespect they often faced back home as the war grew more unpopular. Their plight put my discontent into perspective.

My readjustment to Omaha from reverse culture shock was the result of happy and exciting days abroad. Theirs was most certainly not.

Comparing Omaha to Paris was a pointless equation, yet I was confronted with glaring differences on a daily basis. Paris was sought after by artists for its beauty and light, and by lovers for its romantic allure. Despite its size, each arrondissement had a small-village feel with boutiques, markets, boulangeries, and cafés unique to that quarter. Paris was bustling with fashionably dressed people on foot or hopping on public transportation. Omaha was a sprawling, low-density city where jeans and baseball caps were the norm and everyone drove everywhere.

My constant comparisons were futile. Yes, Paris made me feel more alive, but I thought there must be an energy to tap in my new reality. I stopped feeling forlorn about what I was missing and instead wondered what I had to offer. Omaha seemed small and deficient until I discovered it had charm and hidden gems in its people. With this realization, doors opened to kindred spirits who understood my artistic pursuits.

One such creative portal was Omaha's Old Market. A vital railroad hub in the 1800s, Omaha became a vibrant wholesale produce district with its easternmost section near the Missouri River. It remained commercially viable until the 1950s, when urban sprawl caused independent grocery stores to be overrun by large supermarket chains. During the 1960s, the city started demolishing ornate architectural buildings that were historic landmarks—such as the U.S. Post Office, City Hall, Fontenelle Hotel, and the old Woodmen of the World building —and the Old Market stood in the wrecking ball's path as well. The Mercer family rescued the area, inspired by local artists and entrepreneurs.

Sam Mercer was born in London, educated at Oxford and Yale, and lived and practiced law in Paris as a dual French-American citizen. He had inherited prime real estate in the Old Market from his father. Sam had little interest in the day-to-day management of the large, red-brick buildings and warehouses that he owned, until they were threatened with condemnation notices. He saved the properties by renovating them for new uses. Called a fool at the time, he and his advisors proved to be visionaries.

By the late sixties, the Old Market had become the hippest part of the city, with art galleries, restaurants, bars, and shops. It was a haven for the countercultural set. From my senior year in high school to the time I left for France, I was a habituée of the Old Market's hot spots. After I returned from Paris, I hoped to be an aesthetic asset to its sophisticated atmosphere. Wearing my chicest French outfit, I approached the best-known restaurants—M's Pub, V. Mertz, and The French Cafe—and offered musical entertainment with a European flair. I likened my offering to the cabaret shows in New York supper clubs that feature a pianist and a singer stylizing standards from the American Songbook, except my cabaret program would include beloved American, French, and Italian songs in the pop, musical theater, and light classical genres. M's Pub hired me on a regular basis, while other restaurants engaged me for special occasions.

I called the mayor of the city and asked for an appointment. Mayor Al Veys agreed to meet with me, and I offered to sing for official occasions. He seemed intrigued and rather charmed, and asked me to sing something for him right there in his office. I did, although I don't remember what it was. Before long, the mayor asked me to sing for a function at city hall.

Coincidentally, I developed a special friendship with Sam Mercer's son by virtue of a mutual friend I'd met in Paris while sitting on the outside terrace of Les Deux Magots café. I was sipping *chartreuse verte,* one of my most pleasurable and economical activities, because one glass of liqueur could last for a good hour. Free entertainment was provided by a steady flow of pedestrians wearing the latest fashion trends on the boulevard Saint-Germain, as street musicians serenaded. One late summer evening as I savored my nightcap, the headwaiter led a smartly dressed young Asian man to the little round table hugging mine. We caught each other's eyes a few times—something women learn to evade, unless intentional—and a conversation ensued. His name was Hiro. He was from Japan, had attended university in the U.S., and now lived in Paris. On hearing that I was from Omaha, he said, "I've met one other person from Omaha, whom you probably wouldn't know. He was my roommate at Harvard, Mark Mercer." I laughed and said that everyone in Omaha knew the Mercers, but I hadn't met Mark personally.

Hiro and I got together occasionally for meals at brasseries or drinks at his flat. He enjoyed performing Kau Chim for me, a Buddhist fortune-telling practice. We sat on the floor as he cast out special sticks from a sacred lot. Each stick represented a poetic phrase. Whether the revelations were positive or disappointing, I didn't mind. Hiro was pleasant company. Once back in Omaha's Old Market, I saw Mark Mercer and told him the story. We developed a bond through our mutual friendship with Hiro and our mutual love for France.

Another allegorical passageway that led to Omaha's cultural treasury was the Alliance Française Omaha. When Mark told me there was a French club in town, I found the listing in the phone book and called for information. A woman with a veritable Parisian accent graciously invited me to attend the next luncheon. Genevieve Pullum was the group's president. At the event, she introduced me to members and seated me on her right for the meal and presentation. Genevieve was enthralled to learn that I had sung in Paris, and she asked if I would entertain at the Alliance's upcoming event.

Providing my own piano accompaniment, I sang "Sous le ciel de Paris," "Les Feuilles mortes," and "L'Âme des poètes." Among the sophisticated Francophiles that I met that afternoon was a voice teacher, soprano Diana Morrison, who'd been trained at the the Royal Conservatory of Music in Toronto. She was talented, exigent, and eccentric. Diana came across as an upper-crust socialite, but she was generous and genuine as a friend and teacher. She was full of one-liner social tips, like "Never wear your diamonds to the dentist" or referring to wardrobe accoutrements, "If it doesn't add, it takes away."

When I entered Diana's large colonial home in a chic part of Omaha, it was almost like being back in Europe again. She taught in her living room that was all white, except for the black grand piano and art deco vases on the mantel with exotic flowers. She loved wearing white, which matched her curly, shoulder-length platinum hair that flowed behind her long pale face dotted with soft coral rouge. Diana brought out colors and range in my voice, and a suggestion of stardom, that I'd never experienced. The discoveries were endless under her tutelage. Classical music, with its wealth of languages, poetry, and composers, was an open door to new concepts, cultures, and forms of expression. I practiced assiduously during this special time that I considered a brief hiatus in Omaha, always dreaming of my return to Paris.

Diana introduced me to an element of Omaha's social and cultural scene, a world into which I felt a sense of belonging without making any special effort except to be myself. Among Diana's students were the family members of Warren Buffett, the Oracle of Omaha. Diana was the singing teacher to Warren's wife, Susie, who was actively engaged in her midlife dream to be an inspired singer, to bring joy to herself and the audience. Diana helped Susie work up a full-scale cabaret repertoire. In 1977, I was invited to her show at the French Cafe Underground in the Old Market. Backed by an orchestra of top musicians, Susie lit up the room with her winsome charm and lovely singing.

Susie's nephew, the son of her sister Dottie, was Thompson Rogers, a handsome fellow about my age with a sparkling personality and wit. He was taking singing lessons from Diana as an enjoyable and edifying pastime. Tom and I dated for a while and became good friends.

To my taste, the greatest talent in the family was Tom's dad, Homer. He had a booming baritone voice, an exuberant stage presence, and a heart of gold. Homer never missed my shows and often joined me in concert for a solo or duet.

I admired the entire clan, and enjoyed being Tom's date, whether joining him for a meal at a restaurant, for a family gathering at the home of his Aunt Susie and Uncle Warren, or at parties at his high-end bachelor's pad where the festivities teetered on the wild side. We were young, the alcohol flowed, and all-out binges were forgiven and forgotten by morning.

When I needed a job with flexible hours to sustain my rent and voice lessons, I turned to Tom, who managed a wholesale company downtown. He good-naturedly hired me as his assistant with flexible hours, and he seemed delighted that during my breaks, rather than run to the coffee room, I went to the warehouse to practice my vocalizes.

After I received two years of intense voice training with Diana, she and her husband moved to Washington, DC. My next private teacher was Mary Fitzsimmons Massie to whom I owe my bel canto technique and indoctrination into old-world elegance. Mary was an octogenarian, yet ageless in mind and spirit. She had lost the ability to walk and depended on her live-in caregiver to perfectly position her at the piano before her students arrived. There she would be, sitting on the bench with a warm smile, white permed hair, skin like porcelain, dressed in a pantsuit with coordinated blouse and long dangling earrings. Mary's pedagogic lineage would impress anyone in the music business. Her teacher was Mary Münchhoff (1867–1942), an internationally renowned singer from Europe and prodigy of Mathilde Marchesi (1821–1913), who quite literally wrote the book on the methodology of bel canto singing, the Italian vocal method of singing that emphasizes the beauty of sound.

I rode my bicycle to lessons at Mary's home studio at least twice a week and practiced several hours a day. Her teaching method was all-encompassing. As a masterful pedagogue, she explained each developmental step in clear, succinct terms. I worked diligently to become proficient with the vocalizes, classical repertoire, and languages of Italian, French, and German. Mary poured forth her abundant knowledge and exquisite artistry, and I soaked it up.

An infatuation with music, and my vision of a viable career on the horizon, eclipsed the seduction of having a love life, with the exception of unavoidable crushes here and there. One was for my debonaire Italian tutor, Ercole Cavalieri. I discovered Ercole while searching for a language teacher specifically from the region of northern Italy where the dialect is purest. We worked on lyric diction and poetic understanding of the Italian repertoire. Ercole was a cancer research doctor who loved music and opera and was happy to oblige.

Ercole's best friend and tennis partner was John Bull. They both attended my concerts and never missed my dinner shows at M's Pub. John was an advertising executive responsible for national syndication of *Mutual of Omaha's Wild Kingdom* television program, and he began inviting his clients, reserving large tables for eight or ten people. A February 1979 article in the *Omaha Mirror* showed photographs of a crowded M's Pub with me wearing a long over-the-shoulder gown, standing among the tables with mouth wide open on a high note. The article had pictures and named every who's-who in the audience. I was quoted as saying, "I have my goal set on being an international opera singer . . ."

I remember vividly those cabaret shows in Omaha and being certain that music was my calling. I felt utterly alive. As I looked into the audience, John's eyes sparkled brighter than the table candles. His smile warmed me with a serene glow. As the months passed, John joined the Alliance Française. He was elegant and chivalrous by nature. We spent time together in social situations for almost a year before he asked if he could phone me.

He invited me out for dinner. I wore my white dress with little red polka-dots that crisscrossed at the bodice intersected by a V-neck décolletage. The bias-cut skirt softly flowed from the waist to mid-calf. Black heels and clip earrings polished the classic look. We dined at a fine restaurant and talked for hours, relaxed, intrigued, and already falling in love.

Thus began a beautiful and brief courtship. It was serious from the start. John held me in such high esteem, and vice versa, that I aspired to live the rest of my life worthy of such respect. Quietly, I tried to prepare for marrying an older man. My circle of friends contained no role model with a similar experience. I projected our lives twenty years into the future and envisioned a woman in her prime pushing her husband in a wheelchair as a potential scenario. She was loyal; he was elegant and grateful. I privately held the conviction that if we married, I would never leave him and always care for him, no matter what the future held. I was absolutely certain that I could keep that promise, even though I was totally uncertain what fate had in store.

Surely John was also processing his own ruminations. One afternoon, our private thoughts were given voice when we each imagined the future out loud. I remember citing my father's death at age thirty-four and saying that for all we knew, either of us could die prematurely. Therefore, we must say yes to love. Somewhere in the midst of the conversation, John alluded to our age difference and offered a sort of abstract permission for me to seek outside comfort should the day come. I said that, if I grasped his meaning, he should never mention it again because it would never happen. This was an example of how

John and Anne Marie, engaged to be married, at a dinner show featuring Peggy Lee at San Francisco's Fairmont Hotel. (February 1980)

John's depth of wisdom was commensurate with the shallowness of my innocence. But I was sage enough to recognize true love when it presented itself so authentically.

In December 1979, John proposed and I accepted. Three months later, we married and honeymooned in London, Paris, Cannes, and Athens. John and I began to build a good life in Omaha. I studied and concertized nationally and in France. I was content. Although he knew my heart's desire had been to live again in Europe, I tried to convince him that our mutual happiness was now my priority. But evidently, my artistic goals were part of what attracted John to me, for he had a similar longing—to indulge his lifelong yearning to paint in the City of Light. Within three years of our wedding, we moved to Paris.

4

UNDER PARIS SKIES

One *of my two signature songs*, "Sous le ciel de Paris," is a symbol of romantic Paris. Its lilting melody and waltzing rhythm danced in my heart as John and I, with our Scottie dog, Misty, boarded the *Queen Elizabeth II* in October 1983. For us, setting sail on Cunard's oil-fired flagship was the launch of an experimental European journey that floated into tens of years, homes in two countries and three cities, two distinct careers for me, and the fulfillment of a long-held dream for John—to dedicate his days to painting.

Four-legged creatures were pampered aboard the *QE2* on a swanky deck of their own by the kennel master and attendants. They had common play areas, a visitor lounge, a grooming boutique, and individual shelters for sleeping. John and I could visit Misty at scheduled times to walk and play together on a special promenade deck. On booking the passage, we were forewarned of the strict laws concerning pets entering England: any animal that "touches British soil" must be quarantined for six months. No exceptions. Although only a transitory stop, when we disembarked at Southampton—the two-thousand-year-old port city on England's southern coast first discovered by the Romans, then the

Saxons, and where the *Titanic* departed in 1912—we were forbidden to leash our pup and strut the gangway as a threesome like we did when boarding at New York's harbor. Instead, we hand-carried Misty in a travel crate to the shuttle that would take us to the ferry.

At last, we set Misty free, albeit on a leash, for the five-hour boat ride across the English Channel, or *La Manche*, as the French call this appendage of the Atlantic Ocean, the narrow arm that splits France from England. The channel's widest point measures a hundred and fifty miles and its narrowest, in the Dover Strait, is a mere twenty-one. The waters of our one-hundred-mile route were prone to be volatile. Passengers who were frequent channel crossers cautioned us that the winds and waters can turn rough in the blink of an eye. Evidently, someone blinked mightily, for our boat swayed and pitched the entire way. It was so different from the smooth sailing across the great Atlantic on the *QE2*, where not once did I feel unsafe. On the ferry, I hung on for dear life. Misty got tucked back into her cage. John spent his time at the bar. But we made it.

As the ferry approached the port of Le Havre, our exhaustion turned to exhilaration. In the distance, we saw the Normandy coast and the harbor of the second largest port in France after Marseilles. John, my partner in life, travel companion, and historical reference, explained that Le Havre had been so badly bombed in World War II that three-quarters of the port and city were destroyed. The image moving closer and closer into view was an ancient thriving port town, most of which had been rebuilt in the last forty years.

Once docked, Misty was able to immediately dig her paws into, and do her business upon, French soil. The French customs officials simply asked for proof of vaccination and waved us on. As Argos was to Odysseus, Misty was John's noble hound and best friend. And she was a big hit with the French. Whether walking the grand boulevards or the cobbled quays along river banks, dames and demoiselles of all ages would stop to coo over the sweet tail-wagging black beauty, although I contended they were surreptitiously flirting with her handsome consort.

A train took us from Le Havre to Paris. After eight days of planes, trains, ships, and ferries, John, Misty, and I settled cozily into Les Résidences de Claridge on the avenue des Champs-Élysées. The magnificent tree-lined thoroughfare, with broad pedestrian walkways, spanned from the place de la Concorde to the place Charles de Gaulle, where the Arc de Triomphe proudly dominated the center of twelve radiating avenues.

Two critical missions filled our days: find a place to live and obtain resident permits. We had one month for the first assignment and three months for the second. While our furniture was crossing the Atlantic on a slower cargo ship, we made the Parisian home search our first goal. We pondered what part of the city would become our neighborhood—romantic Left Bank or bourgeois Right Bank. Newspaper ads. Phone calls. Visits. Negotiations. My French language ability was superior for singing French repertoire, excellent for casual conversation, but abysmal for discussing terms of rental contracts. John and I toured cramped, dark, and depressing flats within our budget, and magnificent, bright, and roomy ones far exceeding our resources. Eventually, we met an agent, Monsieur Lepi, and depended on his realtor advice and translation skills. One morning he called about a soon-to-be vacant apartment which he described as a rare opportunity for two reasons: it had not yet been listed, and it was in a coveted location, the Île Saint-Louis. He said the six-storied nineteenth-century building at 29, quai d'Anjou had twelve units, two per floor, the larger of the two facing the river, and the smaller one facing an inner courtyard. The attractive stone structure had been renovated with an elevator. Although the price tilted a little over our budget, we were intrigued. The agent arranged for a showing.

Two natural islands in the historic heart of Paris are connected by Pont Saint-Louis and belong to the fourth arrondissement, but they're considered neither Right nor Left Bank. The larger island, Île de la Cité, was, and still is, an important governmental and religious seat, beginning with the Romans in 52 BC. On this island stands the Notre Dame Cathedral, the Sainte Chapelle, the Préfecture de Police, the Palais de

Justice, the Hôtel-Dieu Hospital, and the Conciergerie. The smaller island, Île Saint-Louis, is a quiet residential and urban oasis and considered a village unto itself, with boulangeries, fromageries, cafés, brasseries, and the famous Bertillon ice cream. Shops have changed hands, but the island has not changed since the seventeenth century.

As we walked toward the atmospheric Île Saint-Louis, traversing the Pont Marie from the Marais district, we could scan the entire length of the small island with place Louis Aragon on the west tip to square Barye at the east end. We were mesmerized by the panoramic site. As he gestured across the river, Monsieur Lepi refocused our attention and pointed directly at the handsome facade a few buildings down from where the bridge ended.

"*Voila! regardez numéro vingt-neuf*... and look up at the fifth story's row of four tall windows . . . that's the place!"

We entered through a colossal red double door and passed through an echoing archway to a set of window-paned doors, beyond which was the concierge residence. Monsieur Lepi pressed a name on the keypad, and we were buzzed into the vestibule. On the left was a staircase and a narrow lift wedged between it and the wall. I opted to climb the five flights rather than squeeze into the maximum three-person elevator.

The current tenant opened the door. Unbeknownst to any of us, this refined Parisienne would become our lifelong friend. With an elegant friendliness, Madame Marie-Françoise Mynard showed us the six *pièces*. The rooms facing the Seine were *un double-living* (combined living and dining area), *un office* (perfect for John's art studio), and the master bedroom. On the courtyard side were a mini second bedroom, a bathroom, a water closet, and a tiny kitchen with compact appliances, plenty of cabinets, and French doors opening onto a balconette.

John and I were completely charmed by the apartment, the layout, and the location. The view and light were spectacular. Everything was perfect, although the size was small by American standards—ninety-five square meters (just over one thousand square feet)—and the price a bit higher than we'd planned on spending. But the pluses far outweighed the minuses. On the second visit, Madame Mynard invited us to sit together for a conversation about the flat, the neighborhood, and the neighbors, as she served Brut champagne with *marrons glacés* from the celebrated Maison Bertillon—glazed chestnuts only available around Christmastime in France.

We were sold.

Our next task was to establish legal resident status. It was ten years since I'd lived in France as a young and single *vagabonde sans papiers*. Everything was different this time. We were a married couple wanting to establish our home, careers, and lives in France. Other American expatriates came long before us—Thomas Jefferson, Benjamin Franklin, Gertrude Stein, Ernest Hemingway, Cole Porter, Julia Child, and Nina Simone—and as with them, the magic of Paris took hold of us in a singular and distinctive way.

While still in the States, we learned from the French Consulate that *cartes de séjour* could only be obtained in-person at the Préfecture de Police within three months of arriving in the country. Several documents needed to be presented: a letter from our bank stating financial viability, evidence of clean criminal records, current passports, and validated copies of our birth certificates and marriage license. The Préfecture building was on the Île de la Cité, not far behind the Notre Dame Cathedral. Appointments could not be scheduled in advance. First come, first served. Armed with the proper papers, we set out after breakfast one fine morning for the fifteen-minute walk. While still on the rue de la Cité, and before turning onto rue de Lutèce, we encountered a queue of people lined around two corners of the massive building. Not sure of their purpose, we passed them all and headed straight to the entrance. There we found the front of the long queue. We asked the police guards for directions to the office that issued resident permits. He said the line formed at the rear, and only those who come very early are likely to get an appointment the same day. It was already mid-morning. We had no chance that day.

"What?" John said, dismayed and indignant. "I will *not* stand outside in a line all day long."

"If I return early on my own tomorrow," I asked the gendarme with deference, "may I obtain the permits for both my husband and myself?"

"Both parties need to be present," he perfunctorily informed us and resumed his duties.

On the walk home, John grumbled, and I silently discerned that standing on his feet for hours must seem daunting for John. I rarely noticed our age difference, except in situations like this. Making no mention of the thoughts crossing my mind, I offered alternate ideas.

"Honey, we could return another day and bring a folding stool for either of us to rest on as we make our way forward . . . or I could go alone, very early, and you'd come later and try to find me in the line."

In that era, there were no cellphones to streamline such undertakings. Neither plan seemed workable. We decided to wait a few days and reconnoiter.

That evening, or the next, we had dinner plans with an American couple we'd met on the ship. They were wrapping up an extended vacation traveling around Europe. We dined at Chez Pauline, a well-known bistro with traditional cuisine and art nouveau decor. During dinner, we related our frustrating attempt for the resident permit. Normally, John was not one to complain, but he related the incident in bemoaning detail. After all, the story was rather entertaining. Our shipmate friends were sympathetic, but admitted to having no experience in the matter. As the conversation moved to another topic, I felt a gentle tap on my shoulder.

"*Excusez-moi, Madame* . . . but we could not avoid overhearing the interchange . . ." said the French woman sitting next to me on the leather banquette that lined the wall of the restaurant. "France should not be so unwelcoming, and we are sorry for the inhospitable reception you received. My husband and I are journalists with a leading newspaper, and we know the head of the Préfecture de Police rather well. With your permission, we will contact him next week and see what he can do for you."

Le Préfet, who reports directly to the Minister of the Interior, has tremendous responsibilities in the city of Paris and environs—the security of Paris; management of police and firefighters; motor vehicle registration and traffic control; registration of associations; protection of the environment; determining the dates of discount sales in large stores which can be held only twice a year; issuing permits to boulangeries for their summer vacation to assure that the bakeries in a given neighborhood are not closed at the same time; and issuing identification cards, driver's licenses, passports, and residential and work permits for foreigners. What I was sure he did *not* do was personally issue permits at the individual level when he had an entire division of fonctionnaires dedicated to this purpose.

And he is going to meet with us? I said to myself, doubting the likelihood.

Nonetheless, with a smile of gratitude, I gave the benevolent couple, Simone and Pierre, our phone number, hoping my dubious thoughts were imperceptible.

Before the end of the week, the phone rang. It was Simone. Pierre had spoken with Monsieur le Préfet who proposed that we phone his secretary to arrange a meeting. I thanked Simone profusely. After writing out and practicing my script in French beforehand so I could make myself perfectly understood, I called the secretary, introduced myself, mentioned the names of the journalists, and modestly gave the reason for our call. She placed us on her boss' calendar.

On the day of the appointment, with heads down, we once again strode past the queue of people and announced ourselves to the gendarme at the main door. He ushered us inside to a bench in the lobby where we were to sit. Someone would come for us. After a brief wait, the secretary addressed us by name and led us to the august office of Monsieur le Préfet . . . *lui-même*. His large, imposing frame was softened by a cordial air as he shook our hands and invited us to have a seat, gesturing toward the two rococo-looking fauteuils across from his enormous desk of the same vintage.

His official questions had a friendly tone. "Why did you come to France? How long do you plan to stay? What will you be doing here?" His English was broken, and we ascertained that my French was adequate to continue mostly in French and translate for John.

There was a pleasant gleam in the prefect's eyes as we answered his questions with sincere enthusiasm about my love for the music of Debussy, Fauré, Brel, and Aznavour, and John's lifelong passion to paint in the land of Matisse, Dufy, and Chagall.

After examining the documents we had given him, he said in English, "Welcome to France. I wish you all the very best our country has to offer."

We were positively grateful. John must have said *"merci beaucoup"* a hundred times over. In the outer office, the secretary completed the forms and imprinted the ink stamps, and John and I walked away, each with our one-year resident permit in hand. The law required annual renewal for three years, after which a ten-year permit could be requested. In each of the next three years, we'd call Monsieur le Préfet, and he would meet us, briefly, graciously, and effectively. John and I discussed the advantage we were given. There was nothing to do but accept it. Simone and Pierre, who initiated this fruitful connection, refused any token of appreciation, although they allowed us to take them to dinner at a restaurant, once. Three years later, in 1986, John and I each got a *carte de résident de longue durée,* valid for ten years. That was the last time we saw Monsieur le Préfet, but we never forgot him.

Immigration policies in France had changed eight years before our arrival. During *Les Trente Glorieuses*—the thirty-year period of prosperity from 1945 to 1975—foreigners coming to the country were favorably viewed because they were vitally needed for industrial jobs. Colonial migrations were most prevalent. Although colonized Algerians were legally French nationals, they were considered French *subjects* and not French *citizens*. The first migration wave to France in the late-nineteenth century were Berber-Algerians, almost exclusively men. In the second wave, around 1947, Arab-Algerians entered France in increasing numbers with their families, surpassing the Berber population that had long dominated Algerian migration. To help with the reconstruction after the war, France granted full citizenship to Algerian men living in mainland France.

During those glory years that began with France's liberation at the end of World War II, the country experienced unprecedented growth. Benefiting from the Marshall Plan, and with Charles de Gaulle at the helm, the modern state of France gave rise to a generous social security system, retirement pensions, and long holiday allocations. France's standard of living became one of the world's highest. Economic growth boosted manufacturing and the need for a larger labor force. This growth led to new laws that brought about the greatest period of immigration to France in the country's history.

But this easy entry into the country came to an end, along with the thirty prosperous years, when the 1973 oil crisis put the brakes on the flourishing economy. France no longer needed immigrant labor. The French population now saw foreigners as competition for jobs and a drain on the social welfare system. France quickly passed laws to stem the flow of immigration. Racism and racial attacks surged. Right-wing nationalist parties spread in popularity, most notably the Front National, headed by Jean-Marie Le Pen.

We had good friends in the South of France who discreetly shared the France-for-French ideology. Colette was a fine pianist and my faithful accompanist when I performed in concerts, recitals, and operetta productions in Cannes, Mougins, and Nice. Her husband, Albin, was a kind and intelligent man and a gifted medical doctor who became our personal physician when we moved to the Riviera.

Our friends were Pied-Noir which literally means "black feet." I thought the term had a derogatory ring, but Colette reassured me that it was colloquially accepted. Pied-Noir referred to people of European origin who were born in Algeria during the period of French colonization from 1830 to 1962. Algeria was only one of France's many colonies and protectorates. In their War of Independence, from 1954 to 1962, Algerian nationalist groups fought for freedom, economic equality, and leadership positions for the Berber, Arab, and Islamic people. France and the Pieds-Noirs fought to hold on to sovereignty of the country and the concept of colonial rule, but they lost. The war led to Algeria's independence, the fall of the French Fourth Republic, and the exodus of European and Jewish Algerians. The vast majority of them headed to the South of France or Corsica, where the land, sea, and climate reminded them of what was once their beloved North Africa.

Our pianist and doctor friends had been part of that mass departure. John and I noticed that, although it had been more than twenty years, Colette and Albin had never fully reconciled the circumstances surrounding their abrupt departure from their birthplace. They often reminisced about the way of life that they, their parents, and grandparents had enjoyed in Algeria. We sympathized, even though we could never truly understand their unique experience.

Colette and Albin were warmhearted in every way, except in their attitudes toward people of color. It was rare when the subject surfaced, but always uncomfortable when it did. One evening, we were invited for dinner with several of their friends on the terrace of their beautiful home in the hills of Mougins. Flowers and fruit trees surrounded the patio, and a light Mediterranean breeze cooled the hot summer air. Colette had painstakingly prepared a delicious gourmet meal, but the soirée turned sour with bitter and offensive prattle. John and I withstood listening to a vituperative exchange about the dreadful immigrants that were ruining the country.

Unable to bear another minute, I spoke up, "*S'il vous plaît*, it hurts to hear the denigration of foreigners. After all, we are immigrants to this country, too."

"*Oh, ma chère*, not you! We're talking about Arabs," Colette boldly and plainly admitted.

"You mean we are accepted because we are white?"

"*Mais non*, it has nothing to do with race. You offer cultural enrichment to us and you appreciate our way of doing things."

I was more than a little sick after this dinner. Neither the meal nor the conversation settled with me. In general, John and I avoided voicing our opinions on controversial issues facing our host country. We knew that the history of the North African population in France was complex. For example, we soon learned that not everyone from Algeria, Morocco, or Tunisia was Arab in ethnicity or Muslim in religion. Statistical information is unreliable because French law and census data prohibit any reference to national, racial, ethnic, religious or linguistic minorities. Philosophically grounded in the motto *Liberté, Egalité, Fraternité,* the law upholds the belief that the state should interact with the individual only, not communities or groups, in order to give equal treatment to everyone. Yet, critics say the law makes minorities invisible and leaves them vulnerable, and it makes it difficult to identify systemic racism. From data based on surveys, polls, geographic origin, or declarations, it was estimated that in the 1980s, around three million Muslims were living in France, about 5 percent of the population. Most were disadvantaged and twice as likely to be unemployed than the general population, and typically worked in coal-mining, iron, steel, and car manufacturing, or as street sweepers, housekeepers, and nannies.

I still hold pangs of conscience that the color of our skin, and the color of our money, afforded us the red-carpet treatment in France. Or at least that my husband and I accepted with pleasure the considerate treatment and, at times, special privilege. There also may have been truth in Colette's riposte—that the admiration we had for French high culture, coupled with our desire to assimilate into the French way of life, was partly why the French opened their arms to us. Perhaps, though, another reason for our advantages was grounded in a deeper connection going back to 1944, when Americans helped liberate France from over four years of tyrannical Nazi occupation. I say this because on many occasions I heard Frenchmen reveal to John, who fought on North African and European soil during the war, that they and their country would be forever beholden to the Americans and Allies for this supreme favor.

I abhor the thought of racism, power, and prejudice; nevertheless, I am guilty by oblivion. When my husband and I, a well-dressed white couple, skipped past hundreds of down-at-the heel brown and black folks waiting in line, it was a power play—an advantageous race card flipped in their faces. However innocent, unintentional, and unconscious our actions were, we sowed divisions and were, literally, out of line. Years later, I would confront a new kind of disparity while living in Czechoslovakia, experiencing the arbitrary hierarchy of West over East.

5

LES CINQ GLORIEUSES

*C*haracteristic of *Les Trente Glorieuses* years in France from 1945 to 1975, ours were *Les Cinq Glorieuses*—five illustrious years in Paris from 1983 to 1988. For John, this was his most artistically prolific period, painting canvas after canvas from his home atelier on the Île Saint-Louis and signing each oeuvre with the nom de plume he had used since the forties: *Jobul.* For me, these glory years were filled with musical inspiration, vocal development, and singing engagements. And for us as a couple, it was our happiest and healthiest flow in time, steeped in intellectual, cultural, and social stimuli that stirred us with delight. We were two artists in love, living in a city that revered art, and we reveled in its beauty at every turn.

This was Paris in the mid-eighties, when the city's magnetic light had lured not only the artist Jobul into its warm rays, but also the Bulgarian-born American artist Christo, who wrapped the Pont Neuf, and the Chinese-born American architect Ieoh Ming (I.M.) Pei, who designed a central entryway to the Louvre Museum. What emerged from Pei's imagination was a pyramid-shaped steel framework sheathed in reflective glass, a concept that blended both ancient and contemporary design. The controversial plan, introduced in 1984 by President François Mitterrand as one of his most ambitious *grands projets,* was the talk of the town. *Quelle horreur! The former palace of the French monarchs desecrated by a modern triangular structure?* But John was instantly sold on the idea and told Mr. Pei just that when we met him at the American Club of Paris.

Founded in 1777 by Benjamin Franklin, who was the toast of Parisian society during his mission to France to secure continued military and economic assistance for the American Revolution, the club was a lifeline for John to make friends with other expatriates. I'd tag along if the club's monthly luncheon featured a guest speaker who caught my interest, such as the mayor of Paris, Jacques Chirac, or the architect Pei.

As the dessert course was served after lunch, the slightly built man with a noble air, wearing his signature round-framed spectacles, approached the podium. The words of his opening statement still ring in my memory: "First and foremost, architecture is art . . . it is the very mirror of life." His sonorous voice expressed his lush ideas on respecting tradition while embracing change. After the presentation, John took my hand and led me to the front of the room to meet Mr. Pei. It was John's custom to shake hands and exchange a few words with anyone he deeply admired or with whom he felt an affinity. John would approach the person in his distinguished manner with a mix of respect and familiarity, as though a mutual recognition preexisted among artists who crossed paths. It was an affinity John and I shared.

We trod the earth similarly and stepped lightly into our chosen city, considering each experience a gift. Where else could we meet notable characters who believed that to create is to point the way to the future? For John and me, to be in the presence of brilliant artists like Pei—whose speech stirred our hearts—emboldened us to regard our crafts as callings.

A similar stirring touched our lives when in August 1985, Christo and his wife Jeanne-Claude carried out a transfiguration of the Pont Neuf, the bridge on the east end of the Île de la Cité that King Henry

III had constructed at the end of the sixteenth century. John and Misty imposed upon themselves a new daily routine for the duration of the project. In the late morning, they took a brief trek along the banks of the Seine to the quai d'Horloge, where John leaned into the stone embankment—his observation perch—to watch scores of organized artists, frogmen, rock-climbers, and carpenters drape Paris's oldest bridge with a golden sandstone fabric and truss it with rope. Sometimes I went along to witness Christo's unique aesthetic expression, which is considered to be environmental art as well as performance art. My ultimate thrill was to see the creative project reflected in the gleam of John's eyes and watch a whirl of imagination overtake him. He'd return to our place intent on picking up his brushes and paints because now even the sky was no longer a limit.

Being true to one's artistry involves audacity. My performance art involved wrapping and trussing myself in glamorous evening gowns, undergirded by restrictive foundational garments, and entertaining audiences with favorite French, Italian, and American songs. I was on top of the world performing gigs at the Paris Ritz Hotel, Theater d'Operette de Cannes, and traveling with my pianist on multicity concert tours. I secured some of those engagements through an agent, and others as a result of an archaic strategy: the in-person cold call.

I would drop in on Paris' top luxury hotels in the evenings to see what types of musical entertainment they offered. For most, it was nothing more than a grand piano in the lobby or lounge with a tuxedoed pianist at the keyboard producing rather bland background music. My next step was to make reservations for lunch—less expensive and less crowded than dinner—and while there, casually ask the maître d' if the hotel ever had live music that featured a singer. I would be a customer during this visit, which obliged the personnel to be accommodating to my queries.

The *crème de la crème* venue was the Paris Ritz, and where I had the best luck. My tactically planned lunch at its Michelin two-star restaurant, La Table de l'Espadon, was a gastronomic and decorative bonus in itself. The other diners and I were surrounded by a magnificent painted ceiling, Bohemian crystal chandeliers, gold drapes, and a majestic fresh flower arrangement crowning the center of the room. At my table, a delicate vase of flowers and imperial gold-motif Haviland china sat on the white linen tablecloth. Waiters glided around the room carrying trays and filling glasses as smoothly as a Balanchine ballet. Yet all of this opulence was purely the setting for the main attraction, the sumptuous and innovative cuisine.

Today a myriad of brands bear the name "Ritz," but this was *the* original Ritz conceived and created by César Ritz. The youngest of thirteen children born into a poor peasant family from a remote Swiss village, César moved to Paris as a teenager where he worked his way up in the hospitality industry. He met the famous chef Auguste Escoffier who became his best friend and prodigious mentor. By 1873 César was twenty-three years old and managing some of Europe's most eminent hotels. With the help of investors, César transformed a prince's former residence on the place Vendôme into the Hôtel Ritz Paris. When it opened in 1898, it was hailed as the swankiest hotel in the world, attracting royalty, artists, and writers. It changed the hotelier world forever.

During my lunch, the restaurant's maitre d'hotel was friendly and conversant on all aspects of his venerated place of employment. He explained that the Ritz offered piano music each evening in the larger Bar Vendôme, but only on weekends in the smaller Bar Hemingway. Occasionally, a harpist was hired for teatime, but in the maitre d's long tenure, never a singer. The maitre d' initiated the suggestion that he might arrange for me to speak with the bar manager who was responsible for the musicians. Halfway through my meal, he jaunted over to my table with a smile of success. The bar manager would meet with me in the Bar Vendôme after my lunch.

A more tepid welcome awaited me at the bar. It was evident that the bar manager lacked imagination, but he politely feigned interest in my ideas, which I only broached cursorily. He said that new concepts needed approval from the general manager, John Roozemond, whose name and phone number he wrote down and handed to me. This was exactly what I had hoped to accomplish.

The following morning, I called and spoke with Monsieur Roozemond's secretary who expressed regret that he was out of the office but she'd be happy to take a message. The kindness in her tone gave me the impetus to share what I'd prepared for her boss. I knew that cordiality and trust with the gatekeeper was the *sine qua non* to gaining an audience with the decision-maker. I knew this firsthand because I had been a secretary. My mother had been a secretary. The position has the boss's ear and controls his calendar. Something I did *not* know at the time was that I would own a staffing company in the future that specialized in placing and training secretaries and support staff, and that I'd eventually become an expert on the subject.

My pitch was well thought through. I offered a European version of "New York-style cabaret," citing the Oak Room at the Algonquin Hotel and the Café Carlyle at the Carlyle Hotel as models. French ears usually perked up when these famous American supper clubs were invoked, even though no one I spoke with, including the GM of the Ritz, had actually been to these hotels or been entertained by cabaret artists such as Julie Wilson or Bobby Short. I had. Many times. John was a habitué of these clubs during his frequent business trips to New York, and after we were married, we went together. Naturally, through John, I got to know the performers personally, thanks to his ability to make friends with the subjects of his admiration.

The essential components of the New York cabaret scene are minimal. An elegant lounge or dinner club, a crowd that loves music, and a singer and a pianist with a program. I proposed some modifications to the New York model to better fit the Ritz culture. Our show would be acoustic, as my voice could carry without amplification. This would maintain the refined atmosphere in the Bar Vendôme and avoid having loud music spill into the corridor. Sets would be short, with breaks in-between, allowing guests quiet time to converse between intervallic live music. And, instead of presenting songs only in English, I'd perform tunes from the Great American Songbook as well as French, Italian, and Neopolitan standards. If the mood and audience called for it, light classics could be thrown in.

Apparently, the secretary took notes in shorthand because she repeated back all my key points in accurate detail to ensure she would relay the message correctly. Finally, I asked if she would be so kind as to arrange a half-hour appointment with Mr. Roozemond, at which time my pianist and I would present a potpourri of the international songs that we believed would harmonize with the elegant atmosphere of the hotel and the tastes of its sophisticated clientele.

The secretary shared with me that, in addition to being responsible for all operations at the hotel, Mr. Roozemond was in charge of the property's total refurbishment and involved in the creation and development of the Ritz-Escoffier Culinary Institute, now known as one of the world's leading culinary academies. In order to preempt my potential disappointment, she laid out all the reasons he most likely wouldn't add anything to his plate, yet she promised to transmit my message and follow up with me personally.

The secretary kept her word and phoned within a few days. To my surprise, she said that Mr. Roozemond was on the other line and wanted to speak with me. I went through my spiel again with him, this time more polished and succinct, given my practice-run with his secretary. He thanked me and extended an offer to meet the following week.

My pianist was the incomparable Robert McCoy, the greatest and most versatile pianist I've ever worked with. Bob was in France on a Fulbright scholarship after earning a PhD in collaborative piano performance at the University of Southern California. He was originally from Iowa, and we were rooted in similar cultural and familial backgrounds. Besides being the epitome of professionalism, Bob was down-to-earth and good fun.

On the day of our appointment, Bob and I met the secretary in the lobby who ushered us to the Hemingway Bar where the general manager and bar manager stood. Mr. Roozemond had a tall, slender frame and an attractive square-jawed face with a full head of hair parted neatly on the side. His patrician looks belied an unpretentious congeniality. After a pleasant verbal exchange, Bob hopped to the baby grand and we launched into the up-tempo "Tonight" from Westside Story by Leonard Bernstein, then performed one verse each of "Smoke Gets in Your Eyes" by Jerome Kern, "La Vie en rose" by Louiguy and Édith Piaf, and "Arrivederci" by Umberto Bindi. Throughout the audition, the managers' smiles and sways to our rhythms energized our confidence. They were sold.

Negotiating the fee and contract in a private meeting with Mr. Roozemond was easy and refreshing. Considering the upscale conditions and high expectations, I stated my fee without blinking—the high-end of my normal fee times three—and he concurred without discussion. On each performance night, my pianist and I were given a key to a luxurious suite for use as our dressing room and green room. This was a perk I didn't expect, but we needed a place to relax between sets due to a clause in the agreement which I'd never before encountered: *Under no circumstances shall the parties sit down with the clientele.* This restriction made it awkward when the Ritz guests, usually couples, would compliment me, engage me in conversation, and invite me to sit and chat for a few minutes. I had to invent excuses that surely sounded lame. But the compliments, smiles, and applause were gratifying. The guests were happy, and our contract was renewed intermittently over a longer period of time.

My professional goals in Paris were not only to perform, but to study vocal technique, expand my repertoire and languages, and become a better performer. Here again, the stars aligned, and as the proverb states, "when the student is ready the teacher appears." I was fortunate to work with a world-renowned singing coach who taught some of the greatest singers of the twentieth century—notably Maria Callas, Teresa

Berganza, Jessye Norman, Placido Domingo, Luciano Pavarotti, Régine Crespin, and Mady Mesplé—and lesser-known, ardent singers such as myself. The way we met was luck or happenstance, and though I'm not sure that I believe in either, there is no other explanation, unless one has faith per Joseph Campbell, that if you follow your bliss you put yourself on a kind of track that has been there all the while.

On Sunday evenings, John and I watched the television program *Le Grand Échiquier*, a popular variety show hosted by Jacques Chancel. One evening, Chancel's premier guest was Placido Domingo. He was accompanied at the piano by someone unfamiliar to me, but with whom I was thoroughly impressed: Janine Reiss. After their performance, Chancel asked Madame Reiss to critique Domingo's singing so the viewers could see what the tenor experienced in a typical coaching session. Madame Reiss politely and assuredly obliged, and Domingo accepted her advice with eager deference. I was struck with a *coup de foudre* for this voice expert as we watched the way she gave vocal and stylistic direction to a world-class opera star. I never would have dreamed that one day soon it would be me standing at the other end of Janine's piano receiving instruction at her home studio.

The introduction came in early 1984 by way of baritone Jacques Rouet d'Huart. We were rehearsing in the south of France for a joint recital we performed later that year in Cannes. I asked Jacques for advice about finding a voice teacher. He reservedly said that his vocal coach rarely accepted new students, but he would ask around. After John and I returned to Paris, Jacques phoned to say that his teacher, Janine Reiss, agreed to have a consultation with me.

Outfitted in my best dress and heels, I arrived at the elegant art nouveau apartment building on the rue de Courcelles and took the elevator to the sixth floor. I felt my heart pound and my hands tremble as I rang her apartment bell. A housekeeper opened the door with a warm greeting and showed me to a sitting room. I glanced around at the old-world furnishings and felt transported into an aristocratic salon of the Belle

Époque. Janine came in, and in our self-introductions, I found myself using every formal French term of politesse that I could summon. She led me into her spacious voice studio, lined with large balcony windows on two perpendicular walls. Her studio, which never really changed over the thirty-five subsequent years, contained a Pleyel grand piano, a settee and chairs with a coffee table, bookshelves stuffed with opera scores, a small antique desk, and walls decorated with *nature-morte* oil paintings in gilded frames. Janine had a gracious and natural manner that immediately put me at ease. She invited me to take a seat and asked about my musical background, how I came to live in Paris, and the conversation flowed. She then invited me to sing for her and accompanied me exquisitely. Janine explained that she was often out of town working on opera productions, but if I could tolerate her periodic absences, she would be pleased to work with me. Elated, I thanked her and we set our next date.

Janine was a master of the French, Italian, English, and German languages, and was exigent about precise lyric diction. Janine loved the human voice and had an uncanny ability to bring out the singer's natural tone. She insisted on musical accuracy and emotional truth, and was sought after and loved by singers, composers, and conductors the world over. As I worked to reach Janine's elevated level of musicianship and authenticity, mastery emerged.

Over the years, I came to know Janine professionally and personally. When both of us were in Paris, we had weekly lessons. There were dinners and lunches at each other's homes and in posh restaurants, such as Maxim's or her favorite, the Crillon Brasserie. Our special bond between teacher and student became a thirty-five-year trusted friendship. And although I'm getting ahead of my story, Janine passed away in 2019 at the age of ninety-nine. From her, I learned that ambition, connections, and fame may be essential for a successful career, but it is hard work, humility, and respect that are the stuff of artistry.

As artists in Paris, John and I settled into the French lifestyle as if our souls had been born there and patiently waited for us to join them.

In our first days of marriage, John often told me with a smile, "For better or for worse, but not for lunch." In the States, he'd enjoyed lunching at restaurants with clients or colleagues every weekday. As a resident of Europe, his noontime outings continued. John frequented the neighborhood cafés and brasseries, and the owners and waiters lit up to see him and Misty come through the door, often catering first to Misty with a bowl of water and sometimes a small plate of meat. John's preferred lunch spot was a little corner café that featured *le hot dog*—a *saucisson* drilled into a fresh baguette with a squirt of mustard inside, served with *pommes frites* and washed down with a cold beer, usually a Kronenbourg 1664. John was in heaven.

On 28 April 1986, John stopped at a kiosk on his way to lunch to pick up his daily *International Herald Tribune*. All the newspapers screamed headlines about Chernobyl. The Number 4 nuclear reactor at the Chernobyl Nuclear Power Plant, near the city of Pripyat in the north of the Ukraine, was burning due to an explosion that had occurred days earlier. The disaster was shrouded in secrecy and became a watershed moment in both the Cold War and the history of nuclear power.

For the Soviets, publicizing a nuclear accident was considered a serious political risk. Only until the meltdown's radiation spread farther north, and officials at a Swedish nuclear plant started asking questions about what was happening in the USSR, did the Soviets finally make a brief announcement. Mikhail Gorbachev and the Communist Party downplayed the incident, both domestically and internationally, describing it as a minor event that required no special measures to protect the population. In reality, this disaster sent four hundred times more radioactive material into the sky than the atomic bombing of Hiroshima.

France, heavily invested in nuclear power, also lied to its citizens. It hid the atmospheric effects of the radioactive fallout from *la nuage de Tchernobyl*. Each day, John and I tuned into the *Météo* on French television where meteorological experts displayed maps of the nuclear cloud's trajectory using geostationary satellites. The images showed the cloud conveniently, almost miraculously, skirting France. Residents of France were told they were in the clear when they were not. While Ukraine, at ground zero, and its neighbors Belarus and West Russia, suffered the most damage from the largest radioactive release into the environment ever recorded. It was a terrible time for all of Europe.

The lethal accident happened thirteen months into Gorbachev's term. Much later, in April 2006, Gorbachev revealed something extraordinary. He wrote in the *Daily Times*, "The nuclear meltdown at Chernobyl this month twenty years ago, even more than my launch of *perestroika*, was perhaps the real cause of the collapse of the Soviet Union five years later."

For John and me, living on the continent brought international news closer to home. We learned better how the French perceive their place in history and their role on the world stage today. Our news sources were of in-depth quality, albeit not always immediate. These were the days before the digital revolution, emails, and internet technology. Instead, we absorbed print editions of newspapers and radio programming from the BBC World Service.

François Mitterrand, the candidate I was proud to help eight years prior, was now the president of France. *My early efforts paid off,* I mused with tongue-in-cheek. In November of 1984, we'd voted for Walter Mondale (former Vice President under Jimmy Carter) in Paris by absentee ballot, and we were at the Democrats Abroad campaign headquarters on election night when we learned of Mondale's lopsided loss to Reagan, who won every state but his opponent's home state of Minnesota.

Regardless of our political party, we agreed with Reagan's main foreign policy goal: to win the Cold War. In the spring of 1983, just months before John and I moved to Europe, Reagan had predicted, "I believe that communism is another sad, bizarre chapter in human history whose last pages even now are being written." Reagan saw the economic crisis engulfing the Soviet Union and heard the rumblings of protest in countries where the Soviets had a stranglehold on human freedom and dignity. On 11 March 1985, Mikhail Gorbachev became the General Secretary of the Central Committee of the Communist Party of the Soviet Union, making him the most powerful leader and policymaker in the Soviet Union. No one knew then that Gorbachev would be its last leader.

During our years in Paris, reportage on the Cold War intensified and focused on the relationship between the two nuclear superpowers. One couldn't live in Europe without being drawn into discussions with strangers on this topic, from taxi drivers to socialites. The Soviet bloc countries were right next door.

Generating most of the buzz was the rhetoric of Gorbachev. Soon into his term, he began addressing his country's failing economy and social structure, proposing daring concepts for economic liberalization, increased social openness, and greater freedom of information. Russian words like *glasnost* and *perestroika* became part of the world's lexicon. John and I read about Gorbachev's pioneering ideas for reform and wondered how this would impact the Soviet's occupied satellite states and the wider global community. But in the mid-eighties, Europe's demarcation lines between West and East still held strong, and no one predicted these to be the pre-revolutionary years that indeed they were.

As a global change quietly loomed, John and I were focused on our artistic pursuits. We were content to flourish inside our Parisian niche on the quai d'Anjou. That is, until we learned that a larger flat on the quai d'Orléans—the south-west bank of the island steeped in the light of the long afternoon sun—would soon become available. It had been almost a year since we'd met Marie-Françoise Mynard, the previous tenant of our flat. We had developed a friendship with her and her husband, cultivated by occasional meals together at home or restaurants or chatting over coffee or tea. Marie-Françoise was part of the executive board at the United Nations Educational, Scientific and Cultural Organization (UNESCO) headquartered in Paris. Jacques was a prominent psychotherapist whose *cabinet* was on the rez-de-chaussée of our quai d'Anjou residence.

Normally, when Marie-Françoise phoned, it was to relate good news or extend an invitation. But not this time. The voice at the other end of the line was low and trembling. Jacques had been diagnosed with an advanced-stage cancer. He fell gravely ill very quickly and could no longer see patients, leaving Marie-Françoise as the sole breadwinner. They were forced to vacate their spacious flat and move to a unit half the size across the courtyard in the same building. She said tangentially that breaking their lease would be costly unless new tenants could be found quickly. And while that was not meant as a cue, John and I picked it up, willingly and thankfully, even though the circumstances that provided us the opportunity to move to a bigger and sunnier flat were heartbreaking. Jacques died within a few months.

It is the custom in France to keep the deceased at home where friends and family can visit. John and I went across the courtyard to pay our respects and sit with our widowed friend. Jacques' body lay on a narrow bed centered in their living room. The scene, the atmosphere, and most importantly, Marie-Françoise, were peaceful. I found it comforting that Jacques hadn't been dragged out of his home after taking his last breath. Instead, he was washed, dressed, and laid out in the parlor. After a full day of loved ones bidding adieu, the corpse was placed in a wooden casket and moved to l'église Saint-Louis-en-l'Île for a funeral Mass before the burial. Time moves slower in the rituals and ways of the Old World.

Our second Parisian residence was *la pièce de résistance*. The spectacular view from the second-floor balcony looked out onto the river Seine and Left Bank. Barges and *bateaux mouches* sailed past. The tall, glass-paned balcony doors streamed light onto John's canvases as he painted in his studio and softly lit the music stand of my grand piano as I played and sang in the living room. Built in 1880, the six floors housed twelve units and the *loge du concierge*. Our flat had a spacious foyer and the dining room and kitchen were the largest rooms of all. We hosted many dinner parties and musical evenings. The wine flowed and spirits sailed.

Jobul painting of the view from our balcony on the quai d'Orléans on the Île Saint-Louis

John had a cocktail vernissage showing his recent and older works at which several friends purchased original Jobul paintings. Admittedly, invitations to any soirée on the Île Saint-Louis were coveted, so I won't deny that our location was half the reason our parties were successful. But John and I were a great team and grateful hosts, happy to make new friends. Our social circle was bound to expand, because whenever we met nice people, we invited them to a home-cooked dinner party and entertained them with live music surrounded by John's art collection.

If only our financial resources had flourished in tandem with our social and professional blossoming. The largesse of our *mode de vie* was not sustainable—upscale restaurants, season tickets to the opera, champagne parties, and travel around Europe—yet we didn't speak of that. "It will all work out. It always has, hasn't it?" was John's response to worries I had of any sort, not the least of which was watching our capital dwindle. In all fairness, nearly running out of money during our nine years in France wasn't caused solely by our extravagance. In the first two years, the U.S. dollar reached an all-time high, and then came that awful Plaza Agreement—a meeting of the G-5 nations at the Plaza Hotel in New York in September 1985—when they decided to realign world currencies. Notwithstanding the enormous impact this had on global macroeconomics, trade relations, and markets, in real terms for us Americans living in Paris, the franc-to-dollar ratio slid precipitously from 10:1 to 5:1, causing everything to double in cost. My singing jobs paid well, especially when I landed tours across France or concerts at high-end venues, but this income wasn't steady. John took part in art shows and exhibitions and sold a few paintings, yet only occasionally.

In blissful naiveté, I took John's reassurances to mean he had a backup plan tucked away. In fact, it seems he did, albeit with a snag. John was a collector and lover of art all his life. In the early 1950s, he purchased an original Henri Matisse drawing while the artist was still alive from the Main Street Gallery in Chicago, a reputable art dealer from where he had acquired other original paintings and quality lithographs by famous artists. During a trip to New York in the early 1980s, I was with John when the Matisse drawing was valued by Sothebys for a very tidy sum. *Jeune femme allongée* was John's backup plan.

John conferred with his trusted friend and owner of an art gallery on the Île Saint-Louis, Monsieur Levy, who thought it was a prime time to sell and had several interested buyers lined up. When he and John carried said *oeuvre* and its provenance documents across the Pont de la Tournelle to the private residence of the one and only authenticator of Matisse works, she deemed it a fake, without elaborating on how or why. John and Monsieur Levy were in disbelief, but nothing could dissuade her ruling. I have since learned that in the field of *objets d'art*, the business of authenticity is inanely and dubiously complex.

Even more complex was my relationship to alcohol, fast becoming an annoying friend. My dependence on it lurked below the surface and commingled with its constant companion, Denial. My husband's reliance on booze was a long saga that was managed on and off over the years. Not so with mine, which steadily progressed. Only when I immersed myself in music, study, and performance did the craving release me from its clutches.

My favorite French poet, Charles Baudelaire, described my unconscious state almost perfectly in his prose-poem "Enivrez-vous" from *Les petits poèmes en prose* written in 1857. His verses resonated so viscerally with me that I learned the poem by heart, which I still repeat when I need to connect with a sympathetic mind. So what if the poet is long dead? The rhetorical artifacts Baudelaire left behind are living and solid guideposts.

His lines begin with:

Il faut être toujours ivre. Tout est là : c'est l'unique question. Pour ne pas sentir l'horrible fardeau du Temps qui brise vos épaules et vous penche vers la terre, il faut vous enivrer sans trêve. Mais de quoi ? De vin, de poésie ou de vertu, à votre guise. Mais enivrez-vous.

Even the best translation of poetry cannot truly express the essence of the original. Sometimes there are words, terms, and expressions that have no equivalency in another language. For example, the French verb *enivrer*. Translated crudely as "to be drunk" cheapens its more subtle meaning—a state of mind where the senses are overcome by something, like being immersed in, or intoxicated or inebriated by, an activity that can be spiritual as well as carnal. My English language approximation:

You must always be intoxicated. All is there: it's the singular question. In order not to feel the unbearable burden of Time that weighs on your shoulders and pushes you down to the ground, you must be intoxicated without ceasing. But with what? Wine, poetry or virtue, as you wish. But intoxicate yourself.

Total immersion has always felt like my saving grace. To pour myself into something, anything, whether wine, poetry, or virtue. All the way—or nothing. This worked well during my Parisian years when my deeply buried fallibilities and addiction came to light so briefly that only occasionally was I struck by the stark awareness of our situation. One that I'd immediately try to forget: our lives sparkled because of John's hard-earned savings, but those funds could buoy us up for only so long. As for alcohol, it seemed more like a friend than an enemy, and up to that point, the friendship was capricious but manageable.

Eventually, these fleeting glimpses of reality began to compound and demand our attention. We were forced to acknowledge that neither 16, quai d'Orléans nor Paris were forever. John had a plan to which I agreed for lack of a better idea. Alas, our five glorious years in Paris turned into an unforgettable and movable feast, as we packed up and headed south.

6

RIVIERA BLUES

T*he idea to move to France's southern coast* was sparked by John's best friend, Deon Sutton, whom he'd met through the American Club of Paris. Around the summer of 1987, Deon and his wife Simone—a former Lanvin model in her seventies still bearing a mannequin's silhouette encircled by an aura of haughty charm—had already abandoned Paris for Nice's warmer climate, calmer pace, and lower cost of living.

Even though we had personal and professional connections in the region, I had never imagined residing in a seaside resort town until John laid out his plan. We were like-minded when considering most decisions. When not, the resolution fell on the person whose proposal made the most sense or who was most passionate about the outcome. I wanted to stay in Paris with all my heart and might have been content downgrading to a Parisian garret, those meager rooms designed as maid's quarters on the top floor of buildings where poor artists often lived. But I never said it out loud because it was only somewhat true, and besides, I had more than myself to consider. I was in a partnership of two loving people with similar goals but increasingly different needs.

John felt at home in the south of France, a painter's paradise. Paris may be called the City of Light, but nothing compares to the shimmering glow that reflects the sea and sky of the Côte d'Azur. Sunlight was important to John. Its warmth soothed his elder bones. Its brightness animated the palette on his ever-more-colorful canvases.

John at home in his art studio in Nice, France

Nice is the largest city on the French Riviera, an eighty-mile stretch of land from Saint-Tropez to Menton. The Mediterranean coast offered John much to do, see, and gain in creative expression. During most of the twentieth century, this beautiful strip and the region above it, Provence, was home to John's favorite artists: Henri Matisse, Marc Chagall, Raoul Dufy, Pablo Picasso, and Fernand Léger. Although a generation older than him, these painters were alive during much of John's lifetime. By the time we moved to the region, what remained of their illustrious lives were their works displayed in museums, theaters, chapels, and chateaux.

In our last year in Paris, signs of diminished health had begun to manifest in John. His stride was slower. The Metro's long staircases wore him out. His vim and vigor waned. And though there was no sudden demise, and his daily routine and positive disposition hadn't faltered, I looked for ways to keep his health robust and convince him to moderate his beer consumption and cigarette smoking. This is why I thought John's plan to live near the sea might be the physical boost he needed, in addition to relieving our financial situation. He could take longer walks year-round in the temperate climate, he could swim whenever he wanted, and he could resume his regular lunches and inspiriting conversations with his friend Deon.

We had brainstormed other options, like the most obvious—return to the United States. But where? We had sold our house in Omaha, a town with slim prospects for a gainful singing career. John grasped at straws, suggesting we move to New Orleans, a place I'd never visited.

"Darlin', you could sing in the jazz clubs, and I would find a job somewhere," he submitted. That proposal was so pitiful, it motivated me to find a way to remain in Nice. Moving back to the States was always an option, but in my mind, a last resort. I had two tenable reasons for staying in France, besides the fact that we loved it there—John's health and my profession.

For a retired American, there were advantages to living in France in terms of health care. As I recall, foreigners with longterm resident status in France qualified for the national health system. The French system gave more complete coverage, including dental, at a lower cost for a retired person than the U.S. health system provides with Medicare and a private supplemental plan. But in any case, we needed an interim insurance policy because Medicare doesn't cover Americans living abroad and the French long-term residency process takes time. We found a policy through the Association of Americans Resident Overseas (AARO). Providentially, the association launched its insurance program at the same time we moved to Paris, and John was their very first customer. The premiums were affordable, the benefits covered 100 percent of medical expenses with no annual limit, and it offered guaranteed lifetime coverage with no age limit, as long as we resided overseas.

Still, the figurative handwriting was on the wall: It was my turn to be the breadwinner. If I was to be the main income generator, my prospects in the music world were better in Europe where artists are esteemed and where I had more connections.

While we didn't belabor the issue, John and I had a serious discussion early in our marriage about our end-of-life wishes. We promised to uphold each other's requests to the best of our abilities when the time came, depending on circumstances within or beyond our reach. As usual, John and I had similar wishes. Should either of us become infirm, we wanted to stay home, remain together, and avoid institutional facilities. With playful sincerity, I assured John that he could never live in a nursing home because I'd have to go with him . . . so that was settled.

In early 1988, we set off for Nice to apartment hunt. The first place we visited was in a nondescript building in the thick of a noisy commercial district. With map in hand, we walked to our second appointment via the promenade des Anglais and the quai des États-Unis to 1, rue des Ponchettes. We stood in front of a rose-colored stucco building that hugged the historic Colline du Chateau, or Castle Hill, which had been the site of a medieval citadel long ago destroyed. Just around the bend was the Vieux Port of Nice, and around the corner in the other direction was the famous Cours Saleya flower and produce market.

We stepped into the airy entranceway and took the elevator to the fifth and penultimate floor. On entering the flat, the bright, clean foyer and large living room were immediately rendered inconsequential compared to the breathtaking vista of sea and sky that stood out like a huge Dufy painting framed by the large balcony doors. We stepped onto the balcony and there before us was a light-blue horizon over an azure seascape. On closer observation, we had a miniature view of the beachfront activities below. Topless women and men sunbathed, swam, and frolicked on the seashore. John was certainly sold. How could I object in the face of such intense natural beauty and an apartment that would cut our rent costs in half?

The layout of the flat was perfectly suitable, with three rooms overlooking the sea: a living room, a bedroom, and a small art studio for John. On the back side was another bedroom, a bathroom, and a *cabinet de toilette*. Just to the left of the entryway was a compact *cuisine* with a tiny balcony so close to the Colline's rock wall that you could touch it. Looking straight down to ground level, about a dozen tightly fitted one-car garages were cut into a stone alcove where residents parked their cars. Our flat came with a garage where I could practice the science of geometric relativity, maneuvering the car by inches inside the cramped space.

For five years we had enjoyed the freedom of not owning a car, but that needed to change if we lived on the coast. Soon after we returned to Paris, John took a signed and numbered Matisse lithograph off our living room wall and carried it to Monsieur Levy, his art dealer on the Île Saint-Louis. Within days, Monsieur was able to sell it for twelve thousand dollars. We purchased a car with a portion of that income. I would have gone for something French and fun, like a Citroën Deux-Cheveaux, but John was a longtime Ford customer and chose the best-selling car in Britain and popular throughout Europe—a brand-new Ford

Escort. Apparently, Prince Charles had given one to Princess Diana as an engagement gift (which makes one wonder). The windfall from the lithograph also covered the transport of our worldly belongings, which by then had known the rumble of moving vans from Omaha to Paris, quai d'Anjou to quai d'Orléans, and now, Paris to Nice.

We packed our Escort with a few essentials, including our adventurous pup Misty, and drove to Nice by way of the autoroute to Grenoble, where we picked up the Route Napoléon through the Alps. The spectacular drive follows the journey taken by Napoléon Bonaparte in his 1815 escape from Elba to Grenoble. John complained that I took the hairpin curves too fast, and I tried to slow down.

The owner of our new apartment had given us a choice—either wait one month to take occupancy, so she could have the interior painted, or move in right away, have it painted in our own good time, and get the first month rent-free. We sent for my brother Joe, a professional house painter, to come from Nebraska. He got a free vacation out of it, and we got our flat expertly brushed with pomegranate red in the foyer-turned-dining room, and *vieux rose* on all the other walls. We also enjoyed time with my brother, exploring our new neighborhood and swimming in the sea, despite John's reluctance to join us at the beach.

The shoreline of the Riviera is mostly blanketed by soft white sand, but to our chagrin, not so in Nice. In this distinctive crook of the coast, the beaches are filled with smooth stones that for eons have washed down from the mouth of the Var and Paillon rivers. Walking on the rocks felt like a firm shiatsu foot massage to me, but for John, the rugged surface hit painful trigger points and threw him off balance. We tried special rubber shoes designed for swimming, but they couldn't alter an uneven terrain. Further, it takes strength to grapple the pulling tide and undercurrents of the Mediterranean Sea, and John didn't always have sure footing even in the best of conditions.

The Riviera has been called the playground of the rich and famous, but I saw it as a last-stop for old retirees from northern climes. A playground, yes, but for transient vacationers who pack the beaches and promenades from June through September. During the official holiday months of July and August, the coast is even more congested with legions of scantily clad visitors milling around town and cars idling bumper to bumper along the seafront roads. One can find glamour, glitz, and luxury in Monte Carlo and Cannes, but rarely in Nice.

This unique geographic location nestled in one of the most gorgeous parts of the world between France and Italy had a tumultuous history spanning from 350 BC to 1860 AD, when the city then called *Nizza* was annexed to France. While a mix of French and Italian influence permeates the city's architecture, muted pastel colors, and cuisine, there is a notably local Niçois culture unto itself. Living among the city's transplants and transients, the indigenous Niçois people have inhabited this strip of land for centuries and speak the native dialect *Nissart.* The Niçois are mostly clustered in Vieux Nice, the city's vibrant Old Town. They work as shop owners, seafarers, and restaurateurs. Only a few restaurants have been awarded *la cuisine nissarde* label with dishes like pissaladière, socca, and ratatouille made in the authentic tradition using local produce. It may be possible to duplicate the recipes elsewhere, but unless the ingredients are rooted in this land, you haven't tasted the ambrosial and earthy *cuisine nissarde.*

Unlike my mellifluous acculturation to the lifestyles in Paris and later in Prague, I always felt like a foreigner in Nice, as if I were on an extended vacation and should be leaving any day for home. This land-locked Nebraska native was never a sun-and-sand girl. While there was nothing wrong with whiling away hours on a beach or drinking chilled Côtes de Provence vin rosé on a shaded terrace as a complement to a succulent lunch, I would have much rather been running for a bus in Paris to make my next singing lesson on time.

At first, I traveled back to Paris regularly to work with Janine Reiss and see friends. However, those trips became less frequent when I came to terms with my new location. I modified my musical offerings and job search strategy to accommodate a casual resort environment. It was demoralizing, but I had some success when I decided to stop making comparisons to Paris and succumbed to taking the role of girl singer in a jazz band.

Jazz is a sophisticated genre of music, but simply not my style. I was able to pull it off because, as a trained musician, I could technically learn its rhythms and improvisational methods. Even more to my advantage, most jazz standards originate from the American show tunes that I grew up on and can sing in my sleep. I met a seasoned jazz musician and asked him to put together a quartet. Together, we had a fine sound, and I was able to score some coveted gigs around the area. During the run of the Cimiez Jazz Festival, *Anne-Marie Kenny and the In-Bloom Band* was the lounge band at The Beach Regency in Nice, the hotel that housed the festival musicians.

I respected my fellow band members. They were devoted to jazz as an art form. When they played inside a loud, smoky bar, they were happy to jam and riff and make musical discoveries for each other, whether or not anyone else listened. But I—who loved opera, art songs, musical theater, melismatic melodies, stylized arrangements, storytelling, languages, poetry—never, ever wanted to create music that droned beneath loud conversations, shrill laughter, and the whizz of blenders at the bar. But that was precisely what became of me.

I wore my elegant gowns and looked fit to kill, but the bar manager suggested I deck myself in something sexier. Vexed and humiliated, I went to the Old Town and found a cheap skin-tight outfit with a large, silver chain belt around the hips. The manager and band members were wild about my new look, but I wondered if the audience knew that I was faking it, that it wasn't me inside the black stretch pants, that my singing voice was devoid of soul.

When the international festival musicians came back to the hotel after their performances at Cimiez, they hung out in the lounge and listened to our group. That should have impressed me, and it did to some degree.

There were a few memorable moments, like when Etta James's drummer jammed with us. When he later invited me to his room, I obliged. I had verily sold my soul, but not my body. That was judiciously loaned with no strings attached.

Les Vendredi et Samedi
Anne Marie Kenny chanteuse américaine
anime les Soirées
de la Plage Beau Rivage

Publicity poster that reads: "On Fridays and Saturday evenings, Anne Marie Kenny, American chanteuse, entertains at the Plage Beau Rivage" (Nice, France c. 1988)

It's a mountainous feat to excavate long-buried feelings that revive the turmoil of my first few years in Nice. To face pungent emotions that accompanied my actions and arrange them into a composite of words. To take care not to compromise truth to abate my humiliation.

What the world calls infidelity began for me in Nice when a smoothly polished banker from Monaco named Paul started to pursue me. We met at the Opéra de Monte Carlo during the intermission of *Il Barbiere di Siviglia* starring a young Cecilia Bartoli in the leading role. Paul was tall and broad-framed, his voice had the timbre of a bassoon. He was with his mother; I was with John. Afterwards, Paul and I met again, and again, for platonic but flirtatious lunches. It was the first time as a married woman that I did anything like this. His delicate advances were artfully crafted. After months of flattering attention, I finally gave in. We spent a day and night together in Paris. Although I was nervous, he proved to be a skillful lover and I slept with a feeling of contentment. Yet no sooner had morning come than he shrugged me off with arrogant disregard. During breakfast in the lobby, as I felt aglow, he commented sarcastically on my crumpled hair. We took a taxi to the airport in near silence as he read *Le Monde*. But most crushing of all, on the short Paris-Nice flight, he sat in first class as I rode in coach. I came home and was sick in bed for a week, overwhelmingly devastated.

Very soon after, Janine Reiss called out of the blue and asked me to join her while she was working with the Chorégies d'Orange summer opera festival near Avignon. I spent a whole day with Janine, and over lunch I told her everything. She listened sympathetically, then paused and said it reminded her of a similar story that Maria Callas had confided to her. Maria told Janine how Giuseppe di Stefano had madly chased after her and once he had made his conquest, he became ugly, critical, and denigrating. It was widely known that the flamboyant di Stefano reveled in his image as a bon vivant and bragged publicly about his affair with Maria Callas.   Receiving this loving response from Janine about my personal tragedy meant the world to me. I thought, if my story has a commonality with Maria Callas, then at least I'm in solidarity with a woman I revere. At least I'm not alone.

And I needed solidarity, then and now, as I piece together remembrances I would sooner let lie. Yet my memories have wings. They land on my shoulders and rest like a weighted yoke. Others squeeze against my heart. A few float in on the hum of an absolving lullaby, and I cherish those.

What I know now, but didn't know then, is that alcoholism warps judgment and is a progressive illness. One can delay its tenacious trajectory, but not forever. Whenever I had an artistic outlet with challenging work, I could shove my drinking habit off to the side and get down to business. But alcoholism doesn't take well to dismissal. It followed me around, waiting patiently, hulking in the corner, ready to pounce the moment my healthy activity concluded.

I managed to carry on, with teetering sanity, some days better than others. One afternoon, John was out and I was alone in the apartment. I sat on the red couch in our living room with a majestic sea view before me, drinking wine, smoking hashish, and alternating between sobbing and praying. Not only was the room spinning, but my thoughts were dark and tangled. I wanted to die. I hated Nice. I hated the mediocre singing gigs. I feared for my future caring for John. I began to imagine how I'd go about taking my life. Like a jolt of lightning, I was stricken by horror at the idea I was plotting suicide. *No, I cannot want this. I cannot do this to John, to myself. But how can I end this unbearable panic and sadness? Should I stop drinking? Maybe I need to moderate. Yes, I'll cut down and see if that will help ease my mind.*

On that one afternoon, the worst afternoon, the confluence of my disease and fear caught up with me. It must have marked a turning point, because I don't remember ever again entertaining an early death. Nonetheless, depression smoldered beneath my attempts at stability and controlled drinking, and there were more dark days to come. Days that were starkly contrasted in a chiaroscuro—light and dark—allegorical painting of our time in Nice.

In the midst of the gorgeous surroundings of the Côte d'Azur, John and I also shared golden moments. Sets of friends and family came to visit. We toured every art museum along the coast more than once. John produced beautiful seascapes, landscapes, and abstract paintings. With our pup Misty, we often took the spectacular short drive to neighboring Italy for lunch in Ventimiglia. The freshest fish, fruits, and vegetables in the world made up our regular diet. I knew these days were special, albeit complexly difficult.

While I don't remember how it was brought to our attention in the summer of 1988, the Victorine Film Studios in Nice (considered the Hollywood of the French Riviera) was looking for extras for the filming of *Dirty Rotten Scoundrels*. John thought it would be something fun to do. We went to the studios for a line-up and were both chosen as supernumeraries in one of the final scenes. There is incessant waiting around on a film set while the sound, camera, and set directors get everything coordinated. During one of these downtimes, John found himself not far from Michael Caine and didn't hesitate to chat with him, or later, with Steve Martin as well.

Months afterward, I auditioned for a larger film project. Three screenplay adaptations of novels by best-selling British thriller writer James Hadley Chase were to be shot in English and dubbed in French: *Présumé dangereux, Have a Nice Night,* and *Want to Stay Alive.* There were only two consistent characters in the series—the leading man and his secretary. Michael Brandon played the former and I played the latter. The other actors changed in each film; among them were Robert Mitchum, Marisa Berenson, and Guy Marchand.

No one was more surprised than I, an unknown in the movie business, to land this small but important role. After a reading, director Jeannot Szwarc (*Jaws 2* and *Ironsides*) called me to his office for an interview. He looked over my résumé and asked where the acting experience was.

"Singers *are* actors. Every song is a new script and a new character to play," I said, without missing a beat.

Monsieur Szwarc was intrigued, and we carried on an interesting discussion around what makes a great actor, like two colleagues exploring ideas. He hired me for all three films. The financial compensation was significant, as were the artistic rewards. A lingering perk is that these films still rerun regularly on French television.

During the filming of *Scoundrels*, John met Shirley, a beautiful woman who, along with her husband, became our close friends. She was married to Michael (Miki) Karoli, a German guitarist, composer, and founding member of the legendary space-rock band *Can*. They owned a house called Le Moulin, a converted olive mill in the foothills of the Alps about a forty-minute drive from Nice. Shirley's mother was Irish and her father was Kenyan. Michael had an elite education in Switzerland, but rejected any semblance of cultural and social conformity, and he abhorred his father's involvement in World War II Germany. To the consternation of his parents, he married a woman of mixed race, took a portion of his patrimony, and moved to the south of France with his bride.

It's just as well that John and I didn't know the extent to which Miki was an international superstar worshipped by rock fans. He and Shirley loved John and me without pretense, and the feelings were mutual. I spent many full days at Le Moulin, and when I was too drunk to drive home, I'd stay overnight. The aesthetic and creative kinship I shared with the Karolis saved me from the deep end of depression. Conversely, the liberal use of drugs and alcohol hastened the evolution of my addiction.

I consciously fought to keep alcohol, worries, and artistic frustration from overtaking me. The idea that nature abhors a vacuum is more than a cliché. The paltry music scene left me empty, and open . . . to whatever could keep me hanging on.

I turned to writing. Poetry, essays, articles, songs, a biography of my father.

I turned to amatory attention. The absence of the intimacy that graced the early years of our marriage became unbearable for me. John and I had spoken precious little about the ebb and eventual evanescence of our sex life, but then again, we didn't always have to talk to communicate. After eight beautiful years of simpatico energy, our biological clocks had begun to tick asynchronously. His was winding down, mine was revving up.

Had I always been sober and clearheaded, perhaps I would have denied or resisted this physical craving. I was in my late thirties, and yearned to be enveloped. I was grateful to the men who came to my rescue. While they came and went quietly, remorse burrowed in and stayed. I remember this much with crystal clarity: at that time of my life, besides quelling a biological ache, I was clutching for sanity. Not love. I had that.

John gave me all that he had materially, morally, and lovingly. Neither of us harbored resentment for what the other lacked, or did to cope. While it was left unspoken, I am sure John was hurt by the situation, by his own inadequacies, and by any inkling he may have had about my escapades. I never lied, nor spoke about them, and he never asked. Years later, it was I who broached the subject, to beg forgiveness.

I turned to the sea. I swam every morning, except when the water was coldest in January and February or if the red flags were flying to warn of whitecaps and rip currents. The exhilaration of plunging into chilly saltwater zaps every ounce of depression, at least in the moment. I learned to hear and trust the voice of the waves. When I finished swimming and was ready to come ashore, the pull of the tide spoke, *Wait for me. Let me take you in.* When the waves swept in, so did I. People drown in the sea along the French Riviera every year. It's a force that will overwhelm or befriend its guests. One must succumb to the velocity and timing of the sea and go with, never against, its flow. The water was my higher power, and it had my attention.

During my swims, I was given the strength to make a resolution, one that I knew I must keep. Like a line in the sand, I sketched a line in my mind that couldn't be washed away. It represented a specific dollar amount below which our bank balance mustn't descend. It was the minimum needed to move ourselves and our things for a new start. Where, when, and how was yet to be revealed. In the meantime, I would try to earn enough to delay the inevitable.

I carried on with occasional gigs that brought in some money. I held to the belief that, when the time came and we had to move, like the voice of the waves, I'd be guided. I continued to drink, have lovers, swim, cook for John, walk with him to restaurants, and hold hands in bed at night and say prayers aloud, a habit we never outgrew.

I've been a vivid dreamer all my life. During the restless years in Nice, a recurring scenario appeared in my sleep state. I'd be riding in the backseat of a car, heading toward a cliff, trying to slow it down, until finally, at one delineated spot, I'd vigorously grab the steering wheel and make a sharp right or left turn.

I awoke. It was the fall of 1989. We were nearing that place in the road, perhaps still a few hundred miles out.

7

THE SONG

For *as long as I can remember*, I dreamed of living in France. I first encountered French music and language through Aunt Rosanne, my father's youngest sister. Rosanne also gave my siblings and me our first piano lessons. She felt it was incumbent on her, in the absence of our father, to ensure that we had an appreciation for the finer things of life. She, too, had lost her father at an early age. My grandfather, Lee Roy Kenny, was an attorney with a promising future when he had a fatal heart attack at forty-four, only nine months after the family upgraded to a stately home in the Dundee area of Omaha.

Nevertheless, my grandmother, Clare Connor Kenny, found ways to maintain a certain standard. Not willing to lose the house or step down in social status, Grandmother's eight children doubled and tripled-up in bedrooms on the third floor so the larger second-floor rooms could be let out to boarders.

Grandmother insisted that her children acquire social graces, possess impeccable table manners, and practice kindness—qualities she deemed paramount to making one's way in the world. Her motto was, "We are poor, but pretentious."

The house swarmed with children, their friends, and the boarders. The dining room table, with all extension leaves in place, was set daily for large sit-down dinners. My Uncle Dave dated Letitia Baldrige, who was often at the Kenny house. She later became an American etiquette expert and author who served as Jacqueline Kennedy's social secretary. I wouldn't be surprised if my grandmother taught young Letitia a thing or two, or at least, emulated the manners on which Letitia would later become the authority.

Rosanne and her sister, my Aunt Moo, learned *le français soutenu*—the most formal register of the French language—at Omaha's Duchesne Academy, an all-girls Catholic school. The prestigious day and boarding school was founded in 1882 by an order of French nuns called the Société du Sacré-Cœur. By any measure, Duchesne offered the highest standard of education in the region at a commensurately high tuition rate. My grandmother was intent on having her only two girls educated there; the six boys would do just fine at Central High public school. Grandmother worked out an effective arrangement with Duchesne's principal. Rosanne and Moo earned their tuition as "char-girls," cleaning the dorms, hallways, and bathrooms of the boarding students. After all, their older brothers held full-time jobs at the Union Pacific Railroad during their high school years and brought their paychecks home to their mother. My father, the second oldest, worked at the rail yards after school on the three-to-eleven shift.

A wrenching twist of fate, or of providence, had abruptly removed the patriarchs from both my father's family and my own family, leaving practically penniless young widows to manage. Through sheer determination, the matriarchs lifted their children out of tragic circumstances to a place of privilege—not of money—but of mind, heart, and spirit. This gifted place appeared gradually along a rough road of loss and suffering.

Gustave Flaubert said, "Life itself holds such *tristesse* that it cannot be supported without some grand alleviation." Writers Flaubert and Baudelaire, born the same year in France, painted modern realism through poetry and prose, never mincing words to depict life's sorrows. In my family, deep feelings were expressed in outbursts, but never examined or talked through. Grief was contained behind the stoic stiff upper lip that was considered a sign of strength. For us Kenny kids, our *tristesse* found an escape route only through the grand assuagements we each created for ourselves.

The mood in our house was dismal after my father's fatal boating accident. Too young to understand what happened, I couldn't ignore the heavy energy or the sound of Mother weeping. It was as though our house had cavalierly tipped upside down and shook so hard that all of its contents shattered, then turned right side up again. We were supposed to carry on without acknowledging our brokenness and pain. Mother almost never spoke of Dad. Each of us children suffered the same loss, each coped differently. We were together, but in many ways, on our own. À la Flaubert, my childhood alleviations gave me wings to fly away from sorrow through dreams, fantasies, and music.

Dreams are cloudy by nature, but a particular dream occurred so often in my childhood that a precise sensory recall is easily coaxed from my memory. From age two and a half—when my dad died—to about age six, nighttime revealed a vivid world where my father waited. He was there to greet me, he took me in his arms, we played and sang and laughed. Then something terrible suddenly happened. My body diminished to the size of a pea, Daddy disappeared, and I freewheeled into a frightening void. My cries and screams woke up the entire household. My mother would come in, agitated and afraid, to settle me down. I would then sleep through the rest of the night. Conversely, all was well with my days.

Another sleep disturbance I had was occasional somnambulism. I'd get out of bed and walk through the house, searching. My eyes were open, but I was asleep, or so my mother told me. She would hear me rummaging around downstairs, often finding me in the refrigerator room where I had set up my doll house. Mother tried to rouse me with

Mom and Dad: Veronica Janda Kenny & Dan L. Kenny (c. 1949)

Christmas 1954, seven months after our dad died. Left to right: Nancy, Joe, Susan, Mary Lou, Anne Marie

cold water or a slap on my face. Finally, she sought professional advice, something not often considered in the fifties. The counselor explained that children as young as two or three can't comprehend the death of a parent on any level except emotionally. Mercifully for me, the counselor told Mother that I would eventually outgrow it, but in the meantime, she should gently lead me back to bed whenever I sleepwalked and not splash or slap me. During the nightmares, she should cradle me in her arms. Unfortunately, the best cradler and cuddler was the parent who died. But, Mom tried. My nocturnal trauma gradually ended, and other mollifications helped soften the distress in my inner world.

I created a veritable home within our home in the company of my two dolls. I was a faithful and doting mother to them, showering them with attention and security. The love felt reciprocal; I was happy when we were together. By the time I started high school, my dolls were no longer my constant companions, but they occupied a special place in my bedroom, and I stayed connected to the tenderness they represented.

The most buoyant relief from the melancholic underpinning in our home was the music that filled every nook and cranny. Mom played her favorite songs on the piano and albums on the record player. The Wurlitzer console was in such constant use from our piano practice that Mom found a free upright for the basement so two budding virtuosos could practice at once. My sisters and I formed a singing quartet under the direction of Susan, the eldest, with accompaniment by Nancy. The Kenny Sisters sang at official functions around town, and we often won talent contests.

Music was no substitute for our father, but it was the trade-off that Destiny handed us, and it came to be our greatest healer.

What my mother couldn't offer in the classical arts, our Aunt Rosanne provided. We were spellbound when Rosanne sat at the piano, dreamy-like, and played Debussy's *Claire de lune* and the *Arabesques* with utmost sensibility, or when she accompanied herself as she sang "La Vie en rose" and "Beau soir" with impeccable French diction. Her speaking voice was warm and rich, and when she sang, her dramatic soprano tone had a supple quality that flowed like liquid honey.

Rosanne's cultural gifts gave me a head start on my French studies at Mercy High School. I came to the class with a love for the Gallo-Romance language, its soft liaisons, gentle gutturals, and nasalized vowels. My French teachers, Mercy nuns, were open to my enthusiasm and gave me creative license to pursue my interests. For instance, instead of writing an assigned term paper, my request to work on a different project was granted: converting an American pop song into French. It was surely a crude translation because after a tedious word-for-word search in Cassell's French-English Dictionary, I attempted to set the verses to rhyme. On the day we were to present our essays, Sister Marilyn raised an eyebrow of apprehension when I strutted to the front of the classroom with my guitar and sang "Harper Valley PTA" in French. It was a big hit with my classmates, but for the life of me, I can't imagine how I translated "the day my momma socked it to the Harper Valley PTA."

The confluence of languages, music, and theater was the greatest discovery in my high school years and became my soulful passion ever since.

I'd frequent local record shops and comb through vinyls and cassette tapes in search of recordings by French singers and composers. I learned the songs of Jacques Brel, Charles Aznavour, and Edith Piaf. French *chansons* touched me like nothing else. The rawness of the lyrics, sometimes gushing with love, sometimes earthy and crude, expressed what I wanted to say. Like the literary genius of Flaubert and Baudelaire, songwriters Aznavour and Brel could turn a universally human story into epic poetry set to music.

I relied on music to assuage pain, to express joy, to celebrate triumphs.

It was one of Jacques Brel's songs—a testament to idealism and love—that rang inside me during the 1989 Velvet Revolution when the people of my mother's ancestral homeland stood up to their oppressors and demanded freedom. The liberation was triumphant, and unexpected.

A new momentum in Eastern Europe had begun to build while John and I still lived in Paris in the mid-eighties. We anticipated an ease of tension on the East European horizon because of Gorbachev's *glasnost,* but neither of us saw the revolutions coming.

According to accounts from those who were there, the phenomenal events rolled out one by one, moment by moment, without prior planning or premonition of the outcome. Even with the political transformation already begun in Poland and Hungary, no one expected the changes to be enduring or of any significant magnitude.

Of course, in hindsight after the revolution, people made claims of having predicted the watershed changes. British historian and writer Timothy Garton Ash was a participant in the revolutions. He wrote about this phenomena in his book *The Magic Lantern:*

> The passage of time produces its own secular distortions. One thing that happened rather quickly in the early 1990s was that history was rewritten—not in the deliberate, Orwellian way of communist states, but through the much more subtle, spontane-ous, and potent workings of human memory. Suddenly, Western politicians "remembered" how they had all along predicted the end of communism. And suddenly, almost everyone in the East had been some sort of a dissident. The ranks of the opposition grew miraculously after the event. Former communist leaders also produced remarkable memoirs . . . some said they anticipated the fall of communism as early as the mid-1980s. Was there a record of this? Well, no. You see, they could not have said this out loud . . .

For those who pretended to have foreseen the revolutions of 1989, I refer to Václav Havel's assertion years later, "I find people completely prepared for history rather suspect."

From our home in Nice, John and I watched on television as the Czechoslovaks took to the streets, formed a brand-new government, and gave a dissident playwright the role of president. I told myself I had to do something. *I was one of them, genetically and soulfully.* I felt an even closer kinship, having read some of Václav Havel's samizdat writings about living in truth. Havel envisioned a post-totalitarian world where the oppressed would regain their dignity.

I thought, here was a man who had no business being an idealist, having lived under constant surveillance, harassment, and years of imprisonment, with his books, plays, and essays banned. And yet, Havel's answer to tyranny was a message of truth, hope, and personal and collective responsibility. When his vision became a reality in 1989, journalists and cameramen gave us and the rest of the world a front-row seat to the festivities.

Our seats, John's and mine, comprised a pair of green leather mid-century chairs placed side-by-side in front of the television set. A magnificent seascape shimmered outside the balcony doors at one end of the room, my black grand piano stood stalwart at the other. Caught in the euphoria of events and the tipsiness of champagne John had popped for the occasion, I stood up as if the piano heralded my next number—"Quand on n'a que l'amour." Brel's original French lyrics speak of a world where the human race cares for each other, where love and forgiveness reign. Its utopian theme is much like John Lennon's "Imagine" or Bernstein and Sondheim's "Somewhere." In Brel's world, when we only have love, a grand voyage is proclaimed, possibilities abound, promises are kept, cannons are met with song, destiny is spurred at every crossroads, and all is possible with love.

I chose this song, or it chose me, because I, too, am an idealist, and it epitomized my jubilation in that moment. The artists and civic-minded citizenry holding candles and clinking keys in Wenceslas Square and Letná Park were my kinfolk, and I was proud of them.

Honoring Brel's prayerful theme and poetic meter, I wrote an English rendition to the song for the occasion of the Velvet Revolution. Unlike

my high-school days, when clumsy attempts at word-for-word translations of song lyrics fell short, I didn't try for a literal conversion of Brel's
poetry. I created something fresh.

It took me a few days to finesse my verses before I typed them on
my portable Canon word processor, folded the sheet into an envelope,
and addressed it to President Václav Havel; Hradčany Castle; Prague,
Czechoslovakia. My cover letter was a message of congratulations to
Mr. Havel and his countrymen, from one of their own of shared roots,
with a humble offering in the form of a poem-song inspired by their
courage and faith.

I expected no reply. This was pure gift.

> When we only have love
> We will share other's pain
> And partake of their joys
> No blame, no shame.
>
> When we only have love
> The battles will end
> And the rifts in the structures
> And cultures will mend.
>
> When we only have love
> Then the world becomes free
> We embrace our neighbor
> True solidarity.
>
> When we only have love
> We speak from the heart
> We stand as one people
> Not races apart.

When we only have love
Then the freedom bell rings
We raise up our voice
In harmony we sing.

Then with nothing at all
But the strength of our love
We'll shine forth our light
As the stars above.

A few weeks later, on a beautiful January afternoon in Nice, as most afternoons are on the Côte d'Azur, John brought up the mail to our apartment with a Cheshire grin. My heart jumped when he handed me an official-looking letter from Czechoslovakia. We went onto our terrace in the sunlight to ceremoniously open it. I held the envelope, made of thin lightweight blue paper used for airmail post, and slid the letter opener under the fold, taking care to keep the return address intact. It was a one-page, typewritten letter which started with, *"Dear Madame Kenny, on behalf of President Václav Havel, who was most touched by your letter and song, we would like to invite you to visit our country and perform at our legendary music club, the Reduta."*

The letter went on to explain how to contact them should I wish to accept their offer, in which case, I should be assured that they would take care of all arrangements. After a flowery complimentary close, it was signed by Mr. Ivo Letov, Director of Pragokoncert.

8

JOURNEY EAST

In my hand was an invitation from someone I'd never met, but with whom I was connected through his writing. My mind darted back to Václav Havel's essays printed in the international press that had so inspired John and me. Better known abroad than in his own country, he wrote with wit, humor, and bravery about living in truth inside a state that governed by fear and demanded conformity. Now, the subject of my admiration, this playwright in the Prague Castle, had read *my* writing, and it moved him to respond. From photos, I knew him as an appealingly shy man in rumpled sweatshirt and jeans (someone who wouldn't think twice about my tangled hair, and might even like it). John and I sat down on our terrace chairs and talked. I held the letter tightly in case a mistral wind kicked up from out of the blue and carried this dream into the Mediterranean Sea.

John was thrilled for me. Once it was settled that I'd accept this golden opportunity, I sprung into action. The first order of business was to call Bob McCoy. By then, Bob had finished his Fulbright tenure in Paris and was on the faculty at the University of Maryland School of Music. Bob jumped at the chance to perform in Prague, providing the timeline worked around his teaching schedule. Once I secured the performance dates, he'd fly to Nice to rehearse prior to our travel to Czechoslovakia. I couldn't confirm the compensation package until I spoke with the organizers, but Bob wasn't concerned. We both felt that our reward was the privilege of sharing our world of music with a society steeped in musical tradition and legendary composers, a society now emerged from a long and dark cultural hibernation. Bob saw it as a once-in-a-lifetime experience. I saw it as the beginning of something great, I knew not what.

The second task was exciting: to phone the director of the concert agency. Mr. Letov was spirited and professional as he verbally reiterated the invitation. He dove into the logistics and venue details of the proposed concert. He exuded pride in his country, culture, and history. It seemed to me—from my end of a crackling phone connection—that his persuasive pitch had a tinge of coaxing in it, which flattered me. He was a good ambassador for his country as he attempted to convince me to accept the engagement and offered information about his people's courageous and complicated story.

His démodé British English was heavily peppered with an accent unfamiliar to me. The syllabic stress consistently and awkwardly landed in the wrong place, and all articles—every *the* and *a*—were missing. (At the time I didn't know the Czech language was devoid of articles.) Conversely, his articulation and crisp consonants were exaggerated, quite the opposite of a mumbler, which helped my comprehension. Eventually, I would come to savor the charming idiosyncrasies of a Bohemian voice in the English language. If only my accent when speaking their mother tongue were half so beguiling.

Letov said the Reduta Club, located in the heart of Prague, was founded in 1957 by frustrated musicians who needed an outlet in the repressed and curtailed cultural landscape imposed on artists. Letov dropped the names of international stars who'd played there in the past, like Louis Armstrong and Marcel Marceau. He regretted that since the

1968 crackdown, the building had been neglected, and musicians from abroad had become a rarity. But the venue continued to be a cultural oasis, a point of resistance, and a place of free expression for the local artistic and political set.

He asked if I would prepare a concert and perform it on two separate evenings. He assured me that the show would be well promoted, and he expected it to attract a public eager to hear an American chanteuse. The director's confident manner wilted slightly when he turned to the subject of money. He guaranteed that our hotel and meal expenses would be covered, and though he could offer us the high-end of local artist fees, it would be a fraction of Western rates. I warmly accepted. Dickering for more money didn't cross my mind. We confirmed the dates of Friday and Saturday, 12 and 13 October 1990.

Letov went on to say that he would be personally at our disposition during our stay, as he'd been for other performing artists like Shirley Bassey, Elton John, Tina Turner, and Johnny Cash, who had entertained at various Prague venues in years past.

He would arrange for two suites at the Hotel International, an establishment that Letov described as quite popular among the flocks of international businesspeople who'd been landing in the city over the last three months since the abrupt transition to open markets. He said the stately hotel had been the preferred accommodations for top Soviet nomenklatura during the former regime. He thought we'd be impressed by this monumental hotel built in the *socialist-realism* architectural fashion known simply as the *Sorela* style.

My interlocutor flew onto the next topic in his courteous and perfunctory manner, but my attention lagged, still processing the surreal conversation taking place, and more specifically, imagining myself entering and staying in a Stalin-era hotel that had been a favored hotspot for high-level bureaucrats who had run all spheres of activities in the Soviet Union and other Eastern Bloc countries. *If those walls could talk,* my mind ruminated as he spoke, followed by, *What was I getting into?*

My focus also dwelled on something Mr. Letov said in passing about having started with Pragokoncert in 1960. I knew his was the *only* entertainment agency dealing with international artists in a country where a centralized command economy ran each business sector as a noncompetitive monopoly. In the last few months, the revolution had opened economic markets to competition—international and domestic—but thus far, Pragokoncert still had the connections, experience, and infrastructure to carry on and hold its own. The ascent to the directorship position for Ivo Letov, who had been with the agency for thirty years, pointed to an upward climb on the rungs of a communist ladder.

I was a naive American conjecturing. I supposed that Mr. Letov fell into the category of people who were politically pressured to choose between professional success or a career of mediocrity. Of course, my thoughts about the entertainment executive who was making me an amazing offer were only my surmised deductions. The subject of communist connections was not my business to broach, and it would have been a grave faux pas had I wondered about his past machinations out loud.

I snapped back to the present moment when Letov asked about my musical program. I described the types of cabaret concerts I'd performed at the Paris Ritz and New York's Eighty-Eights in Greenwich Village. He thought this concept was well-suited for the Reduta and gave me full artistic freedom. We closed by agreeing to remain in contact, and he promised to send me written confirmation via post of the dates and terms we'd discussed.

After our conversation, I mentally scanned the eclectic variety of music in my repertoire and wondered what this special audience would like. Successful entertainers follow free-market business principles: Know your customer and offer the services and goods they want. But this would be a crowd unlike any I'd encountered. I visualized a highly cultured people proud of their world-renowned musical heritage, yet deprived of contemporary Western music for half a century.

I learned later this was only partially true. Some Czechs did have limited access to underground concerts and bootleg recordings of banned local music groups playing "subversive" rock and jazz and heavy metal. There had been a domestic counterculture in which samizdat music, literature, and art were secretly composed, performed, and circulated during the years between the Prague Spring of 1968 and the Velvet Revolution of 1989. There was so much I didn't know, but wanted to understand—how their creative outlets and artistic expression became their truth-telling, their acts of opposition that played an important role in resisting the totalitarian regime. Many claimed the former regime had been finally deposed by the dissident writers, musicians, and artists, including Václav Havel, who had now extended a hand to me.

Another item near the top of my to-do list was to study their Slavic language so that, at minimum, I could greet the audience and introduce my songs in their native tongue. My search for a Czech tutor was fulfilled by a pleasant Moravian woman named Ája who was married to a Frenchman and living in Nice. After memorizing my program script and conversational phrases in Czech, we went a step further. Together, we created a Czech version to my song, which I sang at the Reduta.

Since that time, my poem has been lyrically transformed by Kateřina Klabanová into a new Czech version with fresh cadence. Compared to the French and English, this has become my favorite rendition, because the Czech language has a musicality, a fluctuating natural rhythm that savors consonant clusters and vowel intonations, whether long, short, or silent.

> Jen láska stačí nám
> pomůže strasti nést
> a štěstí druhým přát
> nebude žádná lest

Jen láska stačí nám
boje hned ustanou
sváry se zahojí
národy k sobě lnou

Jen láska stačí nám
dokáže zbavit pout
skutečnou pomoc dát
souseda obejmout

Jen láska stačí nám
ze srdce mluvívá
a to jen jedinou
společnou barvu má

Jen láska stačí nám
v svobodném zvonění
zvedneme svorně hlas
souladem písně zní

Pak stačí jedině
se sílou lásky jít
na cestu posvítí
tenhle náš hvězdný cit

At last, after months of preparation, Bob arrived. John and I picked him up at the Nice Côte d'Azur Airport, which is ranked one of the most beautiful ground approaches in the world. On the descent, both to the left and right, are gorgeous views of the vast azure water, the city of Nice, and the snowcapped Alps. The plane skims above the Mediterranean and seems to land in the sea just before it hits the runway. However jet-lagged

Bob may have been, the stunning landing and the excitement of our upcoming concert in Prague surely invigorated him, although Bob was never short on enthusiasm and verve.

He skipped off the plane with a wide smile. Whenever I saw Bob, I thought he resembled Fred Astaire with his large forehead and receding hairline, a strong and narrow chin, wholesome good looks, and a body that moved with a spring in its step. He was a dream partner for a singer because of his good nature and virtuosic piano playing. Plus, on stage he cut a handsome silhouette in his tuxedo. Whenever we performed together, I'd walk on stage, see Bob at the piano with his winning smile, and assurance was mine, jitters begone.

Bob and I rehearsed all that afternoon. For dinner, John took us to a restaurant around the corner on the Cours Saleya. Everyone had a good night's sleep, and we hit the road the following morning. John and I had decided that driving from Nice to Prague was the most practical mode of transportation because train and plane travel was complicated with multiple transfers. John studied maps of the fascinating route that covered territory we'd never visited before. We planned to spread the estimated fourteen-hour journey over two relaxed days and one overnight with maps and road signs as our guides.

Only in hindsight can I compare the old navigational modes to today's expedient travel apps. Reading a paper map is becoming a lost art, yet cartographic exploration is a visual delight. Our trusted Michelin *Carte Routière* revealed clearly marked routes, historic sites, important places, picturesque alternative roadways, sites worth a detour, and fine dining establishments along the way.

Bob, John, and I climbed into our Ford Escort and headed north and east. We navigated through the countries of Italy, Lichtenstein, and Germany, passing the cities of Genoa, Milano, Como, Vaduz, Munich, Regensburg, and Pilsen, en route to our destination deep in the heart of Central Europe. On the first day, the terrain was mountainous, with winding ascents and descents, occasional tunnels, and a fair amount of straightaways that had been cut through plateaus protected by breathtaking peaks all around.

We spent the night at Vaduz, the capital of the sixty-two-square-mile Principality of Liechtenstein which John had been intrigued about for a long time. This tiny dynastic sovereignty on the Alpine plateau was among the wealthiest monarchies in the world and had one of the highest standards of living. Indeed, it was an impressive place to see. Our hotel was unmemorable, though, and after a quiet dinner and good sleep, we were eager to set out the next day.

We had underestimated the duration of the voyage, not having calculated the time we'd take to admire the mountain views and dawdle over delicious meals, replete with local country cuisine. When we reached the medieval fortified city of Pilsen, we had wanted to see the famous town square, the ancient cathedrals and synagogues, and enjoy a Pilsner Urquell. Most important for John was to visit a memorial dedicated to his fellow American soldiers who liberated the city from Nazi occupation in WWII. Alas, no monument had ever been erected. The communist regime erased this part of history. Anyway, there was little time to linger. We were only ninety kilometers from our journey's end, night was falling and we needed to keep moving.

The final lap from Pilsen to Prague seemed interminable. We were tired and some of us were cranky. (I'll say no more.) Approaching from the southwest on Motorway 5, we saw at last a reflective mist of city lights on the horizon. When the roadway Bucharova turned into Radlická ulice, we knew our maps hadn't failed us. Signs marked "Centrum" pointed the way to the center of town.

Moving in closer, just as we began to cross the Jiráskův Bridge, the smoky brown-coal haze that blurred the skyline cleared to reveal, high on a hill, the outline of the Pražský hrad. It rose mystically from medieval rooftops with its aggregation of the royal palace, churches, fortifications, courtyards, and gardens. We gaped at Saint Vitus Cathedral, the high point in the silhouette. Below was the stalwart Charles Bridge arched across the Vltava River.

I was behind the wheel and slowly pulled the car toward the side of Smetanovo nábřeží. From our geographic point on the right bank of the river, we beheld the view of Hradčany district shown on postcards.

I was captivated at the sight and drawn spiritually by its aura. With few words, Bob, John and I got out of the car to experience the moment. An image of majesty appeared before us, beckoning like a treasured fairy tale. The glow that emanated from the cathedral, castle walls, and bridge was like the light of a soft candle illuminating a storybook. Time stood still for those few moments, and I felt myself curled inside a plush blanket, listening to the soothing voice of my newfound forefather reading to me the legend of a mythical kingdom. The story began with, "Once upon a time, Libuše had a dream . . ."

Libuše was a young prophetess who ruled the Bohemian lands. But the townsmen were threatened by having a woman leader. They wanted her replaced. Libuše said, "Never fear, I foresee a suitable candidate living in a Northern Bohemian village." Soon thereafter, a strong ploughman from the north came and married Libuše. His name was Přemysl. He became the first Czech prince and founder of the Přemysl dynasty that ruled the land for centuries.

Libuše had another dream that envisioned a city whose fame would touch the stars. She identified the rock and wooded ridge above the Vltava River where a castle should be built. Libuše and Přemysl sent their envoys up to the hill. They saw a man carving a wooden threshold, as if the premonition were already coming true. As the word in Czech for "threshold" is *práh*, when the castle was built, it was named Praha, along with the settlement that developed below.

The story was an illustrated legend, complete with a panoramic mural before our eyes. The soft lights of the castle were cast on us, as if to bless our arrival. In that moment, on the embankment where we stood, my husband, my pianist friend, and I entered one thousand years of emperors and kings, a world of myths and fables, Christian and Jewish legends, Kafkaesque ineffabilities, and the melodious winds, strings and brass of Dvořák, Janáček, Mozart, and Smetana. This first sight of Prague's magical beauty was an experience that we three starstruck Americans often talked about afterwards. We were transported into an enchanted world that would never leave us. It became my new, and forever, moveable feast.

On to the hotel, which we feared would be difficult to find in our tired state, and in the dark. Bob hailed a taxi and rode with the driver as John and I followed behind. Through the city, we climbed upward on the winding serpentine road Chotkova silnice, glimpsing spectacular views of the city and castle area. The route meandered toward an elevated plateau called Letenská pláň. While coasting down a hill to Dejvice Circle, we spotted the top tower of the Hotel International. Although the shadowy night obscured our surroundings, the hotel's imposing edifice couldn't be missed. Two sprawling, symmetrical wings flanked each side of a high central tower crowned with a red socialist star mounted on a spike.

We walked into an enormous marble lobby. Straight ahead was a grand staircase girded by marble columns. Our eyes pivoted panoramically to the gilded framed paintings, fancy iron fixtures and railings, and sumptuous chandeliers and wall lamps that sparkled with Bohemian crystal. While John and Bob checked us in, a large tapestry near the open bar area drew my attention. The concierge explained that the woven textile Praga Regina Musicae had been designed in 1954 by Cyril Bouda, a Czech painter, illustrator, and tapestry and stamp designer. He added that it was handcrafted at the Moravian tapestry factory Moravská gobelínová manufaktura which still exists today. Whimsical Chagall-esque musical instruments, birds, and flowered wreaths floated in the sky above the tapestry's colorful depiction of Prague's architectural wonders on both sides of the winding Vltava.

But Bouda's design of Prague's glorious heritage was tainted by a deplorable legacy. A central feature of the textured piece was an imposing monument of Joseph Stalin on the hilltop in Letná Park. As our sagacious concierge continued to unfold the history, I sank into the reality that this otherwise bewitching tapestry was a symbol of Stalinism, a period of terror and control.

While the tapestry lives on, the statue dominating Prague's northern skyline lasted only seven years. Apparently, one day in November 1962, with no prior warning, the population of Prague heard a humongous bang. Pieces of sculpture and plumes of smoke flew above Letná hill as part of Nikita Khrushchev's statue-toppling reform period of de-Stalinization.

The concierge brought history to life on our first night in Prague. This intricately woven artwork had volumes to teach me about the not-so-distant past.

As the porter led us to our rooms, we trudged past the breakfast area which looked inviting even in the dark, given that our meager dinner had been leftover snacks consumed in the car. We had stopped midafternoon for a late lunch in a small village just across the border from Germany. The meal was our first taste of real Bohemian cooking. My little pocket dictionary was sorely inadequate for finding the English equivalent of items on the faintly typed menu. I recognized only the derivatives of a few words. John and Bob ordered *Smažený vepřový řízek* which they discovered were delicious breaded pork cutlets served with a tasty potato salad. The men also ordered beers. John had learned the word "pivo" before we set out. We watched the barman grab two half-liter mugs, and using a side-pull tap, fill them one at a time with pale lager from a massive tank, taking care to put the foam in first, then the beer. John was impressed.

I had wanted to taste the regional red wine, but I was the designated driver. Besides, in preparation for the performance, I'd been fasting completely from alcohol. I also wanted to eat lightly. The only salad on the menu was something called *Šopský salát*. The bowl of chopped tomatoes, peppers, onion, and cucumbers, sprinkled with goat cheese and drizzled with vinegar and oil suited my taste perfectly. On the table sat a basket of rye bread and oblong white rolls with a lard mixture for spreading. I passed on that.

The place was rustic, the food superb, the service rudimentary. Neither the server nor we could communicate except for a few words. We had the distinct impression that the other customers, local rural folks, were staring at us. But we felt comfortable as we ate our meal, tried to be complimentary, and then politely asked for the bill. *Účet, prosím.* We examined the tiny piece of paper for a long time. It was a strip of pale numbers imprinted by a mechanical adding machine low on ink.

We knew the approximate exchange rate was 24 koruna to one U.S. dollar. Something was wrong. The total number on the bottom line was 90, less than four dollars. The barman, the server, and the other customers watched us quizzically pore over the statement. I indicated to the waiter that there must be a mistake. Finally, the barman, who acted like the manager, approached the table, picked up the bill, and with a gruff voice said "*Je to dobré,*" and repeated in German, "*Das ist gut,*" as he put it back on the table and walked away. I'm afraid we started chuckling, amused by the ridiculously paltry sum. The staff appeared offended. Regretting our obtuse reaction, we grossly over-tipped, and left.

We had flunked our first cultural sensitivity test. The wide differential in the cost of living and worth of currency, albeit advantageous for us, gave us a swift comeuppance. We needed to tread more carefully and respectfully when in the company of the residents of our host country. That evening, when we discovered our hotel restaurant was closed, I didn't mind skipping a meal. Our Bohemian lunch and its lesson were still settling.

At our hotel, the porter ushered us to the elevator and we ascended toward the higher-level floors. As we walked down an endlessly long corridor, we eagerly anticipated seeing the suites which Letov had reserved in this remarkable place. Alas, the guest rooms were rueful counterparts to the luxurious common areas we'd traversed moments ago. Our suites were tidy and efficient, but spartan and austere. Everything was brown and dark beige. No other color. No decoration except one dreary framed print. John's and my eyes met with our *whatever* look as he tipped the porter. My artist-husband, who took an aesthetic interest in everything, branded the decor "Soviet-style Minimalism." We had everything necessary to shower, unpack, snuggle into the clean bed linens, and sleep soundly in the warmth and quiet of the unassuming space.

The next morning, we saw Bob's suite. It was identical to ours—same bland colors, same carpet, same room scheme. Creativity and whimsy were not Soviet strong suits. But we were invited guests to this foreign land, and we would express nothing but compliments and appreciation to our host.

Breakfast was in the grand restaurant, naturally lighted by large windows lining a long wall. The waitresses came around with trays of *obložené chlebíčky,* small and savory open-faced sandwiches with a variety of toppings, such as cold cuts, cheese, egg, cream cheese, pickles, horseradish, mustard, and herbs. The waitresses were rather stoic, but an occasional smile of delight popped from behind their timid politeness when I attempted the conversational phrases that Ája had drilled into me. I wondered if the servers were secretly happy that their clientele was changing from decades of bloated and stodgy Eastern bureaucrats to lean and eager Western entrepreneurs.

The hotel teemed with the latter type. In the restaurants, lounges, and lobby, we had occasion to meet several businessmen. Their enthusiastic recounting of the ripe commerce opportunities in this new market lodged in the back of my mind for later reflection. At that moment, though, I had no time to consider anything other than music business. In two days, I was going to make my Prague debut, and in a few minutes, the agent was arriving to meet us.

Mr. Letov breezed through the lobby doors exactly on time. His looks and demeanor matched the voice I remembered from our phone conversations. The fit-as-a-fiddle gentleman upwards of middle-age held himself in perfect alignment. His slicked-back, salt and pepper hair framed a distinctive face with a well-groomed goatee. Letov was all smiles in welcoming us to the country. We sat in a cluster of chairs in the lobby and one of my first questions was whether we would have the honor of President Havel's attendance at either of the two concerts. Letov wavered. He was unsure, but proceeded to give reasons why the president might not be there, to cushion the blow should that be the case. With diplomacy, he reminded me that the playwright-turned-president had a brand-new country to run. Sensing my dejection, which I tried to hide, he quickly added that the president was moved by my poetic verses and pleased that I had come to share my song with the people of Czechoslovakia.

After our discussion about the concert and the weekend activities, Mr. Letov took us on a tour of the city in his low-riding Trabant. The October morning air was chilly. From the car window, we observed the bustling urban life as people walked briskly, rode on buses and tramways, or headed down metro stairs. Of the few cars on the road, most were older models of Škodas, Trabants, and Ladas, so different from the Citroëns, Renaults, Peugeots, Fiats, and Mercedes ubiquitous in France.

Our first stop was the Hradčany castle area and Loreta Square. "This is only quick introduction to Prague," said Letov, sporadically omitting articles, "because, another day, you must take walking tour of Royal Way that begins at castle and takes you across Charles Bridge all the way to Powder Tower." He expounded on medieval history in his animated fashion as he chauffeured us down the steep and narrow Nerudova ulice, which looked pedestrian-only. It seemed Mr. Letov didn't always follow traffic rules. At the bottom of the hill, he dodged the trams on Malostranské náměstí and showed us the magnificent exterior of the baroque church of Saint Nicholas. Then we crossed the river on the Mánesův most, past the stunning Rudolfinum concert hall, until finally we were in recognizable territory—the quai along the Charles Bridge where we had stopped in our tracks the night before. Letov pulled over and parked along the embankment. The daytime view was brighter, but no less mystical and alluring. Once again, it rendered us motionless and speechless. While our lively guide lectured on about the city's history, we could only absorb the city's beauty.

The final lap of our morning excursion led us up Národní třída, past the National Theatre and Czech Academy of Sciences. Halfway up the avenue was the Reduta where Bob and I would rehearse with sound and light technicians. Mr. Letov dropped us off outside the venue and asked us to wait while he found parking. The building's exterior was worn, like all the gray structures on the block. I felt immediately welcomed by the marquee out front that prominently displayed a poster with my picture. The headline and description read:

REDUTA
Studio Theater Reduta
and Pragokoncert Arts Agency
p r e s e n t s
12. and 13. October 1990
Friday—Saturday—19.00 o'clock
A N N E—M A R I E K E N N Y
SINGER—ACTRESS
in the show
"F U L L C I R C L E"

Anne Marie Kenny—USA

Singer, Actress, American origin, is popular not only in her homeland, where she presents her recitals ONE WOMAN SHOW of French chansons, American musical theater and international standards, but also in Paris, which has become her second home.

The singer is accompanied by American pianist ROBERT McCOY, a solo performer and accompanist for leading singers with whom he has performed on the most famous stages in the USA, England, Germany, and France.

In honor of our Velvet Revolution, ANNE MARIE KENNY wrote a new text to Brel's famous melody entitled Quand on a que l'amour. This song will be premiered here.

Reduta

D I V A D E L N Í S T U D I O R E D U T A
scéna umělecké agentury Pragokoncert

u v á d í

12. a 13. 10. - pátek - sobota - 19.00 HODIN

A N N E - M A R I E K E N N Y

ZPĚVAČKA - HEREČKA

V POŘADU

"F U L L C I R C L E "

Reduta

ANNE MARIE KENNY - USA
zpěvačka, herečka, původem
američanka, je populární nejen
ve své vlasti, kde uvádí své
recitaly ONE WOMAN SHOW
francouzských šansonů, melodií
světových muzikálů, světových
evergreenů, ale i v Paříži,
která se stala jejím druhým
domovem.

Zpěvačku doprovází americký
klavírista ROBERT McCOY - jako
sólový klavírista i jako
klavírní doprovazeč předních
amerických umělců vystupoval
na nejslavnějších poódiích
v USA, Anglii, NSR,Francii

Na počest naší sametové
revoluce" napsala ANNE MARIE KENNY
nový text na známou Brelovou
melodii s názvem Když zbývá jen
láska. Právě tato píseň
zazní zde v premiéře.

POKLADNA REDUTY OTEVŘENA DENNĚ
KROMĚ SOBOTY A NEDĚLE OD 17.00,
V SOBOTU OD 18.00 HODIN,
REDUTA, NÁRODNÍ TŘ.20, PRAHA 1
TELEFON, - 20 38 25, 20 38 22

9

PRAGUE DEBUT

The Reduta was closed in the morning, so the manager waited for us outside. Mr. Letov introduced Bob and me as international celebrities. As we made our way into the corridor, the men exchanged small talk while I lagged behind to get my bearings. The place had even more personality than I'd imagined. The off-hours establishment was quiet, but the vibe was sizzling. Smoke and booze infused the air, the walls steeped in jazz tunes.

The manager toured us around and took us backstage to show us our dressing rooms. Mine was cozy with a few chairs, a wardrobe rack, and a makeup table against a lighted wall mirror. I pictured Marcel Marceau applying eyeliner over white-face paint and donning his Bip the Clown costume in that very room where, in two days, I'd slip into my emerald-green gown.

We went on stage to meet the tech crew and rehearse a few numbers. Bob wanted to feel the weight of the piano keys, and I, the stage beneath my feet. I changed into my concert shoes to experience it fully—attempting to move with ease and grace while my heels balanced on tall stilettos and my toes scrunched into a fine-pointed tip.

The sound and light engineers were eager to accommodate. Anything we wanted. They clicked on the microphones and fiddled with the stage lights while Bob played and I sang. The equipment was top-notch. The sound of our music reverberated like waves reflecting off walls and splashing back at us.

I asked for special effects on certain numbers—to shine a spot here, diffuse lights there. We discussed mood tints and glows. The guys agreed without question. Looking back, I can't say whether or not the show's lighting went according to plan because, as soon as Bob and I began, we entered a kind of liminal space, and everything felt perfect.

The concert hall and the country rolled out a carpet toward the unknown, and I felt compelled to walk it. Along the path, people extended their hands. These were Czech artists, writers, and musicians who attended my concerts and befriended me. The immediate attraction was our shared dedication to the arts. But the deeper connection was something else—we were all making a new start. Subconsciously, we saw a future with each other in it.

Journalists Andrea Vernerová and Olga Kittnarová each wrote praising reviews about my show which appeared in leading newspapers. Apart from the interviews, we also met socially. Andrea and Olga were curious about my life as an American woman in Western Europe, and I was interested to learn about theirs in Central Europe. I spoke about my work as a singer, my life in America and France, and my esteem for their country, its president, and the people.

What I first noticed about Andrea when she came backstage after my first show was her graceful manner. A classic beauty, her soft facial features were surrounded by a wavy blonde mane. She introduced herself as a freelance journalist, complimented me on my performance, and invited me to her home for an interview. I went to her spacious apartment in a Neo-Renaissance building on the Hořejší nábřeží in the Smíchov district. The view from her windows overlooked the flowing river. We sat at her dining room table decked with a hand-cut lace tablecloth and porcelain tea service. On my feet were comfortable slippers that weren't mine. In the entryway of her home, I gladly adopted the custom, which was new to me, of removing my outdoor shoes and wearing house slippers provided by the host. In the course of our conversation, I learned more about my interviewer. Andrea was a few years younger than me, married with two children. Her husband was a mariner who held a high-level position at the nationalized Czechoslovak Ocean Shipping.

Andrea was serious about journalism and literature. Her university degree in ethnographic anthropology explained the multicultural perspective she brought to her craft and the flourish in her writing style. Her review about my debut concert dug into my thoughts as a foreigner with Czech ancestry, my impressions about the people and culture. She succeeded in tapping the journal *Demokrat* to publish the article with photos.

Not until decades later did I learn how difficult the post-revolutionary period was for Andrea. During the former regime, she worked for the Československá tisková kancelář (ČTK). In those times, media and public speech were obliged to use specific totalitarian language as tools to shape communist society. This one-way communication, based on ideology, forbade criticism of the state.

Andrea adapted her writing and journalism skills within this system. This wasn't surprising news to me, but on hearing Andrea tell it, I felt a soulful connection to the limitations she endured. She and I shared similarities—born around the same time period, on different continents, with a generous dose of intelligence, talent, and looks. We were serious about our work, not for money or prestige. We wanted to make a difference. At difficult times, each of us had made undesirable professional compromises, lowering values and standards. For me, my compromises were also of a moral nature. I never revealed that to Andrea, but I believe she sensed it. From the very beginning, we offered each other nonjudgmental, sisterly support.

She described how the 1989 Velvet Revolution dismantled the rigid framework of the totalitarian structure. Andrea was overjoyed. She quickly and officially left the Party. Handing in her red book cost Andrea her job with ČTK, but she was finally free of literary shackles. Seeking new work in journalism, she was rebuffed by the writers and independent start-up newspapers proliferating in the new democracy. All across professional sectors were righteous-minded people who wanted to retaliate against former Party members.

But vengeance was the last impulse President Havel wanted his countrymen to act upon. During a TV interview toward the end of 1989, he said that the revolution was "a revolt of decent people against indecent people. And decency also means that no one will take revenge on anyone, no one will persecute anyone." He went on to say, "If we respond to evil with evil, we will only prolong the evil further and further."

The next day, in his first address to the nation on New Year's 1990, Havel warned against casting blame.

> When I talk about the contaminated moral atmosphere, I am not talking just about the gentlemen [of the previous regime] . . . I am talking about all of us. We had all become used to the totalitarian system and accepted it as an unchangeable fact and thus helped to perpetuate it. In other words, we are all—though naturally to differing extents—responsible for the operation of the totalitarian machinery. None of us is just its victim. We are all also its co-creators.

Unfortunately, not everyone put Havel's admonition into practice. People still blamed those who'd joined the Party or aided and abetted it. I admired the way Andrea set aside the rancor of others. Armed with talent, experience, and resolve, she found her way in the new system by freelancing. I hope I'd have done the same.

The other journalist who reviewed my concert was Olga Kittnarová, who held a doctorate of musicology and sidelined as a music critic for radio and press. Almost fifteen years my senior, I addressed her as "Doctor

Kittnarová" in deference to professional and generational protocol. A vivacious intellectual in her mid-fifties, Olga was quick to smile, making her high-arched, rosy cheeks even more pleasantly rounded. Wearing a bouffant hairdo and attractive attire reminiscent of the 1960s—the era when Czechoslovak fashion became stuck in time—Olga spoke with a voice of authority on all things musical, whether composition, history, or theory. She was keen to learn about contemporary American music, of which she'd been largely deprived until now. Yet she showed no shyness in making known that for centuries Prague was considered "the Conservatory of Europe."

For the past eighteen years, Olga had taught at the Prague State Conservatory. She exuded pride in talking about her work with students full of artistic proclivity. She showed me the ornate building founded in 1808 that sits prominently alongside the Vltava, where Antonín Dvořák taught composition and later became headmaster.

Olga's tenure at the conservatory began during the Soviet era. She had no aspirations to assume the role of headmaster or department head, as such a promotion would have required compromising her values and joining the Party. Her calling was to educate talented young musicians. She said to me, "There was nothing political in singing a Mozart aria or playing the cello, piano, or bassoon."

She played the game to a certain extent by joining the Czechoslovak Soviet Friends Club. As an American, I'd never heard of such friendship societies and asked Olga about them. She explained that across sectors, Czechoslovaks were pushed to join clubs that offered cultural exchanges and pen pal correspondents to encourage the integration of Soviet and other Eastern Bloc citizens into a tight-knit socialist world.

After the revolution, Olga stayed at the conservatory for two more years to help bring the school's two-centuries-old tradition into the contemporary world of international music. She then joined the Charles University's faculty, taught a myriad of music courses, and began to publish books. Her music encyclopedia, *A History of Music in Outlines*, serves as my reference guide. The introduction unveils her philosophy:

"It is comforting and amazing to write about the history of music. The annals of this art form, compared with the general history of mankind, never brought any suffering or disaster to humans; on the contrary, it extended only pleasure and entertainment to people."

This was the train of thought that connected Olga and me—the transcendency of music. Whether studying, teaching, or performing in the creative arts, we landed in an intrinsically humanistic and spiritual place that shunned artifice and power plays. We conversed on this plane from our early encounters with each other; it held the promise of an enduring friendship.

Many years later, she told me that I was the first American musician she had ever reviewed. We had both held on to her article *Premiéra americké zpěvačky* that analyzed my Reduta show. An extract from her lengthy piece reads:

> The motivation for her visit is interesting: Her performance is the result of her response to our November events, the Velvet Revolution, in which she wrote new lyrics to the melody of J. Brel's song *Quand on a que l'amour*. The trilingual version of the work . . . was performed by Kenny with a passion for the text's meaning, which calls for the creation of a world without weapons and a society united against evil. She also sang the song, which she sent to President V. Havel, at Charles University and Prague Conservatory, where Pragokoncert arranged discussions with its students.
>
> Her well-supported voice of compelling timbre elucidates her innate sense of the performed music's text and theme, her stage movement is elegant with a natural simplicity. With her performance, Kenny reveals the high-quality training received from her voice coach Madame Janine Reiss and choreographer Andy de Groat.

Although it wasn't preplanned, Ivo Letov asked Bob and me to conduct an "American Broadway" masterclass for the music department at Charles University. We felt honored, knowing the valorous role that generations of Czechoslovak students played during Nazi and Soviet regimes. For fifty years, in the major uprisings between 1939 and 1989, the students were the common denominator, the bounding pulse that drove the tempo.

I knew this much—that on 28 October 1939, at the twenty-first anniversary of Czechoslovak Independence Day, students took to the streets to protest Hitler's takeover of the country. A medical student, Jan Opletal, was shot by police. His death led to even more anti-Nazi resistance. On 17 November, Nazi forces stormed Charles University, executed nine student leaders by firing squad, and forced over twelve hundred students and teachers into concentration camps. Today, this date is known the world over as International Students' Day.

The war and Nazi occupation ended. The rebuilding of a democratic system was rickety.

On 25 February 1948, as a Soviet-backed coup d'état appeared imminent, no less than six thousand university students marched to Prague Castle to fight for democracy, civil rights, and academic freedom. They were met with ruthless violence, and were too late. The communist takeover was already a done deal, launching forty years of Soviet totalitarianism.

By 1968, at the time of the short-lived Prague Spring, Czech students were my contemporaries. In March of that year, while the new Czechoslovak Communist Party leader Alexander Dubček ushered in a period of cultural liberalization, I was living across the Atlantic as a sixteen-year-old American teenager in Nebraska. A junior in high school, I was writing my own music, in love with John Lennon, and when not in my school uniform, feeling liberated in sandals, bell-bottom jeans, and a silky tunic over braless breasts. My country was experiencing its own transition from a patriarchal, culturally conservative mindset to a freer, more permissive way of thinking and living. I was caught up in the hippie movement, as well as women's liberation, antiwar and civil rights movements, all in full swing. And Americans wept through four assassinations: John F. Kennedy in 1963, Malcolm X (from my hometown of Omaha) in 1965, Martin Luther King in 1968, and Robert F. Kennedy in 1968.

Back in Prague, another teenager of my generation, Peter Sís, was keeping a diary. It became a book thirty-nine years later called *The Wall: Growing Up Behind the Iron Curtain,* which today I read with my grandchildren. His journal entry in March 1968 read: "A rally for Dubček! We all march. He is calling for 'socialism with a human face.'" In May 1968, Peter exclaimed on paper, "Censorship is lifted! We can have long hair and wear jeans!" He and his friends could do things formerly prohibited. They held poetry slams at school, played rock and roll, created artwork freely, read foreign literature. Peter got a passport with permission to travel to the West. "Yippee!" he penned. That summer, he left by train to hitchhike around Paris and London. While away, his home country was invaded on 21 August 1968 by Warsaw Pact tanks and troops. Peter returned to a shuttered society.

From everything I've gathered from books and the confidences of friends, the light of freedom brought by the Prague Spring was almost extinguished by the ensuing Soviet invasion. Brave university students went on strike to protest the occupation and demand a continuation of reforms, but to little avail. As weeks and months passed, a crushing of spirits as well as liberties flattened the nation.

Still, the embers of freedom smoldered, and heroism manifested itself. In an intentional act aimed at lifting the apathy that hung over the country, a philosophy student named Jan Palach set himself on fire on the ramp of the National Museum on upper Wenceslas Square. Three days later, on 19 January 1969, the young martyr died from his burns. National demonstrations were roused. Václav Havel appeared on television, calling the act "an appeal warning us against indifference, skepticism, hopelessness." He cut to the heart of the matter: "I understand the death of Jan Palach as a warning against the moral suicide of us all."

I think I get why the Czechs never spoke to me about their most painful history, like Jan Palach's sacrifice. How could a foreigner comprehend what this act meant to them? How each one reckoned with his or her own moral suicide? But Havel's harsh warning, which I heard long after, also struck me, touching at my own hidden moral demise. The guilt from addiction and adultery had burrowed into the basement of my soul, camouflaged by good intentions.

Once again in January 1989, students came out in force with dissidents and fed-up citizens for a weeklong commemoration of the twentieth anniversary of Palach's death. They were met with tear gas, water cannons, and gunfire. Havel was among those arrested. International news covered it, bringing it to living rooms around the globe. What no one knew at the time was that Palach Week was a turning point and harbinger to the revolution later that year.

In May, a petition calling for Havel's release was signed by thousands of Czechoslovak citizens, including Communist Party members like journalist Andrea Vernerová. Helped by international pressure, the authorities freed their famous prisoner.

Finally, on 17 November, buoyed by the fifty-year anniversary of the first International Students' Day and the revolutionary wave sweeping Central and Eastern Europe, students and protesters demanded freedom like never before. Police attempts to beat them back only galvanized their resistance. It was as if the entire nation rose with voices ringing. International journalists televised the ecstatic rebellion for all the world to watch—me included.

Which brings me back to when, less than a year later in 1990, Bob and I were asked to conduct a masterclass for Czech students of music. As we prepared and considered our audience, I thought of the young freedom fighters whose world had recently shifted toward the democratic nation they risked their lives for.

Awestruck, Bob and I took a deep and trod respectfully up the broad stone steps to the venerable medieval university founded in 1347 by

Charles IV, the King of Bohemia and Holy Roman Emperor. We were welcomed by the professors and ushered into a large classroom with a grand piano at the front. Through massive ancient windows, the sun's rays beamed onto sturdy wooden tables and chairs occupied by wide-eyed young musicians.

Bob talked to the students first. He told them about his professorship at an American university and the kinds of courses offered to music majors. He shared about his career as a performing artist and his doctoral degree in collaborative piano performance, a relatively new course of study in American academia. The students were all ears. I spoke to them about my private voice study, the classical bel canto vocal method I practiced, my career as a singer, and my interest in a wide range of musical genres.

Bob and I performed several Broadway songs, prefacing each with a short narrative about the composer. We dedicated our last song "When We Only Have Love" to them because, as I related, their efforts had inspired me to write it. The students were attentive and inquisitive. Their questions turned into lively discussion. After the class, one young person passed me a handwritten note that gave me pause: "Thank you for being a part of our revolution. We had a fear that we would never be accepted by the 'West.' People like you are the ones who are helping to restore our self-esteem."

The day after the masterclass, Bob flew back to his teaching post near Washington, DC. When we spoke on the phone a few weeks later, gratitude and humility lingered from our Prague experience. It never left us.

Among everyone I met during my stay, no one dazzled me more than Zdeněk Merta. The acclaimed composer and pianist, with his toned physique and perpetual twinkle in his eyes, already had an ample share of fans. His wife, Zora Jandová, was a leading actress and singer on the national stage. I was flattered that Zora attended my opening night, given the imminent delivery of their first child. Zdeněk came to both shows and didn't hide his enthusiasm. A pianist himself, he was as enamored with Bob's piano playing as with my singing. On a personal level, Zdeněk and I were the same age and shared a similar energy and playfulness. We bantered back and forth like a pair who had spent their childhood together.

Zdeněk and Zora invited me to return to Prague to sing at their concert slated for the end of the following year. It seemed far off, but I was ecstatic, thinking, *now I have a reason to return.* As Zdeněk gave me more details, his lighthearted affect turned awkward, admitting there was no money in the request. This drawback was promptly counterbalanced with an offer for free lodging while in Prague. An honest discussion followed about the bereft situation for musicians in their newly formed society.

He leveled with me. "My dear Anne Marie, there are very few opportunities anymore in the music business. We are struggling to make our way in a new and uncertain system. No one is hiring. Not Pragokoncert, not the record labels, not the theaters. Zora and I will present a show at the Reduta for a small stipend. Up to now, musicians and theater people survived because the cost of living was very low and the government heavily subsidized the arts. But now, work has dried up. Prices are rising. We must reinvent ourselves."

Zdeněk went on: "There are enormous opportunities in the commercial sector. Foreign companies are arriving by the droves to enter our brand-new market. They are assessing how, where, and when they will set up offices and factories to sell their products. We are fertile, untouched territory for them. We are being overrun by competitive enterprises. This is really something new for us."

I wondered what it must be like for someone like Zdeněk, in his late thirties, to consider starting all over again mid-career. I, too, planned for a professional transition, but of my own free will, not because all the rules in my country suddenly upended.

Zdeněk's perspective was informative and affirmed what I'd gathered. John and I were attentive to news reports and learned firsthand from businessmen at the hotel who were eager to jump into the suddenly new and open market. They expressed both excitement and frustration.

Excitement because the timing was early, the field was wide open, and opportunities abounded. Frustration because of political instability, changing laws, and lack of bilingual business services.

The idea to join the country's business boom crossed my mind. But I had to explore the music field, just in case Zdeněk was mistaken, or wanted to eliminate me from the competition.

In my last few days in the city, John and I were invited to functions where I met local musicians, actors, and artists. The few who had a smattering of English were eager to practice with a native speaker. Beverages flowed at the parties, revealing the wild and crazy side of the otherwise genteel Czech character. I soaked it up and flirted right back. With my work behind me, I wanted to drown in the glory of success with multiple champagne toasts. I discovered *Bohemia Sekt,* a Moravian brut that rivaled French champagne in taste at one-tenth the price. But I held strong against the pull of my baser self and drank only to a slightly tipsy state, for fear my drinking problem, chomping to be unleashed, might be exposed.

After ten days, it was time to leave Prague. Somehow the goodbyes felt more like hellos.

10

INTERMEZZO

John and I drove back through the Alps on our journey home to the sea. I remember nothing of our conversation, only that John knew my heart wasn't where we were heading, but where we'd just left. Somewhere in Prague dwelled the conclusion to my recurrent dream about grasping the wheel and turning away from the cliff. I had changed direction on every level and found myself around a bend, in a place I wanted to call home. The *where* was answered. The *what* would be revealed. It just had to be.

We returned to the Riviera's warm climate and expansive seascape, a geographic contrast to the wintry air of Prague's medieval city. A few days later, I turned thirty-nine. Late by most measures, November 1990 heralded my coming of age. We may not know what the future holds, but for me, random glimpses appeared in premonitions and dreams. I passed the next few months knowing our days in Nice were numbered. Like my legendary ancestress, Libuše, who envisioned her castle before it materialized, our new home was being constructed, not brick by brick, but thought by thought and wish by wish.

We flew to the States for Christmas to see my family in Omaha and John's on the East Coast. My mind was quasi-open to explore options in our home country, but none presented. New Year 1991 rolled out in New Hampshire at the home of Connie, one of John's twins. We confided our situation to her—that France had become too expensive, and we were discerning our next move. Connie extended an unreserved invitation to live with her family for as long as we needed, should we decide to settle back in the States. Her loving offer accelerated my Prague plan. The thought of accepting charity got my derrière in gear.

I asked John to allow me to investigate Prague for potential work, and possibly for our future home. He was hesitant but not resistant. John hadn't experienced Prague the way I had. His ancestors were from Wales, a far cry from Bohemia. He didn't have the artistic success or personal connections I made during our first visit there. But he did feel my excitement, and we fed equally off each other's bright ideas. I didn't have to remind him that we had moved to Nice at his suggestion. When I'd seen his level of inspiration stimulated by the Riviera's great painters and his attraction for the warm climate and the beauty of the sea, I'd been swayed. But in addition to chasing John's dreams, what attracted me to the seacoast were the lower costs.

Now, after three years in the South of France, we were at a new crossroads. Our expenses still exceeded our income, and our funds were approaching that specific dollar amount—the line in the sand I'd drawn and sworn we wouldn't cross.

Without fanfare, John handed me the symbolic baton to orchestrate our next move. In the symphony of our lives together, our final year in Nice stood as an intermezzo between two distinct movements. We had flourished through the fervent romanticism of the first, and were tuning up for the next—a trembling adagio marked by rumbling timpani and emotive strings. And though the tempo quickened for me and diminuendoed for John, we still danced together in the rhythm of our golden mean.

More practically speaking, a change was coming and I was bracing myself. This memoir isn't intended to be a purgative exercise or a tumble into the emotional crater of yesteryear. But I also can't gloss over reality, as I did so well back then, or this story threatens to become the image of who I wanted to be. Keeping my character flaws under wraps, I met the challenges facing us with a "full steam ahead" approach. I was essentially blind to my addiction despite its frequent manifestations through anxious emotional states, slackened sexual inhibitions, and other soul-disquieting ways. Drinking was, for me, an inexorable adjunct to my life, like an unpredictable friend I let in now and then. After all, I could practice periods of abstinence. I'd put the friend in a cozy closet and watch my knuckles whiten, trying to keep the door shut while the next drink scratched its fingernails up and down the dark interior slab until I finally gave in. As these struggles entrenched, love and art and goodness mollified their severity. Those redeeming qualities sometimes lost a bout, but they ended up winning the overall fight. I had too much love surrounding me to give in completely. In this respect, my saving grace was the subconscious knowledge that what my mother always said was right: "God will never leave you in the lurch."

The year 1991 was a buffer between two lifestyles, two countries and cultures, and two separate professions for me. I wasn't risk-averse. Crossing frontiers empowered me. But the next stage was mine to set, and I needed three pillars to hold up the roof—a steady income for me, quality health care for John, and assurance we'd be together no matter the level of his infirmity. My wishful thinking couldn't alter the changes occurring before my eyes. John's condition was diminishing—unsteady gait, stubborn foot wounds, intestinal weakness. His mind was sharp as a tack. His eyes emanated love and intelligence, but a vague fear began to filter through his otherwise confident regard. I hoped to assuage his anxiety. Our anxiety. Our nightly prayer routine helped. At the outset of big decisions, such as our move from Omaha to Paris in 1983, our request went something like: "Dear God, we're about to undertake this plan. If it's not meant to be, please shut the doors as we move forward. We trust you'll guide us." Our prayer of faith in 1991 was much the same.

I made plans for a research trip to Prague in February. I assured John that I'd come home with a detailed report for us to consider, and I promised not to get ahead of myself or come to conclusions without him. John consented, but I suspect his private prayer countered mine, hoping for a miracle that would have us regaling forever on France's warm southern coast.

In preparation, I contacted a few of our good friends in France, successful businessmen, to get their ideas. Jacques Surugue was the director of international recruitment for Bouygues, one of the largest construction companies in the world. Another was Gerard Smits, who'd been on assignment all over the world as a senior business consultant with Booz, Allen, Hamilton. And I spoke with Miki Karoli, the rock star who grew up in the western part of a divided Germany and was well-read in European politics and history, especially as it related to culture and music. My personal advisors—a Frenchman, a Hollander, and a German—were even more enthusiastic than I. They confirmed that the time to enter the Czechoslovak market was *now* and wished they were in a position to do so.

Jacques, Gerard, and Miki gave me something I hadn't expected— they believed in me. They'd say, "Anne Marie, your personality, drive, and resourcefulness are the qualities of a successful entrepreneur. If you find the right business niche in this wide-open field, and stay flexible as the climate shifts, you'll be a sure winner."

More concretely, my informal team of consultants specified what to look for as I conducted my market study. Each advisor shared his knowledge about the new democracies in Eastern Europe. Each had unique tips on how to determine market needs. They told me to listen to what people on the ground were saying. Ask questions. Stay open. They offered to help and advise in any way they could. As I listened, it was evident that opportunities in Eastern Europe abounded in the business sector, but would be harder to gauge in the entertainment industry. Still, music remained on my exploratory agenda. I owed this to myself after devoting twenty years to honing my singing and performance skills.

When John heard about our friends' reactions, his skepticism was alleviated. He also knew that, with the combination of my grit and his blessing, nothing could stop me—except perhaps the hand of divinity.

Singing gigs continued at fancy hotels and nightclubs in Monte Carlo, Nice, and Cannes. I began twice-weekly Czech lessons with my tutor Ája to learn practical conversational phrases that could get me in doors, introduce myself, explain my purpose, express my love for their country and language, and thank hosts and hotel staff.

As I planned for this consequential trip, red wine was my dependable escape when fear tamped my courage. Most nights I controlled my intake, except when moderation flew out the window. In those days, I could start a new day hungover from a night of drunkenness and still manage to swim in the sea, don dress and makeup, and proceed with my projects.

On 28 January 1991, I took a flight from Nice to Vienna and stayed one night at the Pension Pertschy in the city center for 540 schillings, about 50 dollars. The next morning, I taxied to the Franz-Josefs-Bahnhof and boarded the 9:30 train to Prague. Once we started rolling, I let myself relax. My eyes fixated on the landscape whizzing by as I pondered the pioneering journey ahead and wondered what John was having for breakfast.

The train pulled into Praha hlavní nádraží in the midafternoon. It was the first time I saw Prague's main station, built in the late nineteenth-century at the epitome of the art nouveau era. I stepped onto a platform with an ornately vaulted train shed overhead. Gathering my suitcases, I headed to the waiting area and found an exit marked with a taxi sign. I walked with a sense of mission into the brisk, cloudy afternoon. The odor and sheen of brown coal faintly tinged the air.

The cab ride to my hotel was only minutes and a few koruna away. My driver carried my suitcases into the Hotel Praha on Královdorská near the Powder Tower. Constructed in the 1920s as a luxury hotel, it was sorely neglected during the communist era. After the Velvet Revolution, restitution was made to the family of the original owner, who in turn sold it to a small Austrian hotel chain. As the hotel went through significant repairs, some of the unrenovated rooms were available. My spacious bedroom, with comfortably worn furniture, satin-draped windows on two sides, and a huge marble bathroom with tub, cost the equivalent of 18 dollars a night. I hung my clothes in the carved-oak armoire. Dusk wouldn't fall for another hour, allowing me time for a daylight stroll to rediscover the old-world architecture, the mood of the people, and rhythm of the city. Once again, I was captivated.

My days were full. The musicians and journalists I'd met only four months before had filled my calendar with strategic appointments. My plan was to research the cost of living—housing, phone, utilities, food, health care—and scope out the music field and business market to determine whether I could find my niche and make a viable living in either.

My first morning was spent with a realtor who supplied more than just hard-data answers to my questions about apartment rentals. The agent explained that first-time rentals were sprouting in the growing market as a result of new restitution and privatization laws. She provided an overview about the recently passed property laws. Not only was I interested in what the Czechs were experiencing, but because I was considering pulling up stakes in France, moving my elderly husband, changing careers, and investing our savings in this new democracy, I *needed* to know.

John and I read in the international press about former Soviet Bloc countries dealing with a gargantuan privatization process. Each country faced unique complexities. In May 1990, a caption in *The New York Times* caught our attention: "East Europe's Sale of the Century." It was about the region's commitment to free enterprise and effort to lure foreign capital, management skills, and technology. This commitment, and the attitudes of people I met, were promising invitations.

In Czechoslovakia, President Havel and the newly elected political reformers connected the free-market system with private ownership of property. Czech legislators wasted no time in passing economic reform that outlined a stage-based transition from a centrally planned economy to a market economy. But, I wondered, who would ultimately benefit from free enterprise and the influx of foreign investors? The majority of Czechs had little money. Under the former regime, there was no means of investment. Shares in businesses and companies didn't exist. Banks offered a token interest on savings. The only people with access to capital were the communist *nomenklatura* and black-market entrepreneurs.

The real estate agent spoke about the restitution laws that returned private property confiscated by Nazi or communist regimes to the rightful owners. She thought that the restoration of property also helped restore the country's morale and self-esteem.

When I asked about the availability and costs of apartments in the city center, she began by describing how difficult it was to obtain an apartment under the old system, usually based on some higher-up's arbitrary whim. Since 1948, the communist state began to expropriate property, allotting flats to tenants at very low costs. Now, suddenly, as former owners had their properties returned, they also inherited their buildings' tenants who were protected by controlled rents. Free-market prices, based on supply and demand, were only allowed for new and vacated flats.

For foreigners like me, or first-time Czech renters, no cap was enforced on the amount of rent that could be charged. Even so, free-market rental rates were quite low for those with Western currency. I met an American couple who were living on an upper floor of a *panelák*. These functional blocks of prefabricated apartment towers on the outskirts of town were a communist legacy and housed one-third of the country's population. My friends paid the equivalent of 120 dollars per month for their two-bedroom flat, a sum much higher than their Czech neighbors in the building. My friends didn't mind, as a similar place in their home country would've been four to five times more expensive. Conversely, what they paid would have been impossible for most citizens of Czechoslovakia, where in 1991 the minimum monthly wage was 2,000 crowns (74 dollars) and the average monthly wage not even twice that.

The agent's entrepreneurial spirit belied the noncompetitive socialist order in which she'd been raised. She knew I was only gathering information but spent unhurried time with me, gave me valuable information, and would have been right had she hoped I'd become a future customer. She glanced at her file folder and read aloud the current listings. A flat with similar specs and size to our place in Nice would rent for 250 dollars, one quarter of what we were paying. *Noted.*

As for the telecom system, the realtor stressed that finding a property with a private phone line would be an advantage. Households with a telephone often shared a party line with others. I already knew that completing a phone call could take a half-dozen or more tries, dialing the number over and over on a rotary device, hoping it wouldn't go dead. Once a connection was made, the conversation was interrupted by pops, hisses, and static. People without home phones used outside telephone booths.

The realtor felt obliged to tell me that the procurement of a private line in a timely manner involved a bribe. Otherwise, the wait was months, even years. My first reaction was to ask how bribes worked—who should be paid and how much—but I stayed quiet. It felt almost like too personal a question. I naively hoped I'd never confront the culture of corruption and bribery carried over from the former system. The thought of it frightened me. I knew I couldn't move to a country where I'd have to operate in a shadow economy, pay people off, do underground deals. If that would be the case, I'd sooner go broke in France, honestly.

Utilities had been subsidized for decades with little attention paid to conserving energy, making consumer prices low. Heat was cranked up in homes and public places. It was February, and the cold and snow seemed inherent in Prague's wintry aesthetic. People moved about warmed by their woolen coats, fur-lined boots, and hats that covered heads and ears. The protocol in the lobbies of restaurants and concert halls was well established. Inside the front doors was the *vestiare,* typically staffed by a no-nonsense woman who took your overcoat in exchange for a ticket. I learned quickly that to bypass her and wear your coat into the dining room was frowned upon, and to drape it behind a chair at the table was considered even ruder. In fact, there was no need to wear a wrap in the toasty-warm interiors.

Though I savored the radiant comfort inside public places, it had become known that Czechoslovakia was one of the worst polluters in Eastern Europe. Its coal mining plants and city buildings stoked and burned dirty, cheap lignite coal for heat.   There were times the smog darkened daytime hours. My eyes would sting and I'd find myself coughing and congested. I asked how people coped. "We go to our *chatas* in the countryside to flee the bad air," they would answer. I had no country cabin. Air quality landed on the negative side of my pros and cons list.

I scouted out food prices by visiting grocery stores and restaurants. A hearty main course at a pub with a glass of beer or wine cost two or three dollars. Food was cheap, variety was limited, meat was prized, and greens were few. Anthony Bourdain had called Czechoslovakia "the land vegetables forgot."

I was curious why the menu offerings and flavor of the dishes were homogenous from one restaurant to the next, until I learned the glum story of Czech cuisine under communism. During the Soviet's *normal-ization* period, a strict recipe book was created and restaurant chefs were required to adhere to the formula's exact ingredients and measurements. Permission from the Ministry of Health was required to deviate from the 845 recipes. In Prague's international hotels, more elaborate dishes and food varieties could be found at high prices. But since the Revolution, new restaurants, pizza parlors, and other eateries were cropping up around the city.

At home, Czechs had the leeway to prepare recipes the way they wanted, if they could find the ingredients. Farms had been collectivized by the communist state, and vegetables such as asparagus and broccoli were unavailable. Even herbs, onions, and garlic could be hard to find. Root vegetables were plentiful, but sunshine-dependent produce like tomatoes, avocados, lettuce, or zucchini were rarely found except in the summer. A doctor from Prague told me that he once traveled outside his country and brought home two ripe tomatoes in the wintertime. His family was dazed and delighted by the rare off-season treat.

When I was invited to friends' homes, it was usually for a midmorning coffee or late afternoon tea. They most graciously served delicious homemade *koláčky* and *čajové pečivo* that were decorated more beautifully than at high-end Parisian bakeries. An invitation to a Czech home was a special occasion, for the hospitality was graced with old-world charm.

In all, my report to John could not tout the variety of foodstuff in Prague. At best, I might say that the cuisine was limited but changing, and the duck or pork with dumplings and sauerkraut were outstanding. Likening the food markets of Prague to the lush fruits and vegetables on Nice's Cours Saleya would be like comparing a backyard swing set to a trip to Disneyland.

On the subject of health care, I gathered anecdotal information from a few Czechs and Americans. I learned that the country's universal social security system entitled citizens to free medical care. Like all other institutions and industries in the country, the health care system was in a major transition. For foreigners, office visits and medical costs were nominal and easily paid out-of-pocket or through an international health insurance plan.

The Czechoslovak health system promoted preventive medicine. People swore by the curative nature of the country's spas and healing waters. Doctors recommended spa stays of several weeks, fully funded by the state health services, for a variety of conditions from arthritis to mental fatigue. Each spa town boasts at least one magnificent hotel fit for a king and were indeed frequented by European royalty over the centuries. All I could imagine was how John could benefit from the warm mineral springs, hot tubs, massages, and walking trails.

Without explaining my reason, I inquired about salaries for nurses. On my mind was the eventuality of in-home health care. Converting to U.S. currency, an experienced full-time registered nurse in a hospital earned less than 200 dollars per month. On hearing this, I inwardly breathed a long sigh of relief.

Before I left for Prague, John and I had received good news from our AARO health insurance representative in Paris. She had called for two reasons: to tell us that we could live anywhere in Europe and still keep our existing insurance plan, and that she would introduce us to a Paris AARO member who'd recently moved to Prague. She thought we'd enjoy meeting Norbert Auerbach. That was an understatement. I could write volumes about this enigmatic Czech-born Jewish man who, as a child, had fled Prague with his family in the nick of time before the Nazi invasion. He went on to become president and CEO of United Artists, and would become our friend.

My days in Prague were crowded with meetings, and evenings were filled with social events. Whatever the encounter, I took written or mental notes. I called John every day from the hotel phone to give him updates, but our conversations were brief given the exorbitant cost of international calls. He said he missed me and was keeping busy by taking Misty for her daily walks, starting a new painting, reading the newspaper on the terrace, having occasional lunches with Deon, and chatting with Shirley Karoli, who phoned him regularly.

My research into the country's music world started at the office of Ivo Letov and Tomáš Sousedík of Pragokoncert. According to these two entertainment executives, dramatic changes were taking place in the music industry. They said that subsidizations from the Ministry of Culture, once guaranteed, were now uncertain. Artist fees were slow to rise to Western standards. Letov assured me that Pragokoncert continued to manage the Reduta and would organize Zdeněk's and Zora's concert in December. He knew I'd be joining them on stage and he planned to feature my name on the publicity. He might be able to procure more opportunities like this one, offering exposure but not substantial remuneration. I didn't find it necessary to point out the inadequacy of this idea. I thanked the gentlemen sincerely.

At the time, I was unaware of new performing arts agencies coming onto the market. One was established by Michael Kocáb, leader of a rock band that had been suppressed by the communist regime. With Václav Havel and others, he was a founder of the revolutionary political movement Civic Forum, became a member of the Federal Assembly, and helped negotiate the pullout of the Soviet troops from Czechoslovakia. In April 1990, he founded Art Production K, the first private agency to represent Czech and Western artists. Had I known about Kocáb, I'd have tried to meet him, perhaps unsuccessfully, but I'd have made the attempt nonetheless. Stranger things have happened. After all, he was a rocker-turned-politician and businessman, I was a singer with a successful Prague debut under my belt, and in the castle was a playwright-turned-president who appreciated my poetry.

Olga Kittnarová invited me to a concert at Smetana Hall at the beautiful Obecní dům and to an elegant Conservatory Ball at the Lucerna Palace. The Czech orchestras, symphonies, and operas surpassed world-class standards. She also arranged a host of meetings for me with musicologists, authors, composers, and pedagogues at the Czech Ministry of Culture and the Prague Conservatory. The conversations were captivating but left me doubtful that collaboration or solo engagements would be plentiful enough to make a living.

Zdeněk Merta asked me to go with him one evening to the Karlín Music Theatre, an architecturally exquisite neo-baroque building, where his friends were performing. I mingled with actors and musicians at the post-performance party, had a wonderful time, and felt at home. But meeting these performers didn't give me the sense I would become one of them. Although Zdeněk and I had several one-on-one conversations about ways to collaborate, he was at a loss for ideas, other than inviting me as guest singer at his Reduta concert later that year.

But I had an offer for him. Jim Keene from Nebraska, who attended the second of my Reduta concerts, had asked me to launch his Brownville Cabaret Series in July in the U.S. I was gratified to ask Zdeněk if he'd be my pianist for this concert in my home state, with all expenses paid, including airfare and lodging, in addition to a healthy performance fee. He happily agreed.

Compared to Prague's capricious music milieu, the business climate appeared to be roaring. I pursued every lead anyone gave me. They were plentiful, and one led to another. My journalist friend, Andrea Vernerová, introduced me to an attorney, JUDr. Petr Zima. We three met at the sublime Hotel Paříž. Besides his native Czech, Dr. Zima was fluent in English and French. His overview of the country's business situation was just what I needed. He outlined the types of corporate entities and the rules for foreign business owners.

Dr. Zima was a humble person with a sharp intellect and kind demeanor who apologized for not having every answer in the maelstrom of changing laws. He said the country was swimming in the uncharted seas between central planning and free market. The country had yet to create a securities market or a competitive banking system, but this would come in time. He seemed reassured that the government was trying to distribute property to the population in a fair way, most significantly through a voucher plan that would allow ordinary citizens to acquire shares in thousands of privatized companies. He said the playing field had to be leveled for Czechs because they lacked private capital. His concern for equality left an impression on me.

The clincher came when Dr. Zima peered above his spectacles and softly stated in his honest, introverted manner, "No one can be sure—after all, we've just emerged from decades of totalitarian domination—but I believe our country's new political and social systems will remain stable, and business will experience steady growth." Those words from a thoughtful legal mind held more weight than all the predictions of economic analysts put together. I thanked Dr. Zima for the informative meeting and said that I hoped to call on him again when my plans were clearer.

There were also chance encounters. I was poised to jump on the elevator at the office building where I had an appointment with a business referral, when American-accented voices rang from an upstairs hallway. Their conversation and laughter echoed in the otherwise quiet building shortly after office hours. The couple was apparently piqued about being stood up for their appointment. We soon discovered that all three of us had been jilted by the same ill-mannered gentleman. But no matter. I met Phyllis and James Taliaferro, an attractive, generous, and fun-loving couple who would become John's and my closest friends. James was with ČTK's Made in Publicity, the marketing arm of the Czechoslovak news agency. Phyllis was about to accept a staff position as the medical officer for the British and Canadian Embassies in Prague, where she would eventually assemble a roster of doctors and health care professionals who spoke English and were acculturated in Western health care practices. This valuable referral system would eventually lead Phyllis to start a full-scale primary health center that offered comprehensive health services to international and Czech clients in Prague.

To clarify why I said *jumped* on the elevator, office buildings in Prague had passenger elevators called paternoster lifts—an intimidating chain of doorless compartments moving up and down in a loop without stopping. Praguers could deftly step on without even looking and casually step off at their desired floor. In contrast, we foreigners hopped nervously onto the moving target like six-year-olds entering a twirling jump rope, afraid it would tangle at their feet.

Phyllis and James had only lived in Prague a short while, but they were connected and they connected me. That same evening, Phyllis asked me to join them at a cocktail party at the British Club, run by the embassy. There I met British diplomats and interesting business types.

Each encounter was an insight into this nascent country's current state of affairs, whether business, diplomatic, or cultural.

James was involved in the establishment of the American Chamber of Commerce. U.S. Ambassador Shirley Temple Black initiated a meeting of American businesspeople, and Czechs doing business with U.S. companies, to discuss the formation of a chamber. James insisted that I attend this groundbreaking event.

Shirley Temple, a child movie star, was now Ambassador Black. When she was appointed by President George H.W. Bush in August 1989, neither had a clue that within three months, Czechoslovakia would be revolutionized.

Ambassador Black came through the door wearing a colorful Chanel-style suit. Barely five-feet-two, the dark-haired diplomat's stature was better measured by her large life of public service. I immediately recognized her dimpled smile and twinkling eyes from her movies my family watched on TV when we were kids. We loved her songs and had the sheet music to some of her hits. The ambassador addressed the group and gave razor-sharp reasons why American and Czech business partnerships were important to both countries. She invoked the wishes of presidents Václav Havel and George H.W. Bush, who considered both countries as dedicated business partners and trusted friends.

In a relaxed conversation after the meeting at a nearby bar, one of the American envoys told an entertaining story that was corroborated years later on the embassy's website. A few days after communism fell in Czechoslovakia, a seated Ambassador Black called her senior staff together into a private, closed-door meeting. Looking them sternly in the eye, she told them: "I'm only going to do this once, just once." And with that, she stood up, smiled, and pranced around the room singing "On the Good Ship Lollypop."

At this fortuitous event, I received an earful from those who spoke, and those I met casually before and after the gathering. Frankly, I was emboldened. No one actually knew what they were doing. Everyone was flying blind in a muddled system. And yet, people were excited and energized. There were some complainers who seemed annoyed or overwhelmed by the cultural differences and inconveniences. I doubt they ever adapted, and I assume they abandoned whatever reason brought them to Prague in the first place. But the majority of Americans I met wanted to help each other and saw this unimaginably unique situation as a collective adventure.

As I sized up the group of about eighty people with my novice perspective, I noticed several things. The vast majority were men. Of the Americans, most were executives seconded (brought in) by large corporations to scout out or establish offices in Prague. In the minority were entrepreneurs investing their own capital to enter the market. A lamenting refrain swelled from both Fortune 500 executives and small entrepreneurs about the lack of professional business services and the need for customer-service-oriented personnel. My antennae went up at the mention of "need"—and their complaint was duly noted.

It was an altogether informative evening. I walked on freshly fallen snow back to my hotel. In my pocket were a dozen or so business cards from fellow adventurers. I sauntered across the Charles Bridge and had it almost all to myself. Prague in February was devoid of crowds. The ancient city was calm and beautiful. I smiled as fortune dawned on me—my second trip to Prague was as prolific as the first, and I hadn't sung a note.

My admiration for the Czech people heightened during this trip as my knowledge about what they'd been through deepened. I felt their resilience through these changing times. The Czechs were adapting to more than a *transition*, which implies a gradual morphing. The Revolution had caused a sudden *upheaval* on every level. They rose to the challenge, on their toes, willing to learn from Westerners, but at the same time, wanting to share their culture and wisdom with the invading masses in a respectful, intelligent, and proud manner. I was learning from them and distinctly proud to share the same roots. I could see how my own upbringing, my Czech-American mother raising us singlehandedly, stemmed from the culture of my new friends.

I realized that possessing a sensibility for Czech music and language was an inroad to their trust. Eyes illuminated when I'd spiel out my sparse but well-pronounced phrases. One charming Czech trait was their habit of giggling when experiencing a surprised delight. Hearing a foreigner attempt their language gave rise to a soft laughter that was music to my ears.

I waited for golden moments to express my love for the music of Bohemia and Moravia. I'd studied Dvořák's *Cigánské melodie.* I'd heard about the legend of Blaník from which both Janáček and Smetana had based two symphonic compositions. I was curious about the Bohemian legends, and my new Czech friends enjoyed telling the stories. Blaník is a sacred mountain where warriors, led by Saint Wenceslas, sleep until the day they will be summoned to rally and defend their people in time of need. Conversing with Czechs about their fabled stories touched their spirit as well as mine. More than one person told me in a hushed voice that they believed Václav Havel, whose first name means Wenceslas, was that leader, and the people of Prague, the warriors. In their eyes, the Blaník heroes were summoned awake in 1989 after centuries of oppression and took to the streets to rescue the people. I didn't doubt this.

My notebook was filled with material for my report to John. My mission had been to gather information, take notes, but make no determination. The cost accounts and business opportunities spoke for themselves. I penned the report on the train and plane rides home. I made a simple plan that compared costs of living in Prague to Nice. On a separate page, I sketched out a preface to the report, a narrative that I would verbally and softly deliver to John. The words would be important, many of which I'd never before uttered.

My reasoning had to reflect my promise to him, our promise to each other, that we would always be together. For the first time, I needed to explicitly say that his health must now be our first concern and should determine our next move. If his walking became harder, and his body grew weaker, he'd need professional care. We must find a solution where the combined costs of living and in-home nursing were affordable. I needed to assure him there was no sacrifice involved. On the contrary, I was blessed to be his partner and primed to leave music if I found a position that provided us security, well-being, and longevity.

I needed to convey something else, something he already knew—that I loved him, and I knew he'd do the same for me in a heartbeat.

11

AU REVOIR LA FRANCE

On the way back to Nice after my second trip to Czechoslovakia, there was no question in my mind whether I should pursue business opportunities in Prague, but I couldn't make this decision alone. When I got home, John was happy to see me. He hated it when I was away for long. We spent hours talking at our dining room table, on the promenade, or at our favorite café. My written report was simple: two columns listing the costs to maintain a respectable standard of living in two very different cities. The sum at the bottom of *Remain in Nice* was four times greater than *Life in Prague*. We were aware that inflation would change the calculus over the years, but for the foreseeable future, our monthly budget in Prague could be covered by John's Social Security income alone, with some to spare. We'd no longer have to dip into our resources except for one big scoop upfront for moving costs and business start-up capital. Choosing *Life in Prague* would cut our losses and, with luck, refill our coffers with revenue gained . . . if my business succeeded. If it didn't, we had a cushion to make a soft landing . . . somewhere. I was betting on success, not just for us, but for Czechoslovakia.

Nothing was a hard sell between my husband and me. We supported each other's creative ideas. But this proposition was a wild card played for high stakes. With a mixture of excitement and practicality, I tried to summarize everything I learned during the trip—the people I met, their thoughts on the current situation, their hopes for the future. I saw John's skeptical face melt into surrendering admiration. He saw my heart, my sincerity, that I'd done my homework, and that I'd laid out a well-reasoned case.

He acknowledged that the prospects for Czechoslovakia's future looked bright. Compared to other countries in the region, particularly Hungary and Poland, Czechoslovakia was a uniquely attractive market for Western traders and investors because of its highly skilled labor force and the economic achievements it had made before World War II, when it was the seventh most industrialized state in the world.

The other bright prospect that inspired John and me was the moral leadership of President Havel. He was the first leader of the newly democratic countries to visit the United States. On 22 February 1990, a mere two months into Havel's presidency, President George H.W. Bush had greeted the heroic figure and hailed him as a symbol of courage and transformation in Eastern Europe.

When Havel delivered a powerful address to a joint session of the U.S. Congress, which received seventeen standing ovations, John read every word printed the next day in the newspaper. Havel spoke of the difference a few revolutionary days had made:

> When they arrested me on 27 October [1989], I was living in a country ruled by the most conservative communist government in Europe, and our society slumbered beneath the pall of a totalitarian system. Today, less than four months later, I am speaking to you as the representative of a country which has complete freedom of speech, which is preparing for free elections, and which seeks to

establish a prosperous market economy and its own foreign policy. It is all very extraordinary indeed. . . . We are living in extraordinary times. The human face of the world is changing so rapidly that none of the familiar political speedometers are adequate.

John paid attention to the macroeconomics of Havel's visit to Washington, which opened doors to trade, diplomacy, and warm bilateral relations. President Bush lifted former trade restrictions imposed during the communist regime. He set into motion a new trade agreement between the two countries that granted Czechoslovakia the most-favored-nation status, which guaranteed the lowest possible tariffs on its exports. He assured U.S. support for its admission into the International Monetary Fund and World Bank. Bush also pledged to send Peace Corps volunteers as English Education Specialists to Czechoslovakia. Czech lawmakers provided favorable conditions for foreign investment, and U.S. trade missions began arriving in greater numbers to explore possibilities.

While I knew something about these historic meetings because we'd followed them in real time through the media, I never would have believed that the Peace Corps, the United States Embassy, and scores of foreign companies in Czechoslovakia would soon become my clients.

What I was able to explain to John at that time was my understanding of the needs emerging from this ripe commercial environment. Hundreds, if not thousands, of representatives from foreign corporations were descending on Prague, most of them coming and going several times before making a decision to do business in the country—initially for a cursory look, again to explore further, then to find a temporary office, and finally, to set up shop. These executives stayed at the top-tier hotels, which often lacked a full complement of business services or had none at all.

My idea was to establish an office services bureau in Prague for visiting businesspeople. I had sketched out a plan that outlined my company's purpose, services provided, market opportunities, projected start-up costs, and target income. Luckily, I didn't need a formal document to obtain a bank loan for start-up capital. The outline was only for John and me, but later came in handy to register the company.

John was open-minded and, I believe, impressed. I'm not sure the business scheme convinced him entirely, but when I presented my loving rationale—that our commitment to each other was foremost in my mind—it sank in, for both of us. After every aspect was discussed and exhausted, a silent, synchronized moment reigned over us. A look into each other's eyes. A sigh. A smile. A knowing.

We made the decision to move forward in the direction of *Life in Prague*. True to our pattern, we walked forward in faith, no turning back, and offered our plan in our nighttime prayer for God alone to nix. We strode along with a fresh orientation as if we were carrying a safe passage document in our back pockets.

Remain in Nice had lost the contest, but for a while longer, the sunny seaside town was still under our feet and surrounding our view. John spent more time in his bright studio, painting one canvas after another. Several American friends caught wind of our eventual departure from the South of France and came to visit while we could still host and play tour guide. I suggested we might celebrate John's birthday in Corsica, the French island in the Mediterranean which he'd often talked about visiting.

Early in the spring, we took Misty to the veterinarian because she'd become very weak. Already sixteen, we assumed her listlessness was caused by age. The vet said she had cancer and wouldn't live more than a few months. John and I took Misty home and doted on her as we watched her decline, but she still wagged her tail when John called her name. Eventually, Misty's appetite dwindled, her breathing was labored, and she began to whimper and whine as she struggled to amble from one spot to the next. She was in pain, and that in turn pained John, her master, companion, and friend.

One summer day, John dolefully said the time had come for Misty to be released from her suffering. He asked if I'd be with Misty in her final moments. He couldn't bear to see her die. John helped me slide her into her travel cage. He paused for a minute, and said, with teardrops on his cheeks, an indebted smile on his lips, "Goodbye, old friend."

I drove Misty to the animal clinic and laid my hand on her trembling frame as she was brought to rest. A mournful pall lingered in our home for quite some time. John was no stranger to grief in his life, and he carried on good-naturedly. But there were always three of us. Now, only two.

The Brownville concerts were on a July weekend in Nebraska. It was hard to leave John home alone. But we eagerly anticipated the arrival of my new Czech collaborator, Zdeněk Merta. He came to Nice by train to rehearse for our show and relax at the seashore. It was his first time in France and the United States. We flew to New York together and had a few days to see Manhattan and friends. There, Zdeněk had arranged to meet some of his compatriots who'd emigrated from Czechoslovakia to America—one was Peter Sís. I was pleased that Zdeněk invited me to his lunch with Peter.

We went to the artist's Manhattan apartment where he showed us his recent work, and afterwards we walked to a nearby restaurant. I was amazed by Peter's story, how he'd traveled to the United States in 1982 to create a film about Czechoslovakia's participation in the 1984 Olympics in Los Angeles, when the Soviet Union suddenly announced that all Soviet Bloc members must boycott the games. Peter decided to stay in America and was granted asylum.

Since then, the internationally acclaimed illustrator, author, and filmmaker has won numerous awards. Many of his books are on my bookshelf. His stories and images are a poignantly beautiful testament to freedom. In recent years, Peter has reflected on living inside a totalitarian regime and the symbolism of the wall:

> The wall which for many years divided Berlin and the whole of Europe is now, fortunately, only a memory. But some memories need to be preserved. As a message about the past. As a warning to

the future. Even though one wall has fallen, others remain and more are being built. All over the world . . . Symbolic walls, ideological walls, and real walls. Walls of fear, confinement, and suspicion. Walls without which our lives could be freer and happier.

After three days in New York, Zdeněk and I flew to Nebraska, where the experience was bizarre enough to be considered an absurdist comedy. To begin with, expectations were high. When I initially agreed to perform, the promoter Jim Keene had raved about the acoustically vibrant concert venue he'd created out of an old church that had been lifted from one Nebraska town and transported to Brownville, a historic and artsy village seventy miles south of Omaha. Jim had equipped it with a stage, a Steinway grand piano, and a state-of-the-art sound and light system. After a successful year of well-attended classical concerts, he'd decided to offer lighter fare with a cabaret series. I was its first headliner.

When we touched ground in Omaha, a frazzled-looking Jim Keene met us at the airport. He had catastrophic news about the concert hall. During an electrical storm the night before, a bolt of lightning had struck the steeple of the church and set the hall on fire. The stage, the grand piano, and the entire interior were ruined. Jim was devastated, but said the show would go on. He had three days before opening night to find an alternative facility. We wound up on a makeshift stage in the unaesthetic lounge of a steakhouse restaurant located ten minutes from Brownville. During our rehearsal, I complained to Zdeněk that the place smelled of greasy hamburgers. He concurred, but we grinned and bore it.

Both shows were sold out. The audience was demonstrably thrilled with our performances. My extended family, old school chums, and followers of the concert series attended. I had coaxed Zdeněk to play some of his compositions during the interlude, particularly his spirited Moravian folk music. The audience loved the pianist and his music, as I knew they would. Zdeněk accompanied my songs well, although he

Singing my heart out, with Zdeněk at the piano.

After the Brownville concerts, Zdeněk and I relax at M's Pub in Omaha's Old Market district

impishly altered our rehearsed cues to throw me off my game. He would do anything for a laugh, and succeeded. I pretended not to notice or be bothered by his antics and carried on. I'd never before experienced a similar interaction on stage with a colleague. After the show, I blasted him. He feigned an apology while still chuckling.

One of Zdeněk's more typically Czech attributes was an ironic and slightly mocking sense of humor. I wondered if finding a comedic twist had helped Czechs survive the dark periods of their history. Along the lines of the German *schadenfreude*—taking a kind of pleasure over the misfortune of another—Czechs leaned on satire in the midst of insecurity or difficulty.

To soften the blow, I placed this acerbic tendency into the category of absurdist writers like Milan Kundera, Bohumil Hrabal, Franz Kafka, and Václav Havel—authors who availed a metaphorical fantasy to illustrate the woes of an oppressive regime. Their artful works craftily exposed a sad reality through humor, restlessness, and transcendence. They touched the heart of the national collective conscience while pulling the wool over the eyes of the authorities. I met the Bohemian spirit through these writers and, more concretely, through my new friends.

Years later, I was able to view our music tour through Zdeněk's eyes. In his book *Křížem krážem: aneb Dobrodružství potulného muzikanta* (Cross by Cross: or the Adventures of a Wandering Musician), Zdeněk devoted an entire chapter to me with the unoriginal title "Anne Marie Kenny." He credited me with opening doors for him to American connections, which had been my goal. He wrote about first seeing me in 1990 on the Reduta stage with Bob McCoy. With his tongue-in-cheek writing style, he described Bob as a "piano virtuoso" and me as "charming and red-haired," with no mention of my singing, musicianship, or artistry. He recounted our subsequent interactions, and described me as "assertive but witty" and "a little nutty, but without a doubt, very entertaining." I vacillated between regarding his unflattering remarks as frolicsome Czech humor or biting, backhanded compliments. Did the disparaging humor stem from insecurity, jealousy, or resentment? I would never know. I liked him too much to start an argument.

In many respects, Zdeněk wasn't an ordinary Czech, an ordinary composer, or ordinary anything. He was a genius musician with an eclectic taste for all genres of music. On a personal level, he was a good-looking, square-jawed, medium-built Slav with an inextinguishable sparkle. He was a drinker who out-drank me. His warm and flirtatious personality could be disarming, likely intentionally. We had a crush on each other that was never given voice or acted upon.

Not all of his multifaceted traits were glowing. During our Brownville concerts, Jim Keene and Zdeněk met without my knowledge to negotiate future concerts for him and Zora. Months later, I learned that Jim had booked the duo for the following year. I'd been left out of the covert discussions and felt pangs of deceit. No doubt when Zdeněk accompanied me to the U.S., he'd brought his talent and charm along with his personal ambition. Or maybe his secrecy was a lack of trust, attributable to living his entire life under a regime that encouraged suspicion of one's neighbor and spawned whispered conversations. At the time, I said nothing and acted as if everything was normal. I swallowed my hurt, and helped promote their shows. There are no good friendships without occasional disappointments and perceived betrayals. Our friendship could have withstood more than this deception, yet thankfully it was never again tested.

When I think back about the engagements in Brownville, despite the thunderous applause and accolades, the performances had felt lackluster. I couldn't identify the reason at the time. It wasn't only the burned church, the slapdash venue, or my partner upstaging me. I was moving on professionally. My devotion to a field that filled me spiritually but not financially was slipping away. The lightning strike was a symbol, the hand of divinity closing the book on my musical career—an engrossing volume that perhaps I'd pick up again after my new mission was accomplished.

In the last week of September, to celebrate his birthday, John and I boarded ourselves and our Ford Escort onto the Gare Maritime ferry—destination Corsica. We left shortly before noon from the *Port de Nice*, just around the bend from our apartment. Within six hours, we sailed into Bastia, the island's largest port and second most populous city. The harbor was dense with sailboats, private yachts, ferries, and ships. Rising above the waterfront were colorful houses, churches, and citadels with ramparts. We had rented a cabin in a lush, forested area. During the day, we toured the island by car through the mountainous terrain. We visited the town of Ajaccio where Napoléon Bonaparte was born in 1769, two years after Corsica was purchased by France from the Genoese. The unlit roadways in the evenings caused us to return before sundown to our enclave of cottages, where mosquitoes feasted on us through the night.

We drove into the town of Bastia each morning for breakfast, and John picked up the *International Herald Tribune*. His interest in world news was now focused on our future life in Eastern Europe. I was lucky that my partner comprehended the breadth and depth of global affairs, although he considered himself merely a student of history and life.

Indeed, those were exciting times on the European stage and troubling times in the Middle East. Days before our Corsican vacation in early September 1991, a further dismantling of the Soviet Union occurred when the Baltic countries of Estonia, Latvia, and Lithuania became independent states, and the United States reopened its embassies in their capitals. Then the Russian city of Leningrad changed its name to Saint Petersburg. Before the year was out, even greater change would take place. The Ukrainian people would vote to become an independent state, the Soviet Union would officially collapse, Mikhail Gorbachev would resign, and Boris Yeltsin would become president of an independent Russia. It was a big year for Europe and for the world.

At the outset of the year, the U.S. and a coalition of thirty-five other nations launched Operation Desert Storm in the Persian Gulf in response to Iraq's invasion of Kuwait five months earlier. The array of nations formed the largest military alliance since World War II. Kuwait was liberated. John was astonished that, for the first time, war could be shown on television in real time, broadcasting live from the front lines of battle. It didn't seem much of an accomplishment to me. I hated the thought of war.

A full week in Corsica was too long. These were the last days of September and the first of October. The year was running out. We were planning a huge move early the following year. There was much to do, and we were cooped up on an island. Granted, the museums in Bastia and Ajaccio were interesting, and the island's cuisine was delicious. But little other activity took place. Our jaunts were short and slow; we drove rather than hiked. In the evenings, with no television in our room, we read books.

We should have arranged the birthday trip differently. Three days, not seven. A hotel in town, not a cabin in the wilderness. I felt isolated in a barren backwater with no distractions. It was terrifying to be standing still, having just stepped outside of the whirlwind I'd been caught up in for so long.

I found myself wrought with worry—afraid that, at some unexpected moment when the time came to stack up the components of my grand plan, it'd come crashing down. And I'd be responsible because it had been my naive idea. If it crashed, it would not be for my lack of energy, sincerity, or love. It would be karma for my ill-begotten ways. Oh, I did love John and wanted to provide him security and enjoyment in his last years—how many more, I didn't know.

In Corsica, I drank with more fervor and quantity than usual. So did John. I was at my wit's end, but didn't understand it as such. I only knew what I felt, an anguished churning inside. Being slightly inebriated calmed me. If only I could rest at the *slight* degree point. Nirvana lasted for a serene minute or two, like a billow that floated me, until I took another and another drink that kicked me off the cloud, my feet stumbling and words slurring.

One afternoon, I found a different escape. A young man at an outdoor bistro glanced my way. For the hour or so that John and I sat at our table eating a seafood lunch and drinking local wine, the Corsican stranger shyly smiled. As did I. When John went inside to the restroom, I went over to the handsome twenty-something-year-old and said hello. He said hello back like an eager pup. I asked if he'd like to talk later and meet me at the same spot that afternoon.

He was there at the agreed-upon time. We talked. He was timid, robust, and sweet. We went out to a country road in a deserted area that only a local would know. Our short time together was simple. Raw. Wonderful. *Merci, mon jeune homme.* I felt so much better, as though I'd had a long, hard cry that poured my guts out. Every last ounce of panic, doubt, and shame was released in those moments of flesh-to-flesh contact against the hood of a pickup. And sure, shame would come, but not right then. In that very moment, all was good and right.

At the end of October, I took the train to Paris for one last time before our move. While there, I had some dental work done, met with Janine Reiss, and shopped for business clothes. I purchased two classically chic suits from the up-and-coming designer Emmanuelle Khanh in the Marais district. A silk blouse and fitted wool skirt suit with coordinated pumps would give me confidence in my new business role. Mother, who always said to dress the part, would understand that.

My main reason to be in Paris was to collect my nephew David Orso at the airport. He and his brother Mike had visited John and me in France at various intervals. This time, I'd asked Dave if he'd be willing to spend a few months to help as we wrapped up our life in Nice and set up residence in Prague. Although a transport company would pack and move our furniture and household goods when the time came, I was still swamped with logistical tasks before then.

Recently graduated from high school, Dave was an intelligent, well-read, and personable young man who was more than happy to assist his aunt and uncle while seeing the world at the same time. Not having children of my own, I've always held a special love for my nephews and nieces. Dave, the oldest among them, helped us immeasurably.

We gave Dave the spare bedroom in our home in Nice. He and John enjoyed each other's company, played cards, discussed history, and walked around town together. Dave was more than happy to spend time at the seashore where women of all ages, sizes, and shapes frolicked in topless swimsuits.

John and I hosted Thanksgiving dinner early because of my scheduled trip to Prague for my second concert at the Reduta, this time with Zdeněk and Zora. I roasted turkey breasts (whole turkeys were only available at Christmastime in France) and served it with all the traditional trimmings and pumpkin pie. Our table was extended to accommodate seven friends plus John, Dave, and me. I didn't overly imbibe in champagne and red wine because I tried to set an example for my nephew, who also had inherited a predilection for drinking from our shared Irish ancestry. My efforts at model behavior failed more than I wished.

Dave came with me to Prague in mid-November, two weeks before the concert. I had an additional checklist of research items to investigate about our upcoming move while there. Zdeněk and Zora gave us access to a flat in the Žižkov neighborhood of the city for our two-week stay. The fourth-floor walk-up was rudimentarily furnished but fully adequate, located on a tramline and a short walk to the top of Wenceslas Square.

I had prearranged appointments with the general managers of the best hotels. Using the same strategy as I had for the Paris Ritz, I called on the top executives and tried to politely impress their secretary-gatekeepers, who invariably arranged a meeting. No longer peddling musical ambiance, I instead proposed office services for their hotel's business guests, with skilled bilingual secretaries who could make appointments, type documents and correspondence, and provide monthly phone, fax, and mailing address services until the clients had established their own offices. Concealing my crossed fingers, I assured them that my company would be up-and-running in a few months, and that I planned to have offices in the city center.

The hotel managers were receptive to my idea; several seemed genuinely grateful. Even the hotels with business centers struggled under the precipitous demands for a full range of services, or they often lacked familiarity with Western business norms. One of the most memorable meetings was with Pavel Hlinka at the posh Hotel Intercontinental, who offered his perspective on the new market needs. Another was with Martin Coufal at the majestic Palace Hotel, who was certain these essential services were lacking and promised to promote my company to his clients as soon as I gave the go-ahead.

I wanted to leap forward right then—move to Prague, find an office, hire one or two bilingual assistants, create an attractive and clear brochure in English, French, and Czech, and distribute it to every American, British, French, and German company in Prague—but patience and timing held me wisely in place. In the meantime, I listened, observed, and planned. I had some start-up capital that could float the company for three to four months before it generated revenue. But the advice from my friend and management consulting expert Gerard Smits echoed in my head: "Find a way to make money right away." It sounded like an obvious maxim in its literal simplicity, but four months later, when I actually did hit the ground and form a company, Gerard's concept gave me permission to use ingenuity while waiting for my initial concept to take off.

My research trip bore fruit, and I was eager to see John and share the affirmative outcomes of my fieldwork. After the two performances of *Americký Kabaret* with Zdeněk and Zora at the Reduta, Dave and I headed back to France. Soon after our return, John and I settled on an exact date to say *au revoir* to the country that'd been our home for nine years. We notified the owner of our flat that we'd vacate by 31 March 1992, which was conveniently the renewal date of our lease agreement. John and I hoped to return to Nice for a few weeks in the wintertime, an expense I factored into our new budget. We spoke with the concierge of our building who'd been a dependable friend over the years. She was certain she could arrange a short-term studio apartment for us in the building. The thought of being snowbirds on the Côte d'Azur during part of the Prague winter appealed to John, but less so to me. Paris, yes, any time of the year.

Before our final move, I returned to Prague one more time in early February to secure living and office space. The outstanding realtor I'd met with a year earlier was there to show me apartments in the city center. Several looked suitable, but she urged me to see one more place in Suchdol, a northern suburb of Prague. It was a spacious, two-story home with a basement, garage, and garden with fruit trees. Two blocks away was a bus line to Dejvická, a major metro line that sped underground into the center of the city within ten minutes. On the corner was a tiny greengrocer stand. A mechanic lived up the street, an electrician in the other direction, and not far was a clean, family-run *hostinec* with a restaurant that served hearty meals.

"The air is pure up here," coaxed the realtor. "You can walk in the fresh air, have meals on the back patio surrounded by the apple, plum, and walnut trees." I called John that night from the hotel and described the options. We were both in favor of the house. The next morning, I paid the deposit and first month's rent.

During this last brief stay as a visitor, before I'd become an official Prague resident, I packed in more meetings. I saw journalist friends Olga and Andrea, musician friends Zdeněk and Zora, and my new American friends Phyllis and James. I met with prospective clients and attended a gathering of the barely up-and-running American Chamber of Commerce.

One productive appointment was with an American, Steve Kelly. He had office space for rent which he'd advertised in the new English-language newspaper, the *Prague Post*. We met at the proposed office location on Spálená 15 in the former *Knižní velkoobchod* building. The two-room office on the second floor was outmoded and run-down, like many structures in this magnificent city. But a better location couldn't be found. It was just around the corner from the Reduta on Národní třída and almost equidistant from nearby Wenceslas Square and the

Charles Bridge. But before Steve could finalize the sublet to me, I had to meet the new owner, Miroslav Macek, who was out of town for another week.

Regretfully, I couldn't wait and needed to return to Nice. I explained to Steve, "My husband and I will move to Prague the first of April. I've just signed a lease on a house. If you can possibly hold the office space until then, I'd be grateful." He couldn't guarantee, but said he'd try.

John was happy to see me. We had a clear course to follow and made the most of our last few months in Nice. I kept my Sunday gig at the Beach Plaza in Monaco. The manager asked me to play two private galas with my band, which offered substantially more money than the Sunday afternoon concerts with their house pianist. The manager was unhappy when I told him I was leaving.

Our calendar was already getting filled with social gatherings before the year came to a close—a black-tie dinner at the house of friends in Vence, a Christmas Day singing engagement at the Beach Plaza in Monaco, lunch at Colette and Albin's in Mougins, and a New Year's Eve party with friends at their home in the perched village of Tourrettes-sur-Loup.

John and his friend Deon were lunching together on a more frequent basis during this time. After one such outing, John flew through the apartment door beaming brighter than the rays of sun on the sea. They'd been to their favorite restaurant at the Hotel Plaza in Nice, an ornate Belle Époque architectural jewel. The two debonair gentlemen were such habitués of the Plaza that they greeted the doormen and waiters by name, and on occasion, would hobnob with the hotel manager. On this day, John and Deon had chatted with the manager about having an art show featuring a retrospect of John's works in the airy rotunda adjacent to the lobby. Not only did the manager like the idea, but he set 17 February 1992 as the date for a grand reception, the start of the ten-day exhibition. John and Deon brainstormed down to the finest details.

It would be titled "Jobul: Then and Now." John wanted to invite everyone we knew to the reception. He would design a snazzy invitation and mail it far and wide. The manager offered to have the grand piano moved to the middle of the rotunda for background piano music during the reception. John asked if I'd find the pianist and sing a song or two before the presentation he'd give. John selected his best twenty-five paintings to display. He had some of his most recent canvases framed. He worked on a corresponding price list. Mid-February was around the corner and John was in high gear.

The event was spectacular. Many of our friends and acquaintances attended the reception, and brought their friends. People came to honor John. At least a half-dozen paintings were sold. Watching John prepare for and mount this art show, a perfect culmination of his artistic endeavors in France, gave me a satisfaction beyond my wildest dreams.

Six days before we left France, I had written only four words on my calendar. "Be quiet and *tranquille*." I must have heeded the advice because somehow we pulled everything together, with nostalgia for what we were leaving and excitement for what the future could bring.

On 27 March 1992, with John in the front passenger seat and Dave in the back of our reliable Ford Escort, I sat behind the wheel, took a deep breath, and headed up through the Alps and across the plains to Bohemia.

12

LIFE IN PRAGUE

T*he car ride in early spring* brought us to our new world, the third city in Europe we would call home. It was Dave's first time on such a breathtaking excursion. John mapped out a different route from the voyage he'd plotted a year and a half earlier. We passed slowly through distinctive lands that gave us a sense of connection between where we'd been and where we were going. We covered terrain between our bright blue southern French seacoast and the great lakes of Lombardy, through the mountains of Switzerland and forested regions of Germany, to the Bohemian lands of my ancestors.

We headed straight to a hotel in Prague's Old Town district that I'd reserved for a few nights until our house was move-in ready. Our furniture had yet to arrive. My phone calls to the director of the French transport company were met by the voice of angry frustration at the other end of the line. Apparently, our huge container with its camion drivers, who had never been to Eastern Europe, were stuck at a freight holding facility on the outskirts of Prague. They'd been stopped at the border and ordered to drive directly to the customs depot in the capital city instead of to our house, which had been the arrangement.

Well before leaving Nice, John and I got estimates from three moving companies. We chose the one that guaranteed *tout compris,* a door-to-door delivery price all-inclusive of taxes, insurance, and customs charges. Woefully, neither they nor we had a clue about how business was actually conducted in the destination country. Bribes were *de rigueur.* I went personally to the Prague customs depot, determined to have our goods cleared without paying extra charges. On arrival, I looked at the burly fellow behind the counter and instantly recognized a losing battle. I also regretted not having brought along a translator. The agent repeated his sole ten words of English like a broken record: "Pay five thousand crowns for customs, and we release goods." The sum, about two hundred dollars, was equivalent to a healthy month's salary for someone in his position. To any question I posed, the large-framed functionary responded in a rapid Czech blather that sounded like mumbo jumbo to my ears. Another worker, at a desk along the back wall, concurred every now and then with a grunted "*yo*" meaning, yup. It was all very arbitrary. No written invoice. A cash-only transaction.

I understood that cash payments were the norm, and that people received their salaries and made most purchases in liquid currency. It was common knowledge that the entire Czechoslovak banking sector was in the process of transformation and suffered from all conceivable deficiencies inherited from the former central planning system.

Up to then, and for several years to come, most people had no checking accounts or credit cards. Only a limited number of restaurants, hotels, and businesses that catered to international clientele accepted foreign credit cards. Not until 1991 did Czechoslovak banks begin issuing debit payment cards, but they were slow to take off. So I wasn't surprised to be asked for a cash payment, provided it was accompanied by an official bill itemizing services rendered, and followed up with an authentic stamped receipt for proof of payment. My gullible tendencies expected both—or at least one—but I got neither.

I yielded to the payoff for the sake of having a bed for John and me to sleep in that night and to get my temperature-sensitive grand piano and other worldly possessions out of the truck. Swallowing my convictions, I reached into my wallet for the blue-colored *Tisíc Korun Československých* banknotes, bearing the picture of composer Bedřich Smetana on one side, and the Vyšehrad Castle overlooking the Vltava River on the other, and counted out five crisp bills. Before handing them over to the salivating agent, with calm authority I uttered a phrase in exacting Czech that I'd learned for cabdrivers and waiters: *Dejte mi účet, prosím.* (Give me the check, please.) The agent scrawled an illegible shorthand on a blank sheet with no letterhead and no stamp, handed it to me, and that was that. Perhaps, I told myself, it was a legitimate transaction, and my payment was immediately placed in the cash register. The more likely scenario was that four of the thousand-crown notes were slipped into his pocket after having passed one to his sidekick.

Once settled into the house, John and I walked around our neighborhood, a tree-filled residential area on the northwestern edge of Prague that had the feel of a small village. My Czech language skills weren't proficient enough to converse at length with those we passed, but we could greet people and introduce ourselves as their new neighbors. Behind our house was an elderly widowed lady with a chicken coop. She was always smiling and humming. We woke each morning to the cackling call of her rooster. Paní regularly offered us eggs. When the fruit on our backyard trees ripened in the summer and fall, we gave some to her and to the other elderly widowed lady on our east side who rarely smiled but was always polite.

Because John would be at home during the day, reading books, painting, and taking walks, it was important that he felt acclimated to our surroundings. He should know the lay of the land and be comfortable walking to the greengrocer for food, beer, and cigarettes, or simply strolling along the quiet walkways. Without his faithful dog, John no longer had a reason for his daily outings, other than to stretch his own legs or take in the fresh air. Nephew David was an invaluable helper, both as a friend to John and business assistant to me.

Our first social invitation came from Phyllis and James Taliaferro, who invited us to their apartment for a home-cooked dinner. They wanted to meet my husband and welcome us to Prague. Phyllis was so cheerfully attentive to John that he was thoroughly charmed. James and John hit it off immediately. Both men were history buffs. James showed a special respect for John's wisdom, outlook on life, and war experience. At that period in our lives, our longtime friends who knew John in his prime were far away. Now, few people could discover John's qualities unless they sat and talked with him, which James did at length. One day, when I lamented that John had to put up with me as his less-than-perfect wife, James placated me with: "He's been through the front lines of a world war, he can handle you."

Now that our house was in order, I went to work in the city. The research phase was over. It was time to procure an office and license my company. Knowing this was not my first professional go-round in the country gave me confidence. I had already presented a musical package to the people of Czechoslovakia that had been enthusiastically received. Now I aimed to repeat the gesture in a new arena. I would shape a company like I had shaped my concert program—customized for this special audience, orchestrated with tones and rhythms that would strike a chord with their practical needs. The thousands of other fresh business ventures, whether Czech or foreign, large or small, were like mine, trying to accomplish something in the new market. My mission was to provide services that supported these enterprises. I would present myself to Czechoslovakia's burgeoning business world with the sincerity and professionalism I had brought to the country's cultivated musical world. At least, the intention of this altruistic strategy felt right.

Everyone I encountered on the business scene was cognizant that we were part of an extraordinary time in European history. It was humbling. I tried not to push, which was my usual inclination. Just look, listen, and learn from the locals. Tread nimbly on the path unfolding.

Yes, I was idealistic, and my goals often seemed too far-reaching. Although other businesspeople were taking risks, I was an entrepreneur with an idea, limited capital, and no parachute, having moved herself and her husband to a newly formed democracy. My situation was different from that of a corporate executive sent to Prague with prearranged lodging, office space, schooling for family members, travel expenses, a guaranteed salary, and a ticket back home if the assignment soured. I had none of these perks.

Instead, I derived a sense of security from the leader of the country, a philosophizing playwright-turned-president, who continued to guide me with messages that inspired and challenged. My belief in myself—that I could play by ear a new symphonic composition—paralleled Havel's conviction about the role into which he'd been spontaneously cast: "When I suddenly found myself in a political office, I certainly didn't have to invent any political ideals or goals; I merely had to draw on what I'd been thinking all my life."

As in performing improvisational theater, I had drawn from my instincts at the customs office where I first encountered the shadow economy in my new country. But I wondered about corruption's pervasiveness and scope, and its effect on my business. I understood that in the former Soviet Bloc countries, deals played under the table of trade were commonplace, and systematically designed to conceal income from the state's official control and line the pockets of unscrupulous individuals. But it wasn't always that way. The underground economy had been practically nonexistent under Stalin, but began to emerge in the Khrushchev era. By 1964, under the leadership of Leonid Brezhnev, corruption, bribery, and the black market had become pervasive. I would be confronted with these practices in Czechoslovakia as my business developed and as John and I went about our daily lives.

For example, driving around the city in our Ford Escort with French license plates was a dead giveaway to the police that we were foreigners.

Numerous times, we were stopped by the patrol cars. A couple of beer-bellied, uniformed officers would swagger from their car to mine and sternly demand a fine, cash on the spot, of several hundred crowns. The extortion wasn't a large sum, but to me it was the principle of the matter. The first time it happened, I couldn't communicate or understand why we'd been pulled over. I was so shaken, I simply paid it. No receipt. When I told some Czech friends about it, they said it happened occasionally to them, too, and it was better to comply.

I couldn't accept that. I learned to say in Czech, "What did I do wrong?" or "Give me a ticket and I will pay it at the police station." I also could say, as I visibly wrote down the police badge number, "I know the United States Ambassador in Prague, and I will report this." One of these phrases usually worked, but there were times when I needed to spit them all out at once.

While I understood little about the clandestine market, I was sure that its entrenched and corrosive practices were antithetical to the goals of the new democratic country. The collapse of the communist system had been rapid and recent. I was at the ground level when the new government erected a framework to transform totalitarianism to democracy. It was a scramble to quickly and carefully construct a new society with market principles, political and economic reforms, fair elections, civil and human rights, and alliances with Europe and the West. The process was radical, and many people found it painful, but most were full of hope. There was opposition not only from the *nomenklatura*, the old political guard, but also from regular folks who had relied on the black market, state subsidies, distorted price structures, and huge monopolies that limited small business.

I was neither old political guard nor regular Czech folk. I was a guest choosing to live and do business in a country that motived me by its ideals. In his book *Summer Meditations,* Václav Havel gave me not only permission, but a prescription, to conduct business with what he called "higher responsibility."

I am convinced that we will never build a democratic state based on rule of law if we do not at the same time build a state that is— regardless of how unscientific this may sound to the ears of a political scientist—humane, moral, intellectual, spiritual, and cultural.

In spite of my shortcomings, I wasn't deterred from reaching for high ideals. Havel himself often revealed his human weakness and imperfections. In the foreword to the aforementioned book, he admitted, "I have become aware of how immensely difficult it is to be guided in practice by the principles and ideals in which I believe. But I have not abandoned them in any way."

Like any good limping pilgrim, neither would I.

On the thirteenth day of April, two weeks since our arrival, I had an appointment with Steve Kelly to meet the owner of the offices he'd shown me on my last visit. We were to gather in front of the Knižní velkoobchod building at Spálená 15. I got there early. Steve was joined by his partner, Mari Novak. They were a tall, strikingly attractive American couple, businesslike, friendly, and forthright. In other words, I felt like I could trust them, should the deal go through. As we waited for Knižní's new proprietor, Miroslav Macek, Steve briefed me on the story of the building and the background of Macek. I knew we had some time before the owner arrived, so I was all ears, eager to learn how this couple came into possession of the space I was about to see.

Steve said that Macek was currently the deputy chair of the Civic Democratic Party (ODS), and had recently acquired what had been the country's monopolistic book distributorship for the past forty years. The publishing and printing house, Josef R. Vilímek, was founded by its namesake in 1872 when Prague was the capital of Bohemia and a province of the Austro-Hungarian Empire. The privately held publishing and printing house became one of the most famous publishers in the region by the turn of the twentieth century. But the Vilímek family had their ownership snatched from them, first by the Nazi occupation, then the communist takeover. After 1949, the building belonged to the "people's republic" and served as the communist state's central book distributer.

The Velvet Revolution and transition to a free market exposed the company's large debt burden. It owed hundreds of millions of crowns in loans. But it also owned vast and valuable real estate in the city center and warehouses on the outskirts, in addition to thousands of volumes of unsellable old books. The privatization process, viewed in hindsight as overly speedy and grounded in misunderstood liberalism, enabled Macek to purchase the company at a nominal price.

Steve didn't state it directly, but it was clear that the transaction brought into question a conflict of interest about whether Macek's political status had facilitated the bargain. Regardless of rumors we later heard, this was only one of many intrigues that wound around the business grapevine during the economic transformation process. As a foreigner, I hesitated to make judgments based on partial information about issues the lawmakers and courts were trying to sort out.

Mari, in her refined and spirited manner, turned the conversation toward me and asked about my reasons for moving to Prague. As I began an abridged synopsis of my story, we quickly discovered that we both had roots in Czechoslovak soil. Mari's ancestors hailed from the Slovak and Czech regions, mine from Moravia.

Steve and Mari had already begun a business consulting company in the United States when news about Central Europe's emerging markets prompted them to come to Prague in 1991 and register their company, KNO Worldwide, as a Czech entity. They rented offices on Benešovská ulice, and like other entrepreneurs on the scene, looked for their niche in the wide-open marketplace brimming with opportunity. At first, Steve taught English to businesspeople. Mari, who'd been a Peace Corps volunteer in Micronesia after college, contacted the Peace Corps in Prague. Its volunteers had arrived in Czechoslovakia in November 1990 after programs in Hungary and Poland were already under way. While organizing and marketing their core work, project management and business consulting, the couple procured a short-term contract to help with the Peace Corps' Textbook Donation Project, delivering thousands of books to educational institutions all over Czechoslovakia. Mari laughed in recalling that, when all was completed and calculated, their one-thousand-dollar fee equated to an hourly wage pittance. Yet, the project spurred future consulting work with other U.S. government agencies.

Steve knew Macek because he had provided business consulting to him and the interim managers of the book wholesaler building in front of which we stood. They'd forewarned Steve of their insolvency predicament and asked if he'd accept office space as payment. Steve agreed, on the condition he could sublease it, subject to the owner's approval of the tenant. Thus, the purpose for today's meeting with me.

As I stood on the pavement, absorbed in Mari and Steve's stories, my glance strayed beyond their heads to the bending course of Spálená ulice that ended at the large green space of Karlovo náměstí. A few steps in the other direction was where Spálená began at a T-intersection with Národní třída. On that landmark corner was *Máj*, a popular department store built in the seventies. My new friends informed me that the Kmart Corporation, which I knew well because it was the second-largest American retailer at the time, was in final negotiations to purchase thirteen state-owned department stores in Czechoslovakia. The prize was the flagship *Máj*, which stood out architecturally from the other ornate buildings on the block with its post-modern Brutalist style.

Looking back, Kmart completed the acquisition before the end of that year, and the stores became highly profitable. But despite Kmart's victory abroad, within three years, due to financial problems with its parent company at home, it sold its Czech investments to British retailer Tesco.

On that warm spring day, we were three expat Americans conjecturing about the outcome of the Kmart deal before it was settled. Of course, we couldn't know the destiny of this American enterprise in the new market, just as we had no certainty whether our own ventures would flourish, fall through, or one day be sold to the highest bidder.

During our conversation on the patterned cobblestone sidewalk, I felt a heightened awareness of my surroundings, as if my senses were intensely sharpened. The convergence of sound—three voices in soprano, alto, and tenor registers mingling with the pleasing cacophony of car traffic, people walking by, pigeons swooshing down and briskly taking flight, and the intermittent clanging of a streetcar lumbering past—transported my spirit to the Reduta Club, just minutes around the corner.

My encore song "One" from Marvin Hamlisch's *A Chorus Line* began to replay, swelling like an offstage chorus. This quintessentially American show tune of chutzpah and triumph overlaid like counterpoint onto the clamor of the street. Bob McCoy's modulating chord combinations came back, delivering rhythmic texture to the "singular sensational" story line of the song and of my life in that very moment. The aural memory infused my reality: immersed in the bustling culture of Prague, I was standing alongside two other adventurers who would become forever friends, and I was poised to secure the perfect spot for my company.

Miroslav Macek sauntered toward us and extended his hand to Steve before gallantly bowing to Mari and me. He was formal but charming, and outwardly happy to have the opportunity to speak English. "Please call me Miroslav," he requested, yet none of us had the inclination to break old-world protocol to do so. He described himself as a lover of languages and translator of the works of William Shakespeare and Edgar Allen Poe from English to Czech, as well as the poetry of Paul Verlaine from French to Czech. I was impressed.

For a moment, Mr. Macek's eyes focused on me with intensity, and then he asked if we had already met somewhere. I looked familiar, he said.

"Perhaps you attended one of my performances at the Reduta," I suggested.

"Unfortunately not," he reacted with continued bemusement. "Ah, now that you mention music, I saw your picture and read an article about you in this week's *Ahoj na sobotu* magazine."

It was true, journalist Andrea Vernerová had conducted an interview with me a few months earlier, and her full-page spread had just appeared in this popular cultural magazine with color photos. The write-up began with Andrea's observation:

> She has red hair after her Irish father. After her mother comes her Czech origin, and she speaks with a sweet and slightly broken Czech. American singer, poet and actress Anne-Marie Kenny has visited Prague several times in the last two years. Now she is coming to live and work here . . . the Czech blood is returning to the place from which it came one-and-a-half centuries ago.

Inasmuch as I valued the media exposure, I had supposed that the article would do little to promote my new business role for two reasons—it highlighted my former music profession and targeted an exclusively Czech audience. But I was proven wrong. It had left a memorable impression on Mr. Macek.

Mari, Steve, and I followed my potential landlord into the courtyard. The place looked so neglected that I had to shove aside my initial reaction. We climbed the wide and weathered staircase to the second floor. Around the circumference of the landing were three doors leading to offices. The space to be rented housed two adjoining rooms, one larger than the other, as well as an anteroom that could serve as a waiting area where two chairs might fit. Altogether, the space was no more than thirty square meters, if that. Shafts of light streamed in through oversized windows which provided a good glimpse of Prague's urban core in the *Nové Město* district.

I knew the location was perfect, the size was adequate, and the price would be right. I envisioned the smaller room that faced the waiting area as my office. It had a door that I could close for privacy or leave open to view the comings and goings of future clientele. The larger room could hold at least three desks for my assistants; that is, as soon as I could hire them.

Mr. Macek saw that I was pleased. He was amenable to the sublet and confirmed that Steve could negotiate the rental agreement with me. Then he declared, "I plan to occupy the two offices across the hall, although I'll rarely be here because of my other responsibilities in addition to this company." Hmm, a lover of Shakespeare and Poe next door, I mused.

My future floor mate then led us to a large storage area that took up half an entire upper floor. It seemed the privatization process had affected this building like other former state-owned properties—workplaces had suddenly emptied of people and furnishings. Macek said I could choose from the stacks of furniture piled inside. I selected several solid wood desks, tables, chairs, and cabinets. He tagged them for the maintenance man to deliver to my office space. With a little cleaning and paint job, the heavy furniture would be sturdy and functional, albeit far from having a contemporary look.

I hid my hesitancy about the appearance of the place. I told myself that most buildings in Prague needed major renovations. In my mind's eye, I pictured future clients on their approach to my office. They'd walk up Spálená, appreciating the Prague One location in the heart of the city. They'd clearly see number *15* on the handsome exterior of the building and proceed to enter the passageway where they'd encounter graffiti-lined walls and a shabby stairwell as they climbed the steps. Surely no one would turn around and walk away because the short path to their destination was aesthetically begrimed. I believed any negative first impression would dissipate when clients stepped into our bright office environment and saw fresh flowers, smelled the aroma of coffee, and were greeted by friendly faces.

I decided to name my office services bureau "At Your Service" to exemplify our commitment to quality customer service. It was all too evident that under the communist system, the state placed customer satisfaction at the bottom of the priority list. It was sadly ironic how authoritarianism had trickled down to all levels of workers. Be it a coal mine boss, a store clerk, a postal worker, or government functionary, such positions wielded a modicum of authority and power. I saw it myself. At small shops, if customers didn't have exact change, the sour-faced saleslady might just as well turn them away, indifferent about scoring a sale for the state. These attitudes had hung on.

I quickly learned, when I shopped at the grande dame of department stores, *Máj*, that the customer mustn't touch the merchandise. All items were kept behind a counter guarded by a clerk who begrudgingly showed customers one article at a time. She may make the customer wait quite some time while pretending to be occupied with straightening up the shelves. I accepted this as simply the way things were done. Almost like a game, my goal as a shopper was to win over the clerk, approach her ever so politely, and demonstrate respect for her position. Besides, I'd figured out that expressions of impatience or indignance got me nowhere. It wasn't difficult to be sensitive to clerks when considering the country's recent past. Over the decades, the Czechs had experienced deprivation, rations, shortages, long lines, and empty shelves. Some had lived through far worse. They, or a family member, might have known the inside of a concentration camp, prison, or uranium mine, or faced intimidation, interrogation, and torture.

Grumpiness was not intentional, I realized. It was an outcome of lived experience. *A social pattern.* This understanding silently dawned on me and would underlie my interactions and relationships as I built my new business model. I would have to introduce new patterns of business behavior—stemming from the values the Czechs treasured most. This was an awakening for me and would be the key to my success in the service industry. I was on the cusp of discovering how to unearth these values embedded in the charmed Bohemian culture, which the oppressive regime had failed to completely stifle.

After Mr. Macek wished us luck and went on his way, Steve asked me when I'd like to take possession of the space. "Tomorrow," was my reply. He handed me the keys and offered to drop by later in the week to complete the paperwork and collect payment for the remainder of April and month of May. The rent was 250 dollars per month, utilities included. Telephone service—unlike anything I would ever experience—was also part of the package.

The next day, I drove John into the city for lunch and showed him my new offices. It was an effort for John to climb the two flights of stairs. When we reached the second floor, he sat on a ledge to take a breather. I gave a quick tour of the empty offices and described the furniture layout. John saw my elation and was encouraging, but I doubted he envisioned what I did.

We walked down the steps and decided to take a stroll around the vicinity. As we headed toward a pedestrian area, the uneven, old mosaic cobblestones made it difficult for John to stay balanced. Cobblestones can trip even the most surefooted walker. They require a steady center of gravity or the supporting arm of someone to lean on. I provided the arm, but the situation was difficult for both of us. John was embarrassed by his feebleness, and I sensed he had aches and pains he'd not complained about. For me, I'd had no experience as a caregiver. I could perform my duties lovingly most of the time, but sometimes frustration and distress slipped into my actions and words.

On this day, though, I was well. This was a day reserved for us. After today, I'd be at the office for hours on end during the workweek and my husband would be home alone. This represented a completely new lifestyle in our years together. Me at the office. Owner of a business.

I suggested we drive to Betlémské náměstí, a quaint square just a few minutes away. Once there, we parked, and wandered around on a smoother stone pavement. The sun was high, right at noon and time for lunch. Turning the corner on to Liliová ulice, we discovered a new restaurant, V Zátiší. John opened the door for me, and we stepped into an atmosphere as chic as a fancy restaurant in France.

"Good afternoon, Miss, a table for two, please," John asked of the hostess in his chivalrous manner. The gourmet food was scrumptious. The waiters doted on us with pleasant and efficient service. I observed their exemplary customer-focused conduct, something rare in that part of the world at that time, and I took heart in the promising future of my own undertaking.

On the tabletop was a small placard advertising the restaurant's special Easter Brunch on Sunday 19 April, just five days away, which happened to be the date of our twelfth wedding anniversary. John summoned the hostess with his inimitable glance and reserved a special table for us.

At home on that glorious Easter morning, there was a hand-painted anniversary card and a dozen red roses waiting for me at our breakfast table. Apparently, John had secretly called our friend Phyllis and asked her to deliver the flowers while I was away. After breakfast, we dressed up and drove to the English-speaking church service at St. Thomas, a thirteenth-century Augustinian monastery in the Malá Strana district, which would become our parish and church community. After Mass, we enjoyed a delightful brunch at V Zátiší, which would become our favorite restaurant.

At our window table facing the square, we toasted with Bohemia Sekt and recalled our sunny wedding day and the action-packed dozen years of married life since. So many memories and adventures to smile on. John looked as handsome as he did on our wedding day. He was in his element at this fine dining establishment where his social graces fit right in, as natural as the caring, polite manner he displayed every day. We basked in the moment, cushioned between the hectic move behind us and the dire straits ahead.

13

AT YOUR SERVICE, S.R.O.

W*hen John and I rolled into Czechoslovakia* in April 1992, the wheels of democracy had been spinning for more than two years. The fresh air of innovation was intoxicating. Public discourse on the streets, in bars and business settings was lively. There were inevitable comparisons with the other newly freed countries which, some Czechs told me, were progressing at a faster rate. But others said there was good reason for that. Czechoslovakia was the only country that had been occupied nonstop for twenty-one years by Warsaw Pact troops, mostly Russian military. The Soviets called their 1968 surprise invasion a "necessary intervention" to crush the Prague Spring reform movement, saying the socialist order in Czechoslovakia must be "rescued by fraternal international assistance." I would never fully comprehend what my Czech friends went through in 1968 during the Soviet invasion and its aftermath, the long period of *normalization* which demanded submission to an ironfisted regime.

Martin Palouš was there at the time. He was a student who, decades later, became the Czech ambassador to the United States, which was when I met him. He wrote about the situation after the invasion:

I observed this regressive trend with disbelief and frustration . . . even in the student environment, within less than two
years from August 1968, most of my colleagues at the Faculty
of Natural Sciences of Charles University were also displaying a
readiness to follow suit and adapt themselves to the new political
situation, in order to secure for themselves tranquil professional
and academic careers.

I pictured myself in the place of the Czech people, confronting limited
choices after the clampdown: 1) leave, emigrate to another country; 2) stay,
join the Communist Party and play the game with benefits; 3) stay, not
join the Communist Party, but blend in and tow the line; or 4) stay, dissent and protest, and risk persecution, imprisonment, and possibly death.

The dissidents who protested were a small, dedicated minority. By
1977, their convictions were formalized in the human rights manifesto
Charter 77. The four-page typewritten document was less of a political
statement and more of a moral proclamation. It pointed out the country's
violations against basic human rights guaranteed by the United Nations
and the Helsinki Conference to which Czechoslovakia had sanctimo-
niously subscribed.

Copies of the charter were circulated along samizdat channels in
the country and beyond, although some Czechs tell me they didn't
have access to it. Western newspapers published it and international
radio broadcasted it. It aired in Czechoslovakia on banned Radio Free
Europe and Voice of America radio channels. The spokespersons for
the document were philosopher Jan Patočka, international lawyer Jiří
Hájek, and playwright Václav Havel. They caught hell. Interrogations,
imprisonments, and loss of jobs ensued.

Several days after a grueling ten-hour interrogation, the sixty-nine-
year-old Patočka died. He was Havel's beloved mentor, and one of the
greatest philosophers of the the twentieth century. Forbidden to teach or
publish for most of his life, Patočka's instruction had taken the form of

underground lectures and essays in basements and living rooms. Václav Havel's idea of human responsibility in civic society and his quest for "living in truth" were based on his mentor's concepts.

Would I have been one of the 242 initial signers of the charter? Or among the 2,500 who affixed their names to the document over the next ten years? I want to think so, but how can I know? If I'd had the chance to learn directly from Patočka himself in the living room of friends, then yes, I may have had the courage. I want to believe that sitting among other seekers and hearing the philosopher's voice speak about caring for the soul would have strengthened my resolve, would have convinced me to speak the truth no matter the consequence.

Sitting in on some of Patočka's clandestine philosophy lessons was the young Martin Palouš. He knew the risks of signing the charter, but his action was a philosophical and moral decision in line with his personal journey toward liberation. He lost his office job and became a coal stoker in a hotel to make a living. But he was where he wanted to be—in the company of like-minded people who stood up to totalitarianism. In his words, they had "left the protective walls of their private lives, to step into the public space to reach out to others."

By the mid-eighties, when I was living in France and taking freedom for granted, a foreign military still occupied Czechoslovakia. Whereas other Soviet satellite countries had begun modest political and social reforms in tandem with the inroads paved by Gorbachev's *perestroika* and *glasnost*, Czechoslovakia's occupying forces blocked access to such pathways.

Then, suddenly, at the end of the decade, one nation after another fell like dominos, from servitude to sovereignty. Czechoslovakia, one of the last to throw off the Soviet yoke, counted its revolution in days rather than months—twenty-four to be exact. In musical terms, with only a few rebellious days to serve as an overture, the Czechoslovaks leapt from a plodding tempo to *subito accelerando,* suddenly and briskly barreling toward a new society.

Just as suddenly, I was thrown into the accelerando of change. The whirlwind of transformation captured me—the clinking of keys, the song, the invitation, the Reduta concert—and then boom, I was living in Czechoslovakia, a single note in the revolutionary opus.

As a newcomer and neophyte, I lacked knowledge about the region's multilayered history, hardships, and triumphs. To better understand, I relied on conversations, newspaper reports, and more than ever, John's synopsis of his daily dose of the BBC World News and the *International Herald Tribune* (delivered to our house every morning by a teenager on a scooter). For local information, we had the weekly *Prague Post* and daily *Fleet Sheet*—a brilliant concept created by American entrepreneur Erik Best, who published a one-page English-language daily bulletin of tightly summarized stories from yesterday's Czech press.

What was not complicated for me to grasp were the enormous opportunities presented by the abrupt inflow of multinational companies into a city that had been devoid of private enterprise and customer service. That was clear. That I could deal with. Do something about.

I quickly learned that who governed was important to an expatriate entrepreneur. The political talk of the town revolved around the "other Václav" who became prime minister just a few months after John and I arrived. Known as an arrogant Thatcherite technocrat, Václav Klaus's outlook was much different from the Havelian vision that emphasized human consciousness in world politics. Since the inception of the Civic Forum (the makeshift political movement during the revolution), Klaus helped turn the dissident group into a political party with negotiating power. When a new government was formed in December 1989, and Havel became president, Klaus was named finance minister. Less than a year later, he became chairman of the Civic Forum and eventually created an offshoot faction, the Civic Democratic Party (ODS).

Klaus openly voiced his disdain for Havel with references to "the intellectuals in the Castle," and called Havel a "half-socialist . . . in love with state power."

The two Václavs were poles apart philosophically. Havel believed that civic virtue was the underpinning of both political and economic liberty. Klaus argued that civil society didn't exist, that it was merely a leftover fiction, albeit useful, employed by former dissidents to fight the communist regime.   He wrote in the newspaper *Literární noviny*, "I am a liberal economist . . . I have a deep distrust in the centralist thinking of politicians . . . I feel there is no wiser minister, ministry, government party or parliament that can ever substitute for the functioning of the impersonal market."

Political talk aside, the sheer sound of their voices spoke volumes to me. The constricted, high-pitched tone of Klaus's voice matching his strident rhetoric was a contrasting clash to Havel's low, smooth baritone timbre expressing the value of unity and goodwill.

No doubt, my business friends and I indirectly benefited from Klaus's market-based approach that championed capitalism, relaxed business regulations, and devalued the currency. Little did we know that Klaus would be elected prime minister twice and president twice.

On the other hand, so long as Havel was in leadership, I felt safe moving to a nation that was a newcomer to democracy. My mind and heart resonated with what he described as the "enormous human, moral and spiritual potential, and the civic culture that slumbered in our society under the enforced mask of apathy."   At the same time, Havel wasn't naive. He warned that the post-communist transition would be capable of two opposing forces: sowing deep nostalgia for authoritarianism and also creating a stable and democratic nation. He fought for the latter outcome all of his life.

Authoritarianism was attractive to those who had wielded power in the former regime and to those who had lived a quiet life of compliance under it. Of the Czechs I encountered back then, no one admitted to having been a collaborationist or a dissident. They said nothing at all, except when the applicants I interviewed wrote in the narrative section of their curriculum vita: "Neither I nor my family were members of the Communist Party"—as if this statement were a bragging right in the newfound democracy. It was meant, I believe, to indicate that they wanted to be exonerated from the past and were now looking ahead, not behind. Finally, they could breathe an air of hope and future promise.

I met people who were tentative in their response to freedom. Would it last? All they knew—anyone born after 1938—was a society far from free. They had been smothered under the thumb of a brutal Nazi occupation and then decades of Soviet rule. As a foreigner, I understood that gaining their trust would be hard-won. Besides, I sensed their unspoken thoughts. *What would she, an American, understand of our experience?* They would be right. I couldn't really understand. But I hoped they saw my love for their culture and language, my pride in the land of my ancestors, and my belief in their future. About all that, I was sincere.

I knew my business success was far from a given. Instability reverberated inside Europe. Just to our east, Yugoslavia was falling apart rather brutally, starting with Croatia's and Slovenia's secession in 1991. (At that time we already worried, considering our move, but figured that the Balkans was far enough away and of a different mentality. War had broken out and United Nations peacekeeping forces had moved in. In the same first week of April 1992 when John and I were settling into Central Europe, another of Yugoslavia's federated states, Bosnia, proclaimed independence. The European Community and the United States recognized Bosnia's decision as legitimate, as it had for Croatia, Slovenia, and Macedonia months earlier. John and I were glued to the continuous news about the conflict. We learned that the Bosnian Serbs, vehemently opposed to Bosnia's independence, received help from Serbian troops from the wider region and launched an offensive by bombarding Bosnia's capital, Sarajevo. There was no question that Yugoslavia, as it had existed since the end of World War II, was imploding.

By the end of our first month in Prague, before April turned to May, Serbia and Montenegro proclaimed the establishment of a new and truncated Yugoslav, diminished by four republics that had seceded over the previous months. All the while, the Serbian takeover of Sarajevo continued and would become known as the longest military siege in modern history. The city was liberated three years later, but the war had spread across the former country and eventually left one hundred thousand people dead. The city of Sarajevo became the international media's face of a post–Cold War conflict. Territories were changing, countries forming, and others dissolving. We worried. Would this instability spread?

There were milder rumblings in Czechoslovakia, the place John and I had just begun to call home. Slovakia wanted to break away from Bohemia and Moravia. The prospect of a divorce between the Czechs and Slovaks agitated both regions and frightened citizens and foreigners alike. Might Czechoslovakia devolve into a civil war? As it was, John and I received frantic calls from friends and family in the United States who had the geography all wrong. They asked if we were in, or near, the war zone. I gently reassured them (but was mildly annoyed to have to explain) that Yugoslavia and Czechoslovakia were two different countries.

As history unfolded around us, I set up shop. My first call from the office was to attorney Petr Zima, asking for assistance in obtaining long-term residence permits for John and me and a trade license and registration for my company. Dr. Zima coupled his willingness with a matter-of-fact warning:

"Mrs. Kenny, I will move as quickly as possible to establish your limited liability company, which we call an *s.r.o.,* but it will take time. Under the communist system, bureaucratic procedures were notoriously slow. Now the wait-time is even longer due to the influx of foreign entities making applications," he said. "Many will slip an envelope of cash under the table to accelerate the registration process. If you want your company's paperwork expedited through those means, I would not blame you, but you'll need to find different legal representation."

"No, Dr. Zima, you're the attorney for me."

It was the second time I had been struck by Dr. Zima's character. The first was in our initial meeting when he verbalized his concerns about the privatization process favoring the powerful and disadvantaging regular folks. For me, Zima had proven his trustworthiness. For him, the honesty and reserve he exhibited was not a means of proof, but simply who he was.

Dr. Zima outlined activities I could begin while the business license was in process. Renting office space in my name was acceptable, but should be transferred later to the company's name. I could hire staff on a contract basis, begin marketing my services, and work for clients with the understanding they'd be invoiced only after I received an *identifikační číslo osoby* (IČO), the company's identification number required on billing statements and official papers.

Without prioritizing, I set out to find staff, start advertising, and organize the office. I placed want ads for an administrative assistant in two newspapers and waited for my black rotary desk phone to ring with that old-fashioned, extended *brrrriiing* from real metal bells oscillating inside the mid-century mechanism. The sound was music to my ears during its rare emissions, as the apparatus lay silent on my desk most of the day. Later, I discovered that the building's phone system, and the person running it, were part of the problem.

The candidates who called spoke inarticulate English with meager vocabularies (much like me spouting their language outside the bounds of my perfectly practiced phrases). Those first phone screenings were an effective process of elimination. I unapologetically needed a bilingual assistant with whom I could communicate.

Then finally, a woman called who conversed in charming, albeit not perfect, English. She expressed interest in the advertised position because she hoped to work in an international setting and use her organizational and typing skills. I jotted down her name, Dita Hojsáková, and set up an interview for the next day.

Dita arrived five minutes early. She looked neat as a pin with her hair tightly combed into a bun at the crown of her head. Her petite frame was clothed in a pressed white blouse, black sweater, and checkered knee-length skirt. On her feet were practical and polished brown lace-up shoes. Dita exemplified the best of Slovakian culture. She was brought up in a traditional home where one was taught to bow respectfully when being introduced to another. Dita was free only until the fall, as she wanted to resume her university studies. Her attitude, professionalism, and office skills were everything I was looking for. I hired her on the spot.

I asked endless questions about how things were done, where to find this or that, and how to communicate in Czech for particular situations. Dita was resourceful. For questions she didn't have answers to, she'd reply, "I will find out," and promptly call someone—usually her mother, from whom Dita apparently inherited her penchant for efficiency.

We placed ads in newspapers for a full-time assistant to help us prepare for an influx of clients. Dita screened phone calls using a criteria checklist. One of the interviewees was Amira Shehatová. I recall vividly that her résumé distinguished her from other candidates, highlighting advanced-level English, college-level courses, and work experience abroad. When I met Amira for the first time, I was taken by her peaceful manner, soft-spoken voice, and thoughtful responses to my questions. She spoke openly in the interview about being a single mother of a toddler son, which would limit her work time to six hours per day. Regardless of her restricted availability, I hired Amira without hesitation.

Sometime later, during a relaxed conversation, I learned more about Amira's personal story. Her Moravian mother had met her Egyptian father while he was earning a PhD in Olomouc. Amira was born in nearby Hranice, and her family moved to Prague when she was six. Most of her schooling was in Prague, except for a few years when her family lived in Egypt.

I was curious about her work experience in the United States. In early 1989, when Amira was married and five months pregnant, she and her husband fled communist Czechoslovakia. No one could have predicted the revolution on the horizon, and they wanted, for themselves and their child, to live in a free and democratic world. The couple literally escaped in the middle of the night, each taking separate routes at different intervals, and met up in New York City. They made their way to

Denver, Colorado, where their son was born. The year 1989 was pivotal in the lives of millions, and Amira's path had its share of dramatic twists and turns. Before the year's end, the homeland she'd fled had become a new, democratic nation. Not long after, only Amira and her son would return to Prague.

Between the part-time schedules of Dita, Amira, and my nephew Dave, most office hours were covered. This core crew and other part-time helpers were indispensable in the first phase of my business venture.

Dave, the other native English speaker in the office, was a fine writer. He proofread all English text, including my correspondence. Dave was young, wide-eyed, and enamored with the golden city. Prague had become a vibrant mecca for young people from America and Western Europe, many of whom came to teach English and revel in the nightlife. Dave was no exception. Before long, he wanted to spread his wings by working and living on his own, which he did for quite some time before returning back to the States.

To a large degree, employees like Dita and Amira were my teachers. They were at my side like mountaineering Sherpas while I scaled a tall learning curve. At age forty-one, my energy was already revved, and more ignited by the gorgeous city, the transformative environment, and the warm reception of the Czech people.

It was common to hear expatriates complain about the poor work ethic of Czech office workers, shopkeepers, postal clerks, waiters—anyone in the service industry. This sweeping generalization had many exceptions, my assistants among them. They were naturally generous and hardworking. On a practical level, they were motivated to learn English and work at a foreign company, which fully complemented my own ambitions. I was happy that within a few weeks, I'd found downtown offices, reliable legal counsel, and capable assistants.

The advice of my friend Gerard Smits echoed in my head: "Find a way to make money right away." While having lunch one day at a small restaurant near the office, I pulled out my pocket dictionary to translate the food listings. Most restaurants only had menus in Czech or very poor translations, and bilingual waiters were a rarity. As I stared at the menu, an opportunity struck me. After my meal, I asked to speak with the manager. Luckily, he spoke a bit of English. I explained that I was the owner of At Your Service, s.r.o., an office services bureau around the corner, and we could create an attractive English and French version of his menu.

"Great idea." he said, "In the past, we had only Czechs as customers. Now there's a surge of foreigners and only just a few of my waiters can communicate with them beyond a greeting." However, he went on to say that money was a problem. The volume of customers had increased since the revolution, but so had expenses. He modestly proposed: "Instead of currency, would you accept meal tickets as a barter?"

Ano, jistě! "Yes, of course!" was my resolute response since I couldn't officially invoice yet, anyway.

I called on other restaurants and asked: "*Máte jídelní lístek v angličtině nebo francouzštině*?" "Do you have a menu in English or French?" The answer "*Ne, nemáme*" inevitably turned into a work order. Prestigious restaurants like *Obecní dům*, and the fourteenth-century *U Supa* utilized our menu translation services, as did smaller cafés and snack shops. The number of meal vouchers corresponded to the extent of the menu's text. It was a long while before I opened my wallet for lunch, and I often hosted my staff and prospective clients.

Each menu project got easier because dishes from one restaurant to the other were similar. Amira and Dita fastidiously researched each item using the single and dual-language dictionaries on our bookshelves, most of which I'd brought from France. Dave or I edited the final drafts before the menus were formatted and laminated.

As our word processor and fax machine buzzed with steady use, I began to worry about the other apparatus, the telephone. During the office sublease negotiations, I had understood there were no direct lines to our rooms, but was assured we'd have two reliable extensions.

Yet, the phone seldom rang, even when friends or my husband said they'd called at a certain time. Outgoing calls usually went through. Since one of my company's services was to offer a "phone, fax, and mailing address" to visiting businesspeople, any phone malfunction was concerning.

Finally, the impeding issue was revealed. The building had a few main phone numbers that fanned into a maze of extensions connected to dozens of offices (most of which were empty since the revolution). In a closet-like workroom on the first floor sat a lady facing a circuit board of plugs, patch cords, and sockets on an antiquated switchboard. She controlled which incoming calls went through and which ones she didn't feel like answering or connecting.

One evening, John told me he'd tried repeatedly to call me that day, but the cranky person answering didn't understand him, even after he'd clearly and slowly said my name and company name. He'd heard a grunt of some sort before a deadening click. The next morning, I headed to the switchboard room, fuming as I marched down the hall. Before I turned the corner toward my aim of attack, common sense halted my fury. I made a U-turn and went upstairs to find Amira making our morning coffee.

"We need to befriend the switchboard operator," I said, as a preface to explaining the situation. Together, Amira and I took the stairs down one level, tapped on the operator's half-open door, and invited her to our office for coffee and *koláče*. She flashed an indignant look and hastily declined. We attempted lighthearted conversation. The operator softened slightly as I explained, with Amira interpreting, what my company did, and offered our services free of charge should she ever need something translated or typed.

From then on, while it wasn't a bribe per se, but rather good old-fashioned schmoozing, we often stopped to greet the operator and share our office snacks with her. Amira taught her some English phrases, how to recognize our company and personal names, and respond to callers with, "One moment please while I connect you." It worked. Calls started coming through.

Translating menus occupied the time while we prepared for our core business activity. I spent weeks creating a logo and drafting a brochure, narrowing the content to the fewest but most descriptive words to present my company's services in English, Czech, and French. We searched for a reliable printing company. The brochure was our key marketing tool; it had to look attractive and reach the right audience. To my surprise, that would be the easiest part.

The embassies of the United States, Canada, England, Ireland, and France were accommodating when I made appointments with their commercial sections. I asked for their lists of businesses in Prague, and they handed me printouts of all registered companies owned or managed by their citizens, complete with company name, address, phone and fax numbers, and name and title of the top executive. In 1992, there were no email addresses or websites. Communication was conducted through postal service, faxes, phone calls, arranged meetings, cold-calls, chamber of commerce events, and expat hangouts.

While we waited for the three-fold brochure to be printed—which took longer than expected—my assistants addressed hundreds of envelopes, and I composed a welcoming cover letter. Still waiting on the brochure, I designed an interim flyer to hand-deliver to select hotels for their clientele in need of business and secretarial services.

The flyers gained us traction. In particular, Martin Coufal from the Palace Hotel sent over a number of clients who brought us work—typing letters, making appointments, collecting mail, and answering calls.

Like the menu translations, the office services concept was an apparent need in Prague, and a service I knew how to provide. Each day held promise, but nothing in those first weeks foreshadowed the pivot we'd soon make to meet a greater, more profitable market demand. From day one, glimmers of promise flickered around my venture, and the light touched a bliss within me. Once again, I was affirmed that the mythologist Joseph Campbell was right—*There is a track that has been there all the while, waiting for you, and the life that you ought to be living is the one you are living.*

I resolved to remain focused, drink minimally, and work harder than I ever had. Lovers begone, there was no time. Besides, I had a rule never to flirt, no matter how subtle, with a client or subordinate. I simply had to succeed and not become distracted or let alcohol or unprofessional behavior sabotage what seemed to be the answer to our prayers. I knew John would understand the long hours. When I returned home in the late afternoons, my heart broke a little to see how relieved he was to see me. We had a system where I'd tap the car horn as I pulled into the garage. It gave John time to rise from his chair and walk to the front landing to greet me with a smile and a kiss. His look of gratitude when I walked through the door gave me a warm yet sad feeling.

I'd make a quick dinner. We'd sit at the dining room table to eat, talk, and drink Moravian red wine. John had decades of experience as an advertising executive for large firms, and he'd managed plenty of employees during his career. He provided an attentive ear for my stories of the day and offered astute ideas about my quandaries.

John was lonely, although he didn't say it. I struggled to find more time for us. I thought I was attuned to his needs, but apparently I had missed something grave concerning his health. A few weeks into our new adventure, in early May, as my business was gaining momentum and I was riding high, John collapsed.

While I remember precise details of other important events, this episode blurs in my mind; only some flash points of the dreadful picture are clear. I came home from the office—either at my usual time or earlier, as I may have gotten a call—and found John at the house with our neighbor lady, paní Nováková, the frowning one who lived to the east. She had compassionately stayed with John until I got home. Our neighbor blurted in Czech what had happened, little of which I understood, and yet I surmised the meaning by her gestures. She said she'd been shopping at the grocery stand when she saw her new neighbor wobble, then fall flat on the sidewalk.

John chimed in. He remembered walking to the shop and feeling faint as he waited in the queue. The next thing he recalled, a young man and the neighbor lady had lifted him off the ground and walked him back to the house. Paní Nováková insisted on coming inside so as not to leave him alone. As I listened in utter distress, I saw that John was flushed and trembling. He confessed to having a scraped hand and sore hip, but he remained adamant that he was fine. I thought that unlikely. He put on a brave front as he spoke of the episode, seated in his favorite chair with a cigarette between the index and third fingers of one hand, clutching a cold beer with the other. With tears in my eyes, I thanked paní Nováková and walked her down our inside staircase to the front door, then watched as the good woman traipsed to her place next door.

Running up the steps, I threw my arms around John and said how sorry I was this happened. He pretended all was well and responded, "I'm really okay, Darlin', what's for dinner?"

At the top of my master to-do list, written while still in France, was to investigate doctors for John and me. Now the task was urgent. Exactly how I found an English-speaking doctor, I'm not sure. It may have been through Phyllis, who hadn't yet set up her medical referral practice, but had some contacts. Within a few days, John had a checkup by a doctor who ran some tests and recommended that he be admitted into the hospital for a thorough examination.

We then called his daughters in the States to let them know about the situation. The next morning I drove John to Na Homolce hospital, a large facility built in the 1980s for the Czech *apparatchik* and Soviet elite. There, we saw how far behind the developed world the country had fallen in the realms of medical practice, technology, and materials. Transforming the corrupt, top-down communist health care system to a patient-centered modern framework was one of the greatest challenges of the post-revolutionary era. Unfortunately, we experienced the old system stuck in a most undesirable stage. With only slight exaggeration, we were about to enter what John's eldest daughter, Eugenia, called a communist adaptation of the American TV series, *The Twilight Zone*. Our episode would have spooked even Rod Serling, famous for screen stories that combined horror, science fiction, drama, and comedy.

14

GROUNDED

W*ithin view of the expansive medical structure,* we sat in the car to get our bearings and delay entering the front door from which only one of us would exit that day. If I had to measure who was more afraid, it would be a toss-up. By then, John was physically weaker than me, but he'd always been emotionally stronger. Yet, as we waited in the parking lot, I felt his trepidation about leaving our new home for a medical facility in a strange country. I don't remember our conversation, except I'm certain my words would have tried to comfort, with something like, "I'll be here every day, before or after work, or both. And your daughters will fly in soon."

After calling Eugenia, Connie, Patty, and Carole to explain the situation—that their dad had collapsed, seen a doctor, and would be admitted to the hospital for diagnostic tests and recommended treatment—they dropped their work schedules and family obligations and made plane reservations. Knowing the girls would be visiting warmed our hearts and eased our fears. Their presence would be a huge help to me. After the relative ease of organizing the international move, getting settled into the house, and starting a new enterprise, I was suddenly thrown into crisis mode. We weren't prepared for this, for John being sick. Was it a grave illness? Did I need to abandon my plans and tend to him, and if so, how would my business ever get off the ground? I had set my company on a runway, and it was coursing at a steady speed. Slowing it down moments before takeoff could well halt the engines.

John and I simultaneously took a deep breath and made our way toward the hospital. The entrance was unmistakably indicated by a tacky provisional-looking white sign with large black letters: NA HOMOLCE. Two years prior, the complex was the Státní ustáv národního zdraví (State Institute of National Health). The temporary sign was symbolic of the incomplete changeover to which we would fall prey.

John held my arm. The quiver of his being vibrated against my frame as we walked shoulder to shoulder. We entered a spiritless lobby. The Celsius was high but the atmosphere had a chilling vibe. The location of the registration counter was not evident. Once we found it, we were asked to wait for an English-speaking clerk. That person searched a good twenty minutes for the admittance records from John's doctor. I wondered if this poor first impression was indicative of the hospital's overall inefficiency. However, since I was nervous, I held my judgment.

The clerk escorted us to John's room. The architecture of the single-block building deceived the eye from the outside; it was actually an intricate composition of mutually joined spaces. We walked from one long hallway to another in eerily quiet surroundings, passing room after room of closed doors. I wondered whether the rooms were empty or filled with patients. I expected to see a nurse station buzzing in a hive of activity or a waiting room with conversing family members. There was nothing of the sort within sight or earshot.

John's room was good-sized with two beds. The clerk assured John that he would be the only occupant. A big window with open taupe curtains provided ample light. No extraneous decor. Two beds, two chairs, two wardrobe cabinets, a small television, a bathroom. John set his transistor radio, thick novel, and reading glasses on the nightstand.

The clerk told us to settle in, and that he'd inform the floor attendant of our arrival. Our misgivings quelled when a white-capped nurse breezed through the door with a clipboard in hand. She was a stocky, middle-aged woman whose good-natured demeanor was comforting. While she checked John's vital signs—blood pressure, temperature, and pulse and respiration rates—she chattered about what to expect during his stay. The nurse's English was scantly adequate, and yet, adequate at that moment was sublime. John returned her welcoming words with an intelligent charm that was so *him*. All the things I loved about my husband surfaced at times like these. Unexpected crises that spun me out of control brought out the steady calm in John. On this day, though, the man I always depended on to make everything all right was now depending on me to stay on top of things and advocate on his behalf. I could not let him down.

We understood the nurse's instructions. She showed John the call button (which periodically malfunctioned), how to turn on the television (black-and-white all-Czech programming), and told him the times when dinner would be brought around. She said the doctor would come the next morning and each weekday morning thereafter. He'd determine the schedule for tests and therapy sessions. "For now," she smiled, "just relax." With that invitation, John asked if he could smoke, to which she quipped, "Absolutely not."

When dinner arrived, a cold beer was on the tray with an appetizing plate of traditional Bohemian cuisine. The meals served over the course of his stay—pork roasts, goulash, creamed chicken, dumplings, potato pancakes, sauerkraut, cakes and *koláče*—were the kind of down-home fare that pleased John.

I channeled my acting skills to radiate cheerfulness as I prepared to leave my husband alone that first night. We said our prayers, I promised to return first thing in the morning, and with a kiss I wished him a good night's sleep. I walked down the long hallways to the elevator, through the lobby, and outside to the car. With my hands and head on the steering wheel, I sobbed for the longest time before driving home. I did not drink, but thought about it. Instead, I went straight to bed, exhausted.

In the morning, I dressed and headed to the hospital. We waited in vain for the doctor who had admitted John and said he'd be there on the first day and follow John's progress thereafter. It was almost noon when a different physician, a young Czech man proficient in English, appeared and introduced himself as the doctor taking over John's case. He spoke about scheduling a battery of tests over the next week. He asked John questions, then shifted his focus on me to solicit my observations. I wanted to authentically introduce him to the unique person that John was—the war hero, the father of four, the retired advertising executive, the great painter, the loving husband. Instead, I gave the doctor the here-and-now information he wanted. I explained that John's strength had declined over the past few years, and since his fall last week, he was even weaker.

"Doctor, we moved from France to Prague a few weeks ago. Could the stress of the disruption have been too much?" I asked, almost in tears.

Feelings of regret surfaced from deep in my heart. I hated this period of our lives—my husband was suffering, and everything felt out of my control. My only consolation was that John was in the care of a medical team in which we simply had to place our trust, in hopes they'd discover the problem and offer solutions.

With a smile of assurance, I kissed John goodbye for the day. I sped to the office by way of Plzeňská ulice and across the Legií bridge where the Hradčany castle beckoned my gaze as it reigned supreme over the city. The granite bridge continued straight into Národní třída. As I whisked past the Reduta club, the memory of my Prague premiere brought with it the majesty of music which, in turn, reopened a wound I had ignored. I hadn't sung in months. I hadn't grieved my withdrawal from the world of music. The wound flared like a stinging rebuke when, in that mystical moment, it was as if the doors to the Reduta redemptively opened and poured forth my lyrics to Brel's melody "When We Only Have Love." In that split second, I remembered that *love* had led me to Prague. I had rejoiced through lyrical poetry in the country's newfound freedom. My song of *love* spurred the country's president to invite me to sing at the Reduta. And *love* continued to be the undercurrent that rescued every fear in my core and flaw in my character. True to its nature, it washed over me again as I whirled through the streets of Prague.

Whipping around the corner on Spálená, I drove down the alleyway to park behind the premises, where my office building's official entryway (once grandiose, now covered in graffiti) led through the Pasáž Spálená to my stairwell. I ran up two flights of steps, unlocked the office door, and sat at my desk. The life-giving song lyrics still played in my head, especially the coda where the melody ascends to a high peak: "Then with nothing at all, but the strength of our love, we'll shine forth our light, as the stars above." I was aware of the magic, as it had happened before, when lines of a poem strike deeper than prayer.

I looked around my office. The song faded in a gradual diminuendo, then hushed inside a long and final fermata. Alone I sat in silence. I shuddered at my present reality—my husband in a godforsaken hospital, and here I was, passing myself off as a business entrepreneur while shutting the door on music, the one profession I loved and had gotten really good at. Painful emotions—worry, fear, grief—swelled and clashed with my feelings of love for my husband and excitement for the venture I had undertaken.

Confusion threatened to crush me until I spotted my long to-do list. I started at the top and knocked off one task after another. Inside the nucleus of intense activity, I could lose myself and forget about our precarious situation. It was a productive day. After work, tired, I headed back to the hospital for a short while, then home to drink somewhere between a glass and a bottle of ruby red Frankovka, and off to bed. This routine repeated for three days.

On the fourth, I drove to the train station to pick up Patty and Carole who'd flown from Boston to Vienna, then traveled by rail to Prague. We went straight to the hospital. From the glow in John's eyes, one might imagine that his darling angels had floated into his room from celestial clouds. I went to the office while the girls stayed with their dad, talking, reading, and playing cards. In the evening, their presence at home curbed my alcohol intake. We talked late into the night.

When Eugenia and Connie arrived a few days later, all four daughters overlapped in Prague for several days before Patty and Carole left. The girls brought solace to John and made his hospital stay bearable, even pleasant. But they couldn't erase the inefficiencies and failures of the overall experience.

To this day, John's daughters still talk about their harrowing hospital stories. One Thursday, John had complained that his bladder wasn't emptying properly. He told the nurse on Friday of his discomfort. She said to wait for the doctor to arrive on Monday. By Saturday, John was in terrible pain. No nurse or doctor could be found. No one in the hallway. No response to the call button. Connie, Eugenia, and I walked up and down corridors, hallway after hallway, searching for someone, anyone. We called out, "Is there a doctor here?" Only an echo returned our cries. We began to wonder how safe we were, how safe John was, in this deserted fortress. We were at the panic point. I had the notion to put my husband in the car, but where would we take him?

At long last, on another floor, we found a lone doctor, a male intern from Hungary on an exchange program. He was sympathetic to our dire concern and followed us to John's room. The large Hungarian with bushy hair agreed that John had a serious bladder infection. He inserted a catheter, a painful procedure that brought immediate relief.

The intern stated, as if it were the norm, that few medical personnel worked on weekends, and our regular doctor and core medical staff would return on Monday. We begged him to come back the next day to check on John. We wondered if a tip/bribe was in order. But even without it, he came back to see John on Sunday for a quick visit.

What he didn't say, which we discovered later, was that John was an unsuspecting cog in the wheel of a defunct system undergoing major change. Across the nation, health services were being decentralized. Hospital ownerships were being transferred. Health leaders, hospital directors, and department heads had been replaced.   At Na Homolce, reputed to be the country's most luxurious medical facility, the old guard had already evacuated and left a vacuum which sucked us into its disorganized abyss.

After the first week, John's test results were inconclusive. His doctor recommended a longer hospital stay for more tests. We consented. John spent the second week reading, eating, and visiting with his girls. Tests were infrequent. Physical therapy was nonexistent. The nurses made irregular rounds on weekdays, and from Friday afternoon to Monday morning, the place practically emptied.

Na Homolce Hospital was built only a handful of years prior to the revolution with an exclusive mission to serve party elites and foreign diplomats. Its name derives from Homolka Hill where the structure sits on a north-to-south slope. It was the one and only hospital in the country with the newest equipment, yet still far behind Western Europe. Had John been a patient at Na Homolce before November 1989, it would have been staffed with the best medical personnel in the country, who could marginally push boundaries within the rigidity of the Soviet-style system, which included some entrenched practices dating back to the Austrian monarchy.

Our episode took place in the nebulous post-revolutionary era when, as described years later by a doctor friend, the new lawmakers had metaphorically "shut down the lights for five minutes" to intentionally create an entr'acte devoid of laws so people with money and connections could move fast and scoop up the deals. People with communist connections and resources not only had a head start, but also knew in which direction to run. As our doctor friend saw it, they simply turned in their red books and dove into capitalism.

After this grab-and-go period, the country moved toward a more transparent system of privatization by wrapping new legislation around the chaotic process. Laws were written and passed that gave citizens more health care rights, laid the foundation for a universal health insurance program, and allowed medical professionals to enter private practice. John and I would witness major reforms in the health care sector later in the 1990s. We'd ultimately find a caring and competent Czech physician who spoke fluent English and French and who'd recently started his own private practice.

But in early 1992, we were lost in a system fraught with problems. One afternoon, Connie, Eugenia, and I sat with John at the inhospitable facility where he'd been stuck for two weeks already. We all were disillusioned by the lack of quality care, but we held out hope that the tests would reveal the reason he had lost consciousness and fallen to the ground.

His daughters and I spoke privately and concluded that when John came home from the hospital, he shouldn't be left alone all day. I asked my secretary to place an ad in the paper for a full-time nurse. Although our need for in-home care happened sooner than I expected, my plan to move to Prague had been made in light of this eventuality.

Going into John's third week of hospitalization, Eugenia and Connie went home to their jobs and families. We devised a master plan before they left to which John fully agreed. If there were no conclusive diagnosis in short order—whether or not the doctor blathered on about John staying longer or spouted "blah, blah, blah" about more tests—I would bring John home.

On Wednesday 27 May, an array of blooming fruit trees greeted us as John and I pulled into the driveway of our house. It was a strain for John to climb the six outside steps and six inside steps, but he went slowly and seemed to find the arduous endeavor exhilarating. Home at last.

The next day, Dita had lined up three interviews for a nurse. John and I enjoyed meeting the candidates who came to the house, even the duds. The first was a tall buxom woman who spoke English rather well in an authoritative manner. Well-intentioned, she was certain that a regimental schedule of good eating, morning walks, and afternoon naps would rebuild John's strength. With the voice of a school principal, she offered to cook nutritious lunches and expected him to eat everything on his plate. We thanked her kindly and promised to contact her with our decision after we interviewed others.

"Definitely not her!" John exclaimed the moment she exited.

Another was a man, a physical therapist by trade who growled a bit when he spoke. Off he trudged after an abbreviated conversation.

Then along came Adéla. The moment the lithe blonde walked in the door with her beautiful smile, intelligent eyes, and gracious manner, the room seemed to brighten. Adéla was a registered nurse in her late thirties who had worked nearly two decades in Prague hospitals. I read my secretary's interview notes and learned that Adéla had a preference for daytime hours rather than the alternating night shifts of her current job. She would also be grateful for any increase in her current monthly income, the equivalent of less than two hundred dollars. Adéla knew very little English, but said she sincerely wanted to learn. She and John established an immediate rapport. They communicated with few words, but relied on each other's facial expressions and gestures. Adéla's health-conscious sensibilities attuned naturally to John's needs.

We offered a 30-percent increase to her hospital salary and guaranteed fixed hours from 8:30 to 16:30. Adéla seemed overjoyed, and so were we. She would start the next Monday on the first day of June. It would be the two-month mark of our move to Prague.

By the end of June, John and I were still waiting for the hospital bill. I needed to submit it to our insurer. This was the first time I had filed a claim since signing up for the Association of Americans Resident Overseas (AARO) plan in 1983. At the outset of John's hospital stay, I'd alerted the insurance administrator in Paris, who'd reassured me that we were covered anywhere in Europe.

I stopped at Na Homolce's business office on the day John was discharged. The woman at the desk seemed flummoxed. She didn't have the invoice prepared, but said she'd send it to our home address. After weeks of waiting, I made an appointment and went back to the hospital. Again, the billing office had nothing to present. After a frustrating discussion, the clerk finally admitted they had no record of John being there. I found myself in the Kafkaesque situation of trying to prove John had been a patient. I told them to contact the doctor who had handled his case and ordered all those tests. (I wondered, with a sinking feeling, had there been any tests?)

The clerk responded, "Oh, that doctor is no longer here. He was temporary anyway and left to start his own practice."

I prevailed on the billing clerk to believe me. I gave John's room number, the precise dates, the names of the head nurse and Hungarian intern. It dawned on me that I had no hard evidence, had been given no paperwork during registration, and had no copies of John's test results. In the middle of this surreal discourse, as the clerk repeated that there was no record of his stay, I began to doubt my soundness of mind. Was I in the middle of a bad dream, or, as Eugenia described, lost in the Twilight Zone?

My frustration must have turned to tears, because something snapped in the clerk's autocratic attitude. She threw down her pen and looked straight into my eyes for the first time. Her tone mellowed from stridently rude to an apologetic whisper as she began to speak to me as if I were a friend.

"Of course, I believe you, but ever since the hospital turnover process began, our systems have been in disarray. I am determined to find your records, and we will send you a bill."

One month later. Nothing. John and I were concerned that, with no closure, this wild and dubious incident might haunt us later. What if, two years down the road, a collection agency knocked on our door about an overdue bill we had never received? John and I wanted to conclude the hospital experience as positively as possible. After all, no harm had been done. In fact, some good had come from the three-week respite: the girls' visit, and our decision to find home help. And during the stressful time when I was alone, I took a tumble once or twice with a handsome Czech acquaintance who thought he was God's gift to women. In my case, he was a gift, a temporary salve that somehow reinforced the emotional thread from which I was hanging.

I returned to the hospital's business office and said I wouldn't leave without a bill in hand. The same clerk from a month before sheepishly asked me to wait as she left the counter. Finally, a bedraggled gentleman wearing his workplace slippers, tired pants, faded shirt, and a musty, argyle woolen vest, who looked like an overworked administrator plucked out of retirement, emerged from the back room. He laid a bill on the table with a total amount in crowns comparable to around three hundred dollars. I started to point out that the sum was too low for a hospital stay of over two weeks, but instead, I simply said, "Thank you very much." My recollection is that I paid cash and walked out with an officially stamped statement bearing words to the effect, "All medical services, tests, procedures, and room charges entirely paid. No balance due."

On the drive home, as I processed the absurdity of our health care experience, I thought of something that might bring genuine healing and joy to John—a puppy. It should be a Scottish terrier. While I'd not seen any Scotties in Prague, I'd noticed a pedestrian walking a gray-colored terrier with drooping ears and turned-down tail, unlike the perky ears and tail of a Scottie.

I turned to my staff for help, and they asked around to relatives and friends. They told me that the pup I saw on the street was a Český teriér, a mixture of Scottish and Sealyham terriers. This special crossbreed was created in the 1940s by a geneticist and Czechoslovakian hunter named František Horák to help him hunt hare, fox, and red deer in the Bohemian forests. The Českýs were undeniably cute, but I knew John would prefer a Scottie.

Sooner than I expected, my assistant came to the office one morning beaming with pride. She'd found a breeder of Scottish terriers in a village in eastern Bohemia and had already called them. The breeders had a terrier about to birth a litter, and when that happened, they'd be in contact. Before long, when the newborns were sufficiently weaned, my office got a call. Equipped with a map and the directions my assistant got from the breeder, John and I set out for the hour-and-a-half drive to the beautiful Pardubice region along the Elbe River.

We found the cottage on a large strip of land tucked into the countryside. We were only halfway up the walk when the owner and a flurry of pups came to greet us. As John reached out to them, one tiny black hound licked his hands and jumped for joy. She was ours. We called her Miss Two, a variation on the name of her predecessor, Misty. The next day at our house, when Adéla met her new charge, it was love at first sight for her, too.

Miss Two at home in Suchdol

Although Adéla was hired to be John's nurse and companion, to care for his health and living needs, monitor his vital signs, prepare his midday meal, and walk with him in the fresh air, she did so much more, without us ever asking. She kept the main level of our house spotlessly clean. She took charge of John's laundry, and in the Czech tradition, this meant washing, hanging dry, and pressing everything, including ironing his underpants and socks. When John read or napped, Adéla sat at the kitchen table near the window and studied her English phrase book to better communicate with him.

She often arrived on Mondays bearing dishes and desserts that she'd cooked over the weekend for her family. She found a barber nearby and made John's monthly haircut appointments and accompanied him there. She spoiled Miss Two with homemade dog food made of lentils, ground beef, carrots, and grains. But most important, Adéla's innate kindness and medical expertise were fitting complements to the chivalrous, erudite gentleman to whom she provided great care.

With John settled and happy, my business, which was already up and sputtering, could now take off. And it did, like a rocket.

15

A DISTINCTIVE NICHE

The second half of 1992 was tense with political and cultural dissonance. The talk of Slovakia's potential secession was troubling. My expat friends and I moved forward with our enterprises, but not without trepidation. What we dreaded was that our adopted country could break apart and spiral into chaos, or worse yet, a bloody war like in Yugoslavia. Serious unrest would have sent us running, losing everything. In retrospect, I liken the restless atmosphere to the music of modern Czech composer Bohuslav Martinů, who saturated his instrumental masterpieces with clashing intervals and wrought tension before easing into a restrained consonance.

I look back on the wild post-revolutionary era from the viewpoint of a foreigner on the ground at the time, an artist who became a business-woman. Far from being a historian, I could only piece together parts of the full picture.

From birth to death, the country I inhabited was synchronous with my husband's lifespan. John was born in 1917, Czechoslovakia in 1918. When the Austro-Hungarian empire dissolved at the end of World War 1, Tomáš Garrigue Masaryk and Edvard Beneš teamed up with their counterparts in Slovakia in a marriage more of convenience than love. Their new union, První československá republika, was commonly called the First Republic (until the Munich Agreement in 1938), as well as Czechoslovakia. In 1992, John and I witnessed Czechoslovakia's final exhalation. He would outlive it by four years.

As John's life began, and waned, so did this country, with struggles and triumphs that paralleled ours in its last years. It made me aware then, and more so now, that each person in his or her own place and time becomes an inherent part of history's tapestry. It takes stepping away from the picture and looking back to see the interconnections threaded within the weave.

Czechoslovakia's noticeable undoing had begun with the crumbling of another empire, the Soviet Union. The sounding of the 1989 freedom bells had aroused a swelling of Slovak national spirit and desire for independence. I heard complaints among the Pragois that the rapid privatization of the country's state-run industries was slipshod and corrupt. The negative consequences disproportionately affected the Slovak region.

President Havel respected the Slovak sensitivities and ambitions. He admitted that the top-down relationship of the two regions had to change. One manifestation of the rancor was the haggling about the name of the country. Within three months of the revolution, the official name was changed to Česká a Slovenská Federativní Republika. We had to write the acronym *ČSFR* on official documents, but everyone still used *Czechoslovakia* in conversation.

Havel wrote in his memoir that, throughout 1990 and 1991, "we spent thousands of hours in various political meetings looking for the optimal model of coexistence between our two peoples in a common state." A satisfactory model never emerged. Havel's moral arguments fell on the deaf ears of leaders prone to populism. In June 1992, Vladimír Mečiar was elected prime minister in Slovakia and Václav Klaus to the same role in the Czech region. The two republics, still one federation, had two forms of government, two prime ministers, two coats of arms, and two national anthems. Klaus and Mečiar, men with vastly different visions, were already negotiating to split the country. Depending on whom I spoke with at the time, one or the other prime minister deserved more blame for not trying hard enough to keep the country intact.

I found both men to be severe in manner and conviction. Klaus was labeled an arrogant opportunist, eager to rid himself of the poorer eastern region of the country. Mečiar, a former heavyweight boxer, communist, and lawyer, was the leader of the People's Party Movement for a Democratic Slovakia (ĽS-HZDS) and a die-hard nationalist. He was seen as an uncompromising sort who lusted for power and, to my ear, intentionally modulated his raspy voice to rile national fervor in his countrymen.

On 17 July, the Slovak parliament adopted a declaration of sovereignty, giving its regional government more power. The Slovaks had never experienced genuine independence, and although this move didn't bring complete autonomy, it was reason for celebration. Havel resigned as president, more as a symbolic than political gesture. His rationale was that "someone who had taken an oath to defend the constitution of a particular country cannot then sign into law an act dissolving that country." He was reelected a few months later to a country with a new name.

No one I knew in Prague liked the idea of a country breakup. Ordinary Czechs wondered why there wasn't a referendum on the matter, why they had no say in the backroom card games the officials shuffled and dealt.

The rest of Europe anxiously awaited the final decision. Would nationalism spill into other parts of the region? My entrepreneur friends and I, admittedly neophytes, kept watch on the political situation as we kept piling up our own building blocks in the business arena—hopeful that the political dissonance would smoothly resolve into a Martinů-like consonance.

I can glibly write today about the uncertainty and worry we felt thirty years ago. At the time, as expatriates, we neither made light of the situation nor let it paralyze us. The Czechoslovak people had so much more at stake. I hadn't experienced the trauma they had lived. Russian tanks had rolled into this country without warning just two decades earlier. The older ones had lived through the horrors of Hitler's and Stalin's tyrannical rule. Very recently, their neighbors in Romania had executed their leaders by firing squad, which they televised for all to see. And now, neighboring Yugoslavia was splintering into shambles in a bloody civil war. Given these prevailing circumstances, there was reason to worry about an infectious spread of nationalistic instability. But, with Václav Havel's moral compass and the Czechs' levelheadedness, I felt a sense of security.

Nonetheless, when Mari and Steve revealed to me their emergency exit plan, I wanted in. Compared to the expats who were safe under the wings of multinational corporations, we were among the few small business owners with no security blanket, risking our own resources, and frankly, operating by the seat of our pants. Mari, Steve, John, and I agreed to keep each other alerted on major issues. We were registered at the U.S. Embassy in Prague, but were doubtful it could contact, let alone evacuate, more than two thousand Americans by means of telephone landlines and letters. Other measures we put into place were to keep a full tank of gas in our cars, and store passports, documents, and valuables in one handy place. I had a can filled with Deutsch marks, French francs, U.S. dollars, and Czech crowns buried in our backyard.

If chaos erupted, the plan was to call the other couple at home and the office. If we had to leave a message, we'd enunciate clearly a code phrase, which I've completely forgotten because it was never used. I only remember that it made me chuckle, something like, "Don't forget to feed the dog." Our rendezvous point would be the recently opened McDonald's store on Plzeňská ulice, the thoroughfare leading out of town toward Pilsen and on to Germany. The plan was effective in terms of bringing us peace of mind and an *esprit de corps* with our new friends. While our getaway plan was never needed, the buried can of cash bought me time later during an unexpected banking crisis.

With this as a backdrop, we tried to cultivate a social life as well as a business network. In July, John and I had our first dinner party in our new home. Soon after, we hosted a cocktail party in a grand style that harkened back to our days in France. I invited the most interesting

From left to right: Mary Jochim (seated), a guest whose name I've forgotten, Petr Zima, and James Taliaferro. Singing around the piano are: Dave Orso, Phyllis Taliaferro (behind Dave), Zdeněk Merta, and Mari Novak, with me at the keyboard.

Norbert Auerbach and Steve Kelly

Phyllis Taliaferro, Mari Novak, and I dance to the music of Zdeněk Merta at the piano.

people from my new professional world. Our Pragois suburban house wasn't nearly as glamorous as our Parisian flat overlooking the Seine or our Niçois apartment bordering the Mediterranean Sea, but the walls of the living-dining room, lined with John's art collection, rang with the sound of music. These soirées held the rare merging of my old and new careers. I played the piano and sang until our guests unwound and crowded around the piano to bellow out show tunes and jazz numbers. Food, libations, and fun abounded. I was serving and singing more than drinking, happily surrounded by new friends.

July also marked a turning point in my business. Dr. Zima personally delivered the registration papers for my company. Now I could invoice clients. Now I could register my office assistants with the social security agency, elevating them from contract workers to employees with full benefits. We were official.

A week later, a client from the Palace Hotel brought us an order that required masses of typing, pages and pages of documents. We had also received from various embassies their lists of companies doing business in Prague, which I wanted to have compiled and typed into a master list, with a select shortlist typed onto my Rolodex cards. I turned to Amira, "Try reaching that shy girl we interviewed last week who doesn't speak much English but types really fast."

Jana Křivánková took the job and breezed through the workload. More typing orders and menu translations came in. By that time, we knew the names of nearly every Czech culinary dish and their English, French, and German equivalents. No one typed and formatted like Jana. She was meticulous, correcting errors that weren't even noticeable. She was organized and tidied up the entire office, including my desk. Along with her goodheartedness and natural smile, she was a perfect asset to my business.

Jana was as scrupulous about getting everything right as I was about bringing quality services to clients. She wanted a career in the new international business environment of Prague. If the only drawback was language, I thought, it could surely be developed in this capable person eager to learn.

I worked with Jana on the essential dialogue needed to answer the phones, and she taught me how to say the same phrases in Czech—phrases the Dušní students would not have learned. "May I ask who's calling, please?" "Certainly, Mr. (or Mrs.) Smith, I will connect you." "Ms. Kenny is not in the office right now, but I will be happy to take a message." "Would you kindly spell your name?" "Please speak slowly." "I will be sure to give her the message." "Thank you for calling."

Each of these phrases and other teaching and testing tools for office personnel eventually became the basis of a training curriculum that would benefit thousands. But I couldn't see the future at that time. On the surface, which still felt shaky, I was addressing day-to-day challenges as they came, unaware of the solid foundation being laid under our feet.

Then, a spotlight shone on our unique place in the emerging market. Our brochures were finally printed and looked top-quality. When our mass-mailed brochure and cover letter hit the desks of international managers, the phones began to ring. The switchboard operator in our building had finally caught on and promptly routed our calls. (Eventually we'd be given a direct phone line, but not yet.) One afternoon, only days after we'd mailed the brochure, Jana came into my office with a flustered look and said, "I am on the phone with someone talking very fast in English . . . I think he said his name was Mr. Johnson Johnson."

I took the receiver and spoke with the cheerful country manager from the American health care corporation, Johnson & Johnson. He spoke quickly, even to my adapted ears, recounting how his company had just opened operations in the Czech Republic, Poland, and Russia. He said he was impressed with my brochure and liked that I was a fellow American.

"Ms. Kenny, I see that you offer secretarial services. I need a bilingual assistant and other clerical staff in my office, as soon as possible. Like, today!"

"Let me see what I can do." I replied, "Please sit tight. I'll call you back in fifteen minutes."

I turned to Jana, whose eyes widened at what must have been an intractable flash in mine. "Jana, would you go work at Johnson & Johnson on a temporary basis, only for two or three days, until I can replace you?"

"What?" She glared at me as if I were trading her on the new commodities exchange.

I launched into the concept of temporary and permanent job placements, a respected and lucrative service in market economies. I told her, "I myself worked as a receptionist and secretary in an employment agency years ago." (An experience I'd forgotten about until that moment.) "This may become the future of our business," I continued, surprising even myself by this abrupt awareness. "It stands to reason that the companies we sent our brochure to are already established and not in need of our phone, fax, and mailing address services. What they *will* need are secretarial services provided by their own employees in their own place of business."

I pleaded and cajoled as Jana teetered before reluctantly giving in. I called Mr. "Johnson Johnson" back to say that my personal assistant was on her way until I could find someone more permanent. As Jana gathered up her purse and jacket, I wished her a good experience, but asked her to please not enjoy the assignment too much, noting, "I need you here!"

This was the moment our market niche landed in my lap, when AYS became an employment agency specializing in administrative workers.

Our want ads sprang a steady stream of inquiries, candidates, and interviews to our office. Callers were totally unfamiliar with employment agencies, a nonexistent entity during communism. We explained it this way: "We will work with you in your job search, give you options, and help match your skills and goals with the right company and position. You're not obligated to go on any interviews we propose, or take any job you're offered. You pay nothing for our service. We are paid by our client companies, if we find them an employee. We only ask that, should you agree to go to a specific interview, you will be there on time, dress professionally, and put your best foot forward. Please call to tell us how your interviews went and inform us if you start working there within six months of the introduction."

What I believe made us successful was the trust people placed in us. Our written agreements were secondary to the genuine desire we demonstrated in wanting others to succeed. We often advised someone not to take the first job offer, unless they were sure of it. We would forfeit our commission rather than push someone into a position for which they weren't well suited. My staff saw the results: happy customers spoke highly of us and recommended us to their friends.

Candidates were tested for typing, languages, and writing composition. Test scores were then put on every résumé, which my office specially formatted to an attractive international standard. The traditional Czech narrative-style curriculum vitae were appealing with their paragraphic form and storytelling flair. But unfortunately, foreign companies lost patience scanning the florid text containing information they considered irrelevant, such as where the applicant's parents were born, whether the family had or had not been members of the Communist Party, or where their family farm or cottage was located. My staff pulled key points from the candidates' résumés, interview answers, and skills tests, and created a slick, one-page sheet for each candidate. Agreements, résumés, and confirmations were faxed to the client and followed up with a phone call.

Word soon got out among the international companies about our new service, AYS Placements. Our only advertisement was the one-time brochure mailing and my ongoing networking efforts. Company executives referred other executives to us. Among our first clients were Johnson & Johnson, Conoco, Procter & Gamble, Price Waterhouse, Coopers & Lybrand, Schering-Plough, Atrium Hotel, Palace Hotel, InterContinental Hotel, Squire Sanders & Dempsey, the Peace Corps, the Mellon Institute, and Prague Investments.

Another early client was William Lobkowicz, who walked into my office like any regular American newcomer in search of personnel. Without a whiff of arrogance, he explained his need for a high-level, bilingual assistant as he tackled the restitution of his family's castles, land, artwork, and music collections that had been confiscated by the Nazi and communist regimes. I listened, speechless.

One late summer day, my phone rang and a congenial voice with a Southern drawl greeted me, saying he was calling from Louisville, Kentucky, at the recommendation of Steven Miller of Prague Investments.

"Well, it's nice to hear from you, and how may I help you?" I responded.

"My American company is set to launch several stores in Czechoslovakia. I'll be in Prague next week and will need a right-hand person to help me arrange appointments and accompany me to meetings."

"Of course, we can help with this," I said with assurance. "Please give me the exact dates, and by the way, what is the name of your company?"

"Kentucky Fried Chicken."

I lost my composure and howled with delight. "My husband loves KFC, and I can hardly wait to tell him this news! We'll be your best customers!"

And so it went. As companies entered the market, AYS was there to help them get started and expand into the future.

It was no wonder that my staff didn't recognize the names of famous global companies, like Johnson & Johnson or Kentucky Fried Chicken. Although these companies were household names internationally, private businesses hadn't been allowed to operate behind the Iron Curtain. But my employees learned quickly, and so did I, in a crash course of discovery.

AYS was one of the first employment agencies in Prague, and the only one exclusively focused on support staff. In time, more and more agencies and headhunters hit the market. I knew my niche was distinctive and bet that no other staffing company would elect to focus so narrowly. Most agencies, mine included, calculated their commissions on a multiple of the candidate's starting salary, and naturally leaned toward higher-level positions that rendered heftier commissions. I understood from the start that if we dealt only with support staff—secretaries, assistants, receptionists—we'd need volume.

I also had to stay abreast of the new labor laws, statistics, and salary trends. Unemployment was another new phenomenon in the country. Its steep increase in the early years of the open market worked in our favor. Jana had graduated from Dušní, one of two all-girls secondary economic schools which prepared students for administrative careers in the commercial sector. It was mandatory to learn a foreign language and complete two summer internships in state-run companies. Jana explained that during communism, graduates from these two academies were much in demand and quickly found excellent positions. Now, due to the closing of state enterprises, and the budget-cutting measures of the privatization process, even Dušní graduates were slow to find employment, unless their language and adaptability skills could get them in the doors of foreign companies.

The government took measures to reduce the abundant labor supply. Primary education was extended by one year. Subsidies were given to former state companies to employ recent school graduates. State-run training programs were introduced. Incentives were given to citizens for small business start-ups.

In finding and hiring quality talent, the old state-owned enterprises were hard-pressed to compete with the foreign companies entering the market. The latter paid more than twice or thrice the state's wage, offered more opportunities for advancement, and had different expectations. Language skills and a service-oriented mentality were prioritized over technical or clerical proficiency. Under the former economy, a customer-focused attitude was hard to find. It could only be emulated if it'd been taught or demonstrated, which wasn't the case under communism. While I could teach these skills to my staff, other newly established companies in Prague didn't have the time, inclination, or know-how to do this training. They unrealistically expected employees to hit the ground running, not taking into consideration that the ground had shifted in the new economy.

Clients called with increasing frustration and specificity: "Don't send someone stuck in the old ways, with no work ethic." Or more blatantly, "Only send young people; I won't hire anyone who's worked in a former state enterprise." I knew the recent edition of the labor code, published in English by *Trade Links*, and would call out the client for discriminatory statements like that. But their fundamental point was well taken.

Yet I knew it wasn't age. It was attitude. Not all practices in state companies were bad. But in the former system, office workers were allowed to merely appear to be working. They weren't expected to exert much energy, show innovation, please the customer, or, heaven forbid, ever make a complaint. They'd show up, remove shoes, change into slippers, blend in, and job security was assured.

Work ethic? How could I explain to our candidates this phrase with no equivalency in the Czech lexicon? Could a desire to not only meet, but exceed, the customer's expectations be instilled in a nation with an authoritarian past, a nation of force-fed totalitarian ideologies, a nation with a heightened sense of suspicion? Could pride in one's work be worthy of its own reward?

To find those answers, I abandoned idealism for pragmatism. Before pondering solutions, I had to clarify the questions. What precisely is expected in a multinational work environment? Which Czech cultural norms presented obstacles? What could bridge the differences? Who should make more effort to adjust, the Czech worker or the foreign boss? While that answer should be "both," I felt strongly that we foreigners should adapt more to the Czech culture; after all, they were the end user of all our efforts in this country. Not all foreigners agreed with me. Some unabashedly said their goal was to gain maximum profit from the country's low wages and costs. Others claimed they were heroically bringing Western customs to the backward natives. Yes. I heard this line of thinking so often that I regularly questioned my own motives.

In the meantime, an aspect of our work was to prepare candidates for their interviews. I was loathe to suggest that success hinged only on making a good first impression without stressing the value of genuineness. Czech people have a special antenna to detect insincerity. So, I prepped job seekers on typical interview questions. I gave them a rundown about the multinational work environment, expectations, and customer focus. Then, I left it to each candidate to strike an authentic attitude and formulate sincere responses.

On this fine point—to not lecture, but respectfully explain—was the attitude I needed to maintain. We didn't want the reputation of an input-output factory scoring placements to earn commissions. We wanted to put people in jobs that benefited everyone, the candidate and the enterprise. We depended on each other's success to make our collective way.

As traffic flowed in and out of our office, I'd sometimes see Miroslav Macek in the hallway. He seemed unduly serious, yet dignified. He always wanted to chat in English about music or literature. His name was in the newspapers surrounding a political scandal, but it wasn't a topic we discussed. I never thought of him as Macek the politician or Macek the landlord. To me, he was Macek the translator of Shakespeare and Poe.

Before the year was out, Steve Kelly's office rental contract expired, which voided our sublet agreement. I started paying monthly rent directly to Macek. I was surprised when he asked if I wanted the offices that he'd been occupying. He said he no longer needed them, mumbling something under his breath about the building's privatization process being disputed. He was vague, and I knew enough not to be curious. For a nominal extra charge, we added his large office and a smaller wing to our space, resulting in four good rooms.

At home, John was following the 1992 U.S. presidential race. It was a three-way ticket among Republican incumbent President George H.W. Bush of Texas, Democratic Governor Bill Clinton of Arkansas, and Independent businessman Ross Perot of Texas. In August, I met with Consul Deborah Park at the U.S. Embassy about having a Voter Registration Rally. Consul Park was prepared for Americans to register at the embassy, but when I described the lively rallies held at popular expat venues that AARO Paris organized in collaboration with the U.S. Embassy in France, she liked the idea. Americans could still schlep to the embassy, or they could turn up at a fun social and civic event. To get the word out, we advertised in the *Prague Post* and tacked flyers where expats frequented. Deborah thought it should be held in September, because of the time lag between collecting the registrations and mailing the ballots by November.

More than two hundred Americans showed up at a popular restaurant on Karlova ulice and registered to vote. I sat behind a long table just inside the entrance with another AARO member living in Prague; joining us were Consul Deborah Park and an embassy coworker. It was an evening of lively conversation and plenty of networking.

Around this time in early fall, Mari and Steve's company, KNO Worldwide, included me in their "Train the Trainer" course about how to design and conduct a training program. They knew that my clients were asking me to help prepare candidates for an international office environment. KNO and AYS partnered to create a training course called "The Professional Secretary." Mari and I were interviewed on a television program. Steve won the endorsement of Mark Graham, senior manager of Coopers & Lybrand's Prague office. Mark mailed a personalized letter to five hundred Czech and foreign companies recommending our training program. He enclosed the course flyer, which stated:

AYS and KNO Worldwide introduce one in a series of day-long workshops designed to update the secretary in the skills and knowledge required in an international office environment. Topics covered:

- The Secretary: role and responsibilities
- Customer Service: business diplomacy, greeting the client
- Managing Your Boss: calendars, confirmations, reminders
- Records Management: storage and retrieval
- Office Equipment Systems: descriptions and usage
- Telephone Etiquette: front line of corporate communications
- Personal and Company Image: your role as company representative

The course was held on four optional dates in late November. Reservations filled quickly with executive assistants from leading companies. Our venue was the Loreta/Belvedere Room on the panoramic ninth floor of the Hotel InterContinental Praha. With the full day of training, we offered lunch, refreshments, and a customized 1993 calendar book. I instructed the course on the two days it was conducted in English. For the days it was offered in Czech, I hired psychologist PhDr. Erika Gerlová, the daughter of my musicologist friend, Olga Kittnarová.

Erika delivered the material with aplomb. She was a magnificent speaker and intelligent professional who took pride in her work. Her beautiful smile, wavy blonde hair, and stylish ensembles bespoke a contemporary allure. Erika became my top trainer and advisor on Czech cultural norms, attitudes, and mentality.

The workshop would never have been launched without the guidance of Mari and Steve. But it planted an idea in my mind. After our first successful collaboration, AYS went solo to create and deliver training programs focused on support staff. I quickly realized that training and development were the perfect complements to placing staff. Before long, I changed our company name to AYS Placements and Workshops.

The year was coming to a close. I'd made a promise to John before we moved from France that we'd spend part of the winter in Nice. Luckily, the Prague business scene slowed down toward the end of the year as expats returned to their respective home countries for the holidays. I left my blossoming business with Jana, another assistant, and nephew Dave, while John and I drove to the South of France. Our former concierge arranged for us to rent a flat in our old building on the sea for the month of December. We visited friends and soaked up the sunshine. John's lunches with Deon resumed at their favorite spots. John and I took drives into Ventimiglia for lunch. We passed right through Monte Carlo on the way, and my heart strings never tugged for the hotel where I used to sing, or the banker who nabbed my virtue.

On 31 December 1992, while John and I were still on vacation in France, Czechoslovakia's seventy-five-year-old union was peacefully dissolved in the Velvet Divorce. On the first day of 1993, two independent republics emerged: Slovenská republika and Česká republika. At this consequential moment, *The New York Times* headline was "Czechoslovakia Breaks in Two, to Wide Regret" and went on with, "A multi-ethnic nation born at the end of World War I in the glow of pan-Slavic brotherhood, Czechoslovakia survived dismemberment by the Nazis and more than four decades of Communist rule only to fall apart after just three years of democracy." I sighed in relief. My fears about the country's potential ruin ebbed, and my faith in its abilities flowed.

On the second day of 1993, after a month of sunshine, John and I headed back to a country with a new name: the Czech Republic. I drove the route I knew so well. It had been two years since my Reduta concert and first trip to Prague. It had been ten months since John and I had made this beautiful city our home. Driving along quietly, with John resting, my thoughts flew back and forth, oscillating from past to present. I reflected on the upheaval and drastic changes in Central Europe that brought opportunity to so many people. As I drove through forests, mountains and valleys, I silently admitted that I was proud of myself, and surprised, that my efforts were producing one small success after another. An assurance washed over me that the decision to leave France for Prague had been the right one.

I couldn't help but ruminate on the love affairs I'd left behind when we changed countries. Although I had intended to keep it that way, my drinking affliction had followed me like a snag on a hemline that unraveled little by little. During the first weeks of establishing ourselves in Prague, I'd pushed excessive drinking to the side. The tasks at hand had been overwhelming and would have crushed me had I not stayed alert. Then when John's health crisis occurred, I glided into autopilot mode like an actress onstage, playing the role and looking the part. My ability to run through lists of duties with compartmentalized confidence was accomplished only by the grace of God, or love for John, or plain grit.

Yet alongside this fragile cover, panic stood by, waiting for me to falter. I drew rigid boundaries that specified when and where I could drink. Only after work. At an expat bar. At home. Never during office hours. Only one glass of wine at lunch. To the same extent that I remained faithful to these boundaries, I could shatter them within seconds. Something would snap, and I'd be convinced that a drink was the only remedy.

But *a* drink became two, three, and more. I could no better keep alcohol in line than honor my decision to leave passionate desires behind. Alcohol and sexuality were my touchstones to sanity, a provisional cure. Looking back, booze was slowly destroying me. Slowly, because my addiction and anxiety were constantly mitigated by outside influences of goodness and grace—the extraordinary beauty of the ancient city, the buoyant atmosphere of the historic times, the love of my husband, and the friends coming into our lives.

Soon into my Prague days, I stumbled on a life-giving encounter which soothed my ruffled nerves, warmed my shivering fears. A man entered my life who was gentle and accommodating. He asked for nothing in return, nor did I, except the few hours we took from each other's day from time to time. He was someone to rely on, to be there, to hold onto. Nothing about forever was spoken. We didn't fall in love. But affection was present, a kind of endearment offered by an understanding friend without fanfare or calculation. A space where one could cry after intimacy and not explain. Or laugh carefree. He was there for me for quite some time. He held a place in no other aspect of my life except as a silent partner, a subduer of longing and builder of strength. The relationship eventually ended when my drinking careened way out of control. But that would not be for a while.

16

NEW MARKET SYMPHONY

I *couldn't believe my luck* as the door to 1993 opened to a flock of clients. Our recent training programs were intended to help Czech workers adjust to Western business practices, but they did so much more. The courses made a name for my company. The workshop participants, from a variety of business sectors, returned to their workplaces with a new confidence, sharing rosy reports about what they'd learned. Their managers, many of whom were Fortune 500 executives, noticed an augmented level of professionalism in their employees and began calling me for their staffing and training needs.

As orders flew in, I added personnel. We began a wider search for more candidates to fill permanent and temporary positions in our clients' offices. Our recently established temp business carried particular challenges. I thought of the delicate equipoise between supply and demand as an art form similar to balancing a dexterous countermelody. The dual forces of job seekers to job orders required attention and *intuition*, lest either side outweigh the other and throw everything off. Furthermore, companies needing temp workers wanted the perfect person for the job, and *now*.

I mused to my staff, "If only we had a coterie of skilled multilingual clerical workers sitting on shelves ready to hop off and dash to a client's office at a moment's notice." Thankfully, a number of interviewees preferred short-term positions and gladly accepted the on-call nature of temporary assignments.

In the training arena, psychologist Erika Gerlová and I conceived a series of workshops. On this subject, I wasn't improvising solely by ear. The needed training topics came at me like the shrill of a brass band. Business managers sang in unison a refrain commending their employees' admirable qualities and bemoaning the skills they lacked.

I, too, was in basic training. My attorney and accountant were my boot camp instructors guiding me through the regulatory and accounting framework surrounding our three core services—permanent placements, temporary placements, and training. Attorney Petr Zima explained key points in the new labor code and warned that legislation was in continual flux. He designed a template for my employment contracts, but was puzzled by our service that "farmed out" workers to other companies. He said this form of employment was unheard of and fit no previous hiring model.

In the former system, there was no need for the intermediary services of a staffing agency. The state bureaucracy had absolute control over the labor force and was the sole provider of jobs. It set wage rates, outlined rules for advancements, weakened the relationship between performance and reward, and planned the schooling of future workers. With the ultimate goal of full employment, one didn't have a *right* to work—it was a *duty* to work. Loyalty to the regime was favored over expertise and high performance. The system lacked competition, leaving no room for entrepreneurship except among black-market profiteers. Freedom in job choice came with strings attached. A young person could request a particular school or career path, but these luxuries weren't assured, unless the family had joined the Party. The inability to choose one's profession held true across sectors, including the performing arts, the field that first took me to Prague.

Czech musicians and writers told me that the arts had been propped up by the government as a means of control, which led me to believe that if musicians, actors, artists, and writers acquiesced to certain conditions, they'd have secure salaries and career advancements without fear of diminishment or censorship. But when communism fell, artists were kicked off the dole to fend for themselves. The consolation prize was the freedom to sing the songs, paint the pictures, and write whatever they longed to express.

This double-edged freedom also hit office workers as they adjusted their stride in the galloping new market. It required reinvention for those with the skills and mindset to adapt to the new playing field. I discovered that Czechoslovakia had a highly educated workforce. I interviewed young women seeking secretarial jobs who had advanced degrees in nuclear physics or structural engineering.

"Why would you leave the science field in which you've worked so hard?" I'd exclaim.

A typical response would be, "I never wanted to be a nuclear physicist. It was chosen for me after taking an aptitude test in high school."

Brilliant individuals like my physicist candidate wanted to be part of the international influx, to be connected to the world that had been cut off from them. My job felt like a privilege, to find employment situations where these job seekers could prosper. At the same time, I needed to attract and retain talented employees for my own venture. After all, my staff took in job requests on a daily basis from multinationals with tempting offers. I needed to pay wages slightly above those of my clients and, because we were in a rather dumpy building (though in a great location), I needed to create a workplace atmosphere that was attractive in spirit, mission, and innovation. Another valuable incentive I could offer my employees was cutting-edge training programs that set the standard for business etiquette and protocol in this new setting.

After Dr. Zima carefully examined the temporary services conundrum, he determined that I must hire temp workers on my company's payroll and pay them a contractually agreed-upon hourly wage only when on assignment. But whether they were active or idle, I was obliged to pay the employer's contribution of their social and health insurance. The added expense narrowed our profit margins, but on a conscientious level, I thought the worker-centered law was right.

Without exaggeration, *everyone* living and working in Prague during these transitional years was adapting to a brand-new market, a transforming legal system, and wider social and artistic boundaries. The energy emanating from those who were there sounded like an unrehearsed orchestra of virtuosos, each with his or her own score, but somehow converging into intricate harmonies never before heard. The baton that led this orchestral symphony was not in the hands of foreign enterprises. The frontline players driving the tempo were the Czech people. They were powered by a determination to bust open the doors to the outside world which, for anyone under age forty, had been closed all their lives.

I found it exciting to see the Czechs step out and into the embrace of the free and democratic world. As they reencountered their neighbors to the West, it was like rekindling a long-lost friendship after years of estrangement. President Václav Havel, although uncomfortable with the ceremony of public office, opened warm diplomatic ties with nations near and far. He led the push for the Czech Republic to join the European Union (EU)—then called the European Communities—and the North Atlantic Treaty Organization (NATO).

As early as 1991, Czechoslovakia unequivocally stated its desire to become part of the European family. I learned much about the process through seminars at the American Chamber of Commerce in Prague. The path to EU membership would require a process called *harmonization*—approximating Czech legislation to the standards of EU law and its goals for a common market.

Further, the Czech Republic, Hungary, Poland, and Slovakia had already applied to join NATO, the intergovernmental military alliance, to which they already felt an intrinsic sense of belonging. It would take years, but they were on the path.

No one illuminated the importance of global affiliations better than Václav Havel in an essay John and I would have read in the *International Herald Tribune* in October 1993. We thought Havel satisfied his evocative opening question, "Why the post-Communist countries of Europe should seek membership in NATO," with three crowning reasons:

> First, the Czech Republic lies in the very center of Europe, which has traditionally been a crossroads for different spiritual trends and geopolitical interests ... Our experience has taught us that we must take an interest in what goes on in the rest of Europe, for, like it or not, such matters always affect us more than they do many other countries. This is why we have a heightened sense of obligation to Europe. Our wish to become a NATO member, therefore, concerns more than international security guarantees; it grows out of a desire to shoulder some responsibility for the general state of affairs on our continent. We don't want to take without giving. We want an active role in the defense of European peace and democracy. Too often, we have had direct experience of where indifference to the fate of others can lead, and we are determined not to succumb to that kind of indifference ourselves.
>
> This relates to a second reason: we have always belonged to the western sphere of European civilization, and share the values upon which NATO was founded and which it exists to defend. We are not just endorsing such values from the outside; over the centuries, we have made our own contribution to their creation and cultivation. Why then should we not take part in defending them?
>
> The third reason is geopolitical. We have vivid memories of the Munich crisis in 1938 when, without consulting us, part of our country was bargained away to Hitler. Munich meant not only the failure of the Western democracies to confront the growing Nazi

evil—a failure for which the West had to pay dearly—but also the collapse of the European collective security of the time. This experience tells us how important it is for a country so exposed to be firmly involved—in its own interests and the general interest—in a working system of collective security.

Havel's essay continued, with focus on what his country could *give*, not just *get*, by joining with other democratic nations. The notion of harmonizing values as well as laws was at the heart of the accession process. The Czechs I knew—friends, clients, and candidates—wanted to align with the West and leave the past behind. The foreign businesspeople I knew considered the security of NATO membership to be a business advantage.

Come to think of it, I never heard anyone defend the old system, save for the occasional denial of personal responsibility that went something like, "It was a complicated time, and besides, does membership in a group or party affiliation make one responsible for its worst crimes?"

While many fared well in the free-market arena, others were weighted down by a past they preferred to keep hidden. Historian James Le Sueur, writer and director of the musically laced documentary film *The Art of Dissent*, proposed in an essay that, "the Velvet Revolution left behind a complex set of questions, as well as stark class differences, political scandals, and deep corruption. It never really came to terms with the legacy of the communist past; there was no reconciliation program, as in South Africa."

But I beg to differ. There was a major ruckus in 1992 when efforts to reconcile the communist past caused contentious finger-pointing at former party leaders and collaborators. Someone from inside the secret police (StB) stole sensitive files and handed them over to Petr Cibulka, a dissident-turned-crusader and journalist. In turn, Cibulka published the lists, revealing two hundred thousand names of citizens believed to have spied on their friends, neighbors, coworkers, and families.

Shortly before the release of the Cibulka dossiers, Czechoslovakia had become the first country in the post-Soviet region to adopt "lustration" laws. The enactment, passed by the Czechoslovak Federal Parliament in October 1991, set a five-year employment ban on former communist officials who sought any government or private managerial post. These protected positions were soon extended to teachers and other workers. Two things were required to apply for a protected post: a lustration certificate that cleared the person's name and a personal statement declaring the person had never been a high official of the Communist Party, a member of the People's Militias, or a student of certain high schools.

President Havel had opposed but quietly acquiesced to the lustration laws. According to Havel during an October 1991 interview, he opposed the process because it caused the democratic state to judge people "on the basis of internal documents of the StB as their decisive criteria." Yet he acquiesced because "if unscrupulous people of the totalitarian regime . . . remain in their high positions, stay set in their ways, and are as arrogant as before, it will not awaken trust in democratic institutions."

The lustration campaign was a muddled and devastating procedure. It ruined careers and lasted far longer than five years. Thirteen years into the process, the government would release its own list of seventy thousand people who, presumably, weren't simply *potential* informants, but had *knowingly* collaborated with the StB. Of these, three thousand were collaborators from abroad who had informed the secret police about Czechs in exile.

This mentality of pitting neighbor against neighbor was frighteningly strange to me. Had I been old enough to have observed my own country's political persecution during the McCarthy era, or the incarceration of Japanese Americans during WWII, I might have better understood.

The laws of reckoning in the early nineties were one of the major topics bantered around my business and social circles. The fear of being blacklisted by a capricious document took a toll on the Czech people.

It reminded them of the old days when the accused was presumed guilty until found innocent.

As I met candidates and helped them find jobs, I had no interest in knowing who'd been associated with the former StB or Communist Party or who'd spied on whom. It was common knowledge that the secret police had used coercion tactics and made false accusations. Still, I would learn more when, over the years, my once-new acquaintances turned into old friends and sad disclosures poured from their lips. I would listen with attention. How could I, an outsider, pass judgment? What would I have done living year after year, decade after decade, in an oppressive system, having the creativity wrung out of me?

I would have shriveled up.

John and I discussed the changing times. We shared observations about the Czech way of life and the country we now called home. Sometimes we made comparisons between the French culture we'd been immersed in for almost ten years and the culture, mindset, and behaviors in our new surroundings. We decided that, compared to Americans, both the French and Czechs had more reserved and formal mannerisms, which we found refreshing. But the French loved a lively discussion and good-natured argument, while the Czechs edged toward secrecy. We sensed an inner conflict in the Czech spirit and chalked it up to their inability to assess their place in history so soon after winning freedom. It would take time, we thought, to eschew suspicion and shake off the Iron Curtain mentality.

Unlike my husband, I felt a visceral bond to our new land. The kinship between me and the Bohemians, thanks to my mother's lineage, influenced my affection for them. Beneath their diffident facade, I connected with something laudably deep, a representation of survival through grace. Even now, my grasp of their lugubrious experience may seem simplistic, but I believe the people of Bohemia survived the pressure of tyranny's thumb by clinging to their land, their cottages and gardens, and their cultural heritage in the form of music, arts, and literature.

As a people—whether brave dissenters or ordinary folks who went along to get along—they preserved a long view of history for their nation and its accomplishments in architecture, artwork, literature, and music. While living through a kind of collective hell, they pressed close to their hearts everything they held dear. These national treasures comforted like the gentle caress of *Babička's* maternal hand over the wounds of shame and oppression. I, too, was embraced by some of these treasures. Anyone who's walked across the Charles Bridge surrounded by romantic legend, or laid eyes on the shapes and colors of a František Kupka canvas, or read Josef Škvorecký's novel *Dvořák in Love* (*Scherzo capriccioso*), or heard Bedřich Smetana's "Má vlast," can't help but fall in love with the Bohemian lands, for better or worse, richer or poorer.

Upon reflection, I know that the Czechs lived through an experience that was not my own. For that reason, I was content to glean vignettes— intimate accounts, some buoyant, some weighty—that glimmered through everyday moments. I cherished the trust that accompanied an unassuming remark or heartfelt revelation that others entrusted to me.

Years after working together, a highly regarded employee revealed, "Anne Marie, we were taught all our lives that Americans were the enemy, and all of a sudden I was working for the enemy . . . and to my surprise, I loved it."

Another story almost broke my heart.

"You never knew this, Anne Marie," began the tremulous voice of Jana Křivánková during a phone conversation several decades after she'd been in my employ, "because I was never allowed to talk about it. My grandfather was imprisoned by the Communists. He was working as a tram driver and liked his job, until someone reported him to the secret police for something he didn't do. My grandfather's case was lumped in with the sham trial of Milada Horáková in 1950 that was meant to demonstrate that the new regime would stop at nothing, including sentencing women to death. Grandpa, born in 1910, was a forty-year-old married man with kids when he was condemned to hard labor at the Svornost Mine in Jáchymov."

With a lump in my throat, I remained silent. My mind flashed on what I'd heard about those camps. How in the paranoid environment of Stalinist Czechoslovakia, anyone suspected of being capable of committing a crime or opposing the regime could be forced into the "Czech Gulag." Hundreds of labor camps dotting the country were run by a macabre social system, including prisoners guarding, and oftentimes mistreating, other prisoners. Within the eighteen camps around the Jáchymov, Příbram, and Horní Slavkov region alone, where Jana's grandfather was sent, the growth in the number of inmates spoke for itself. The region had two hundred prisoners in 1949, and fifteen thousand in 1953, at the peak of Stalinist repression. They worked under dangerous and extreme conditions with little protection against radioactivity as they mined uranium for the Soviet Union's nuclear weapons program. Most prisoners developed lung cancer. Many died from torture or disease.

Jana continued with a dejected tone that I'd never heard from her before: "Grandpa's wife and children, including my mother, were also banished. They weren't allowed to live, work, or go to school in the capital city. Communist Party officials took over their comfortable home in the Motol area of Prague, while my mom, her brother, and my grandma were made to reside in a remote country village while Grandpa was in prison. My uncle and mother weren't allowed an education past elementary school."

I felt a mix of anger and sorrow as Jana poured forth one revelation after another. "A neighbor secretly taught my uncle the locksmith trade. My mom wanted to be a hairdresser, but was forbidden any career pursuit. When Mom talked to me about my grandpa, I wished I could have met him to say how proud I was of him, and how sorry I was for what he went through. But he died of a massive heart attack after he left the mines and before I was born. As I was growing up, my grandma always told me, 'Never talk about any of this. Be invisible.'"

I listened to Jana's story, frozen in my chair, as she spoke swiftly in an English charmed by rolled *r*'s and a punctuated accent. She then paused, permitting a lingering breath of air to dissipate the heavy burden she'd released. Suspended moments ticked away until the silence was broken by a warmer, softer tone. Jana reduced her tempo as if to underscore something she'd always wanted me to know: "So now you understand, Anne Marie, why I have always been shy. I was told never to speak to anyone, ever, about anything personal or about my family. And dutifully, I didn't."

While building my company, how could I have known the extent to which hardships suffered during the totalitarian regime affected the personality of individuals and the collective culture of the nation? Even my ancestral kinship would have been incapable of bridging this historical and cultural gap. I could only listen and absorb. Their stealthy, painful experience was as foreign to me as my privileged idealism was to them.

My accountant, Václav Jiruš, who had his own stories, was born into Czechoslovakia's First Republic when chivalry and etiquette were *de rigueur*. Every so often, he would speak nostalgically about his childhood years when his parents thrived in a prosperous, cultured, and democratic society. He was a teenager in 1939 when Nazis took over the Czech lands. He celebrated the end of World War II by resuming his studies at the university. The start of his professional career coincided with the communist coup d'état in 1948, when his democratic country was declared a socialist republic. Jiruš said little about working and living during the communist era. He had subsumed his career ambitions into the state apparatus and maintained one steady accounting job throughout his adult life. Under constant surveillance, he stayed out of trouble by diligently following the rules, regulations, and laws autocratically promulgated by central authorities. Forced to retire at the appointed age (sixty for men, younger for women), Jiruš planned to live in lean comfort on a small pension in his rent-controlled flat in Žižkov.

But it wasn't the end of the line for him. The winds of change that stormed the country after the Velvet Revolution brought Jiruš a new lease on life. In his mid-sixties, certain that his skills were still sharp, he perused the want ads. One spurred his attention: "Bookkeeper needed for small American-owned company."

I had placed the ad in February 1993 after my attorney alerted me to the approaching tax filing deadline. AYS hadn't been in business a full year, and I hadn't yet created a record-keeping system. Frankly, I didn't know how. All bills were paid, but copies of financial records, bank statements, receipts, and invoices were haphazardly stowed in my desk's bottom drawer.

While I knew exactly what questions to ask a secretarial candidate, I was clueless about conducting an interview for a bookkeeper. Neither they nor I had experience with the financial management of a private company. The first two interviews were ill-fated, with stuffy accountants who spoke broken but adequate English. Each applicant appeared aghast at the inside of my desk drawer and nervously wrapped up the interview. I was about to call a newly established firm that outsourced accounting services, when Václav Jiruš phoned.

He arrived at the meeting exactly on time. His stocky frame shuffled a bit when he walked; his smile and twinkling eyes were kind. His excellent command of English was laced with a British, old-style formality. He said that since retirement, he'd been studying the new business and accounting codes as a pastime to stay on top of the changes. While I explained the nature of my company, its services, income, and expenses, he nodded affirmatively. Mr. Jiruš assured me that he would either know or could readily find answers to any financial and tax questions we might confront. *So far so good, but do I dare open the bottom drawer?* I reached in and placed everything on the table, like laying down a miserable poker hand. His eyes widened. His mouth started to drop before his dismay turned into a smile. "I think I'd better start tomorrow morning."

Jana and I carved out a corner niche by the window with a desk and filing cabinet for our new part-time employee. Our first year's taxes were completed on time, and every year thereafter. Mr. Jiruš was as steadfast in manner and dress as he was in punctuality and loyalty. Each day he arrived in varying shades of brown slacks and beige button-down sweater-vests over a pressed, white shirt. He didn't hesitate to admit how happy he was to be working, while his former colleagues had since retired to live off their state pensions. In the days before computers, accounting software, and spreadsheets, he was an old-school, pen-and-paper accountant with an impeccable ability to legibly write tiny numbers inside tiny squares on ledger sheets. On payday, he'd hand-print on one-inch slivers of *výplatní pásky* (payslips) which he tore meticulously with the help of the ruler from his black book, to be given to employees for their records.

In the kindest of manners, he educated me in accounting practices and taught me how to analyze a profit-and-loss statement. He took delight in explaining the art of double-entry bookkeeping, describing it as the most elegant system for efficiently avoiding the bane of any accountant's existence: mathematical error.

However, I dreaded when payday came around because of the precarious payroll system. While the Czechs adapted quickly to new business practices and the rapid liberalization of financial markets, their banking practices were slower to change. Ordinary people may have had savings accounts with Česká spořitelna, but none of my employees had a checkbook or credit card in 1992 and 1993. Yes, companies paid invoices by direct bank transfer, but it was a cash economy for payroll and most other transactions.

At the end of the month, Mr. Jiruš calculated each employee's salary down to the smallest *heller* and tallied the totals. He handed me a list of the exact number of each type of *koruna* banknote and the exact number of *koruna* and *heller* coins to withdraw. I then traipsed out the office door with the list tucked in my purse and rode public transportation to Citibank across town. The teller counted out the banknotes and coins one by one in a whispered voice and placed the cash in several envelopes. Putting the envelopes into my large purse, I walked away in a state of paranoia . . . had anyone seen me at the teller window? . . . was I followed into the lobby? . . . was someone on my trail as I exited the building? I worried about the reported pickpockets all over Prague. A purse snatcher would have hit the jackpot had I been the target of a random theft. If that happened, my planned defense was to shriek an operatic high-C. But the threats never materialized. I boarded the metro or tram clutching my purse, assumed a nonchalant pose, and made it back to the office, payroll in tow.

Once there, Mr. Jiruš and I tucked each employee's wages in a small, specially designed payroll envelope. On the top front of the pouch was the employee's name and below were twelve lines listing each month of the year with space for the salary amount, the employee's initials, and date. After taking their cash, workers initialed and returned the pouch, which became the official record of receipt for us to reuse on the next payday. I don't remember Mr. Jiruš ever being even one heller off in this exacting process.

Living in a cash economy had its moments of absurdity, yet we followed the custom, strove for fairness, and paid good wages. It's a bold but true assertion that I avoided paying bribes or under-the-table payments, practices some other businesses engaged in—out of necessity, they told me. I was privately proud of my clean record and tried not to hold anyone else responsible for theirs. Under the guidance of a scrupulous accountant and attorney, we stuck to the rules. The ever-changing laws of the land weren't unreasonable; and besides, I had chosen to live in this land. Within six months of start-up, I was earning a healthy living wage and sinking profits back into my enterprise. More staff. A computer. Another computer. Extra offices. A few new desks. A bronze-plated company sign on the building.

Worklife, homelife, and our financial situation twirled in a quick-paced waltz that swept me forward. I was experiencing success, yet I kept on drinking. I couldn't explain why. By that time, my drunken binges had no rhyme or reason. The craving for alcohol took on a life of its own, having set up camp inside my body and psyche. It was like a squatter who slithered under the floorboards whenever I tried to confront it. Better to live with it, I figured, as I hit the bars after work more times than I care to recall. I would often be the last one to leave the office, turn out the lights and lock the door, with every intention of driving straight home. If my car made it past Malostranské náměstí, I was home free. But occasionally, the steering wheel would involuntarily make a left-hand turn, park on the square, and I'd mindlessly walk the two-minute path to Jo's Bar. It was a favorite hangout among expats, especially the young, footloose, and fancy-free crowd. Not a likely place where I'd run into higher-level executives who could be my clients. I'd go in for one quick drink and, hours later, stagger out.

Swirling below my confidence and hard work were troubles I felt but couldn't name. I suspect they included an unremitting worry that my company wouldn't survive. So much was riding on its success, mainly, my ability to keep earning a good enough living to support John and me. Paradoxically, this uncertainty paralleled my excitement as the business took off. In fact, I did have the right idea in the right place at the right time, but I wasn't sure of that then.

I also couldn't face the hard truth that John's health was failing fast. He was suffering but he never complained. He didn't have to; I felt it. I remember sitting on the couch across from him as he leaned back in his black leather chair. I had to acknowledge that the debonair gentleman who'd always had a lilt in his step now had difficulty walking. My soulmate was still my partner in love and life, but so much had changed.

Moreover, I was wrestling with an intimately personal issue to which I could devote a chapter. As my fortieth birthday passed, an unexpected realization hit me that I would be childless forever. When we were first married, even though John was willing, I made the decision not to have children for two reasons—my husband's advanced age, and my blossoming career. Why had an overwhelming regret for this decision come so late? It pressed with an immense force on the other agonizing emotions stagnating in the low waters of my otherwise thoroughly productive days.

By night, whether out or at home, I would drown myself in Moravian wine. The next day I'd wake to renewed determination. *Never drink during work hours.* That was the promise I made to myself, a pitifully low bar. For the time being, it kept me clearheaded as a business owner and permitted my company to prosper in tandem with the burgeoning business environment and swelling confidence of the Czech people.

It was as if we were on the global stage together, in a dream where the players were naked and had lost their scripts, and rather than bolt offstage, they start ad-libbing. We stood in raw spontaneity with only our struggles, talents, and chutzpah. We were creating something out of chaos, something bigger than ourselves.

That's why the concept of harmonization, the overarching task of the times, presented layers of meaning for me. On the personal level, it was what had saved me up until then—the four-part harmony my sisters and I sang as children, the blanket of harmony I desperately wove to smother my addiction, and the harmony of freedom in my song which led me to Prague.

> When we only have love
> Then the freedom bell rings
> We raise up our voice
> In harmony we sing.

On the collective level, it was a time of dreaming, renewing, and starting over. While businesses and people made adjustments toward accession to EU and NATO, I felt the mood in the country change. The Czechs engaged with their Western neighbors and discovered they were not the enemy after all. Together, they hummed a new tune, sometimes in dissonant harmony, but cohesively. I was one voice in the new market symphony, alongside Czechs who were consummate musicians with or without a score. I still hear the resounding polyphonic chorus of movers, shakers, and dreamers. The spirit of the Prague Nineties still moves me.

17

RODINA MOJÍ MAMINKY

M*y mother had traits* that were quintessentially Czech, traits she possessed from girlhood, long before she married and was widowed. She was gifted in the art of baking and sewing, had a love for music and nature, and was inherently resourceful, frugal, hardworking, and modest. Mom delighted in the finer things of life, many of which cost little—hosting dinner parties with homemade cooking and a beautifully laid table, taking a millinery course to create her own hats, attending charm school so she could teach her children deportment and etiquette, and dressing fashionably in her own hand-tailored clothing.

When I first arrived in Prague and didn't know what to expect, I found myself surrounded by people with my mother's values and attributes. I warmed to the Czech ways like a baby nestled in a womb. The land and people belonged to me and I to them, or so I felt. My mother's influence on me had never shone brighter.

As my siblings and I grew up, Bohemian tradition was ingrained in us. The earthiness of our mother's cultural ways seeped through the eyelets in the lace curtains of our dad's Irish lineage. By some trick of fate, Dad died when we were very young. We touched our Celtic roots through his sisters, brothers, and mother. Our Kenny aunts, uncles, and grandmother represented a witty sophistication and progressive mindset quite unlike the provincial ways of our mother and her family. Still, our upbringing was the sole responsibility of a third-generation Czech-American woman whose grandparents crossed the Atlantic in the late 1800s. Like most immigrants in those days, they would never return to their homeland.

Bearing their sacrifice in mind, and on their behalf, I wanted to return not only to the prominent city of Prague where my ancestors may never have visited, but to the place from where they hailed.

One Sunday in early 1994, John and I packed our car with a map, snacks, and water and set out for a day trip to Moravia. We were heading to Plešice, the village where one of my great-grandfathers and his clan had lived. It would normally be a two-hour drive, but we planned for longer to enjoy the countryside along the way. After about an hour, we turned off the motorway and onto rural roads, entering deep into unadulterated nature. We found ourselves on dirt roads with no signage, and the tiny intertwining lines on our map were useless. We gave up trying to find the village.

Instead, John and I drove leisurely around the Vysočina region, and were enrapt by undulating grasslands, variegated hills and valleys, dense woods and groves, and clear streams and ponds. We stopped near a stream with a wooden footbridge and walked in the fresh air, feeling the fertile land underfoot. A sense of well-being and calm came over us. After having an early dinner at a country inn, we made it back to our Prague home before dark.

More recently, I undertook another Moravian pilgrimage. Joining me were my cousin Joey Vlock, the son of my mother's sister, and his wife Jeannie. This time, I had pored over history books and was armed with GPS. We planned to stay one or two days in Třebíč which sits between the two villages of my mother's paternal and maternal grandfathers. I booked our rooms at the Hotel Joseph 1699, named for the year it became an inn. The town of Třebíč is on the Jihlava river and boasts two UNESCO Heritage sites: the Jewish Quarter and St. Procopius Basilica.

John and me on a footbridge, contented to be lost in Moravia's lush Vysočina region (1994)

The town was founded in the twelfth century with the establishment of a large Benedictine monastery where the basilica now stands. In the fourteenth century, a vibrant Jewish community settled nearby. For five hundred years, the diverse religious communities lived contentedly as good neighbors—until the Holocaust. Today, the town's Jewish ghetto is one of the best preserved in Europe, but it is devoid of Jews. Almost all of them died in the Nazi concentration camps. The handful who survived returned to a shadow of what the thriving quarter had been, and they decided not to stay.

Joey, Jeannie, and I rented a car in Prague for our excursion eastward. As we approached the town of Třebíč, a tall monument to Saints Cyril and Methodius dominated the main square. I set the navigational system for directions to our hotel, apparently only minutes away, but it performed miserably. As we maneuvered the steep inclines, the irritating digital voice steered us up and down the narrow, tortuous streets of the Jewish Quarter, passing dark nooks and vaulted archways. After we were led the wrong way down a one-way path, we ditched the device and phoned the hotel. The front desk attendant asked us to describe our surroundings and knew immediately where we were. He dashed on foot to our car. We slowly drove behind the gallant fellow as he sprinted to our ancient abode situated on the ghetto's peak.

My former assistant, Zdeňka Ledecká, had secured an interview for me the following afternoon with Dr. Rudolf Fišer, a foremost scholar on Moravian history. I hoped he would fact-check my research and shed light on why Moravians like my great-grandparents had left everything behind for a land they'd never seen. Having arrived a good thirty minutes early to the café Fišer had suggested, I sat quietly gathering my thoughts, arranging and rearranging my questions, so as not to appear as ignorant as I was. The café was clean and bright, staffed by one young lady who took my order from behind a glass counter displaying an array of cakes, koláče, and strudels. The sweets looked scrumptious and the coffee was aromatic. I asked for a cup, yet resisted the temptation to order *makový štrúdl se šlehačkou* until my guest arrived, in the hope he'd join me.

Two young mothers with children in tow came through the door and steered their kids and strollers straight back to a small room around the corner that held a shelf filled with toys and children's books. The mothers ordered tea for themselves and chatted together while the toddlers played peacefully. At once, I acclimated to the homey atmosphere.

At the appointed hour, the café door opened slowly, like a steady hand brushing a wide swath onto a canvas. In came a gentleman I recognized from photos on his book jackets. I stood with a smile, and we greeted each other in Czech. Dr. Fišer's formal bearing, thick woolen coat, and genteel manners reminded me of Mr. Jiruš, my former bookkeeper.

Both men were products of an exceptional generation, born at the tail end of the First Republic and raised by parents who'd been enveloped for two decades in a cultivated cocoon of social graces. That was before the war bottomed out everything but the memory of the finer things in life. But many parents had taught those finer things to their children. Some passed the elegance and etiquette down to grandchildren by any means requiring little money, as there was no longer any to spare. They refused to allow the Nazis, and later the Soviets, to wipe away the cultured protocol that had enriched their society, even when being accused of bourgeois tendencies was a punishable offense.

From the biographies I'd read about Dr. Fišer, I knew he'd devoted his professional life to learning, teaching, and writing about the history of Moravia. He'd been a professor at the University of Brno and later the deputy director of the Třebíč grammar school where he continued his research and writing pursuits. After several minutes of our light exchange in Czech, his interpreter and former student, Michael Řídký, scurried into the warm café and quickly shut the door on the cold wintry wind. Michael was an educated man in his early forties from the nearby town of Vladislav. I was pleased that he invited me to use his first name, but I didn't drop formalities with Dr. Fišer, my elder.

We ordered three coffees, and I invited the gentlemen to choose from the assortment of cakes. Dr. Fišer declined, but luckily, Michael ordered a large slice of *medovník*, a honey cake. I chose the strudel, my mother's specialty, and it filled me with comfort and nostalgia.

Dr. Fišer understood why I wanted to learn about the life of my great-grandparents. My mother had little knowledge about what led her grandparents to emigrate. I had with me documents from the genealogical research done by my brother, Joe Kenny —baptismal records, birth certificates, and transatlantic steamship papers—to show Dr. Fišer what we did know.

My mother's parents, Charles Janda (1886–1950) and Marie Toman Janda (1885–1956), were born in Plattsmouth, a small Nebraska town situated at the confluence of the Missouri and Platte rivers. They were married in 1908. Their parents (my great-grandparents) were born in Moravia. Charles's dad, Cyril Janda (1858–1942), was from Plešice, and Marie's dad, Anton Toman (1859–1942), was from Horní Rožínka. Even though these two agricultural villages are only 60 kilometers apart, we had no indication the families ever met before they relocated to Nebraska in the late 1870s.

I asked Dr. Fišer to clarify the hodgepodge of information I'd read about the conditions my ancestors had experienced. Speaking at a measured pace, Fišer began to paint a textured picture of Moravian rural life in the nineteenth century. His low register and adagio tempo fell naturally in sync with Michael's oral translation and my note-taking. With every story he told, I pictured my forefathers and foremothers as part of the scenery and imagined how they'd been affected, how they'd managed.

According to Fišer, the Plešice of today—still small in population but with newer houses—is not the Plešice of yesteryear. Back then, the dwellings in villages were low, one-story structures with shingle roofs. Heat was only in the kitchen, emanating from a big tiled stove where, in the wintertime, children slept near the warm embers. Some of the bigger farms had more than one small house. Since families had few possibilities for work other than farming, their wealth depended on the size of their land and, to a lesser extent, the number of children.

He said that from the sixteenth century to the Velvet Revolution of 1989, the Czech lands of Bohemia and Moravia were controlled by foreign powers, with the exception of a few brief periods of self-rule. Yet the people were creative and industrious, as demonstrated by their music, literature, intellectual pursuits, and architecture. By the late-nineteenth century, the architectural styles in cities and towns were a magnificent blend of medieval, baroque, and art nouveau. Foreign musicians such as Mozart and Beethoven, seeking inspiration, had sojourned here and left a legacy of great compositions. With a smile, Dr. Fišer said the proverb, *Co Čech, to muzikant* (Every Czech is a musician), was true about the Czech predisposition for music.

The Plattsmouth City Band in full regalia for a July 4, 1889 performance. Standing left to right: Anton Janda, Frank Vitamvas, John Bukacek, Cyril Janda, John Bajeck. Seated left to right: Robert Martin, Vincent Ptacek, Frank Janda, Thomas Janda, Hubert Janda (son of Thomas).

I proudly interjected, "Music was in the soul of my Bohemian ancestors, too!" I pulled out a photo taken in 1889 from my notebook. "After my relatives settled in Nebraska, they started the Plattsmouth City Band, a brass ensemble commonly known as the Janda Band because five of the ten members were Jandas." I pointed out the four brothers: my great-grandfather Cyril on clarinet, Anton on tuba, Frank and Thomas on slide trombone, and Thomas's son Hubert on bass drum and cymbals. Dr. Fišer and Michael seemed politely impressed as I added that I, and all my siblings, were also musicians.

"This leads me to believe," I conjectured to the historian, "that these young men had already formed a band in Moravia and must have learned to play all these instruments in their childhoods." I couldn't hide my eagerness to find more clues about their upbringing—the education, dreams, and opportunities of their youth.

To help me see the bigger picture, Dr. Fišer described the key historic events of the times. Based on his summary, and from what I've read, there was deep discontent brewing all over Europe in the nineteenth century. In 1848, a tumultuous wave of revolution flooded most of the continent. It was called the Springtime of the Peoples or Springtime of Nations. Many European revolutionaries fled to America, some to settle permanently, others to raise funds and then rejoin the struggle back home.

In Moravia and Bohemia, urban liberals and nationalists fought the empire for civil rights, constitutions, free press, and regular elections. In Prague, students clashed with Austrian troops who responded by bombarding a section of the Bohemian capital, killing more than forty people. Agrarian communities, like those of my ancestors, fought for freedom from the empire's oppressive practices of serfdom.

With the exception of France, which achieved the final overthrow of its monarchy, and the Austrian Empire, which finally abolished serfdom within all its domains, the 1848 revolutions across Europe failed in the short term and resulted in even more repression. Yet the insurgencies hadn't been in vain. The desire for freedom smoldered and sparked future reforms.

The Czechs began to calculate a set of maneuvers to gain greater autonomy. As one of the most industrialized regions in Central Europe, they knew that the Austrian Empire depended on their high rates of productivity in sugar and coal refining, smelting works, brewing, and railroad construction. Their economic and cultural successes were bargaining chips to negotiate for increased self-rule and representation in government.

In 1867, just when the Czechs were on the verge of establishing their right to national autonomy within the monarchy, Emperor Franz Joseph delivered a humiliating blow. The Austrian Empire became the

Austro-Hungarian Empire, elevating Hungary while moving Czechs lower down on the political and social strata.

The doyen of the Czech national movement, František Palacký, stated: "We were here before Austria, and we shall also be here after Austria." But Palacký wasn't speaking for the thousands of Bohemians and Moravians who'd lost hope by then. Their exodus, which led to a great Czech migration wave to America, was a consequence of three converging circumstances: lack of ability to self-govern, dwindling resources, and opportunity abroad.

Dr. Fišer's words "dwindling resources and opportunity abroad" hit me like a jolt. The conditions that caused my kinfolk to flee the Bohemian lands were the same reasons that I, one of their offspring, returned to this land more than a century later—for the promise of a brighter future. But I said nothing about that; rather, I began to ask specific questions.

"Was there religious persecution under the monarchy?"

"If your ancestors were Catholics," he stated confidently, "they were in good favor, because the Hapsburgs aligned with the Roman Catholic Church."

"Was the Hapsburg monarchy oppressive?"

"That depended on the time period and one's station in life. Most people had become acclimated to autocratic rule," my scholarly companion admitted. Since 1526, the Bohemian lands had been part of the Austrian Empire, and by the nineteenth century, the imperial system was a fact of life for many of its subjects. They were required to speak German, the official language of the empire, while speaking Czech and the closely related Moravian language amongst themselves.

Most rural people immigrated not because of oppression or lack of self-governance but because of poverty, hunger, and uncertainty. The Industrial Revolution was replacing the agrarian and handicraft economies with machine manufacturing. A population influx into urban areas created social problems. Land became scarce as families grew larger. Traditionally, the oldest son inherited the farmsteads, leaving younger sons to make a living by some other means, whether inheriting land through marriage, moving to larger cities like Brno to find work in the textile factories and leather tanneries, or relocating abroad.

Concurrent with these worsening hardships, the U.S. railroads were advertising for workers all over Central Europe. They sent "pitchmen" to lure Czechs with the promise of employment and a lifestyle that preserved their language and customs.

This fit with my family's story. I shared with Dr. Fišer and Michael that before the Jandas and Tomans left their homeland, they already had connections in Plattsmouth, where the Burlington and Missouri River Railroad had begun operating in 1870 and was hiring hardworking men. The appeal was promising—the American Civil War had ended in 1866, the country was rebuilding, and Nebraska had become a state in 1867.

In May 1876, at age sixteen, my great-grandfather, Anton Toman, bade farewell to his home in Horní Rožínka and boarded the steamship *Suevia*. After homesteading a short time in South Dakota, he went to Plattsmouth. A year later, the rest of the Toman family followed. In Plattsmouth, Anton would eventually meet his wife, Marie Chyba (1863–1945), who came to America with the Cyril Janda family.

In July 1879, at age twenty-one, my other great-grandfather, Cyril Janda, left Plešice with his parents, siblings, and his bride of less than two months, Pauline Martínková (1858–1944). The family also brought along three orphaned teenagers from the village—Jon, Josef, and Marie Chyba. The group traveled by land to the port town of Bremen, Germany, where they boarded the steamship *Oder*, destination New York. They made their way to Plattsmouth, where the oldest brother had already arrived a year earlier and was working for the railroad. Now, the entire Janda family was in America. That is, all but one. Cyril's oldest sister, Františka Jandová Čaňková (1843–1918), stayed behind.

The families were welcomed in Plattsmouth. The town was sectioned in quadrants with the Irish on the north, Germans on the south,

"Bohemian Town" on the west, and the roundhouse, depot, and offices of the Burlington and Missouri River Railroad on the east.

My great-grandfathers worked for the railroad, Cyril as a carpenter, and Anton as a blacksmith. The men were also active in their community. They were president and vice-president of the committee to fund and build the town's Czech-speaking Holy Rosary Catholic Church. At its completion in 1890, they remained in leadership. Cyril became the organist and choir director, a volunteer post he retained for forty years.

Overall, Czech immigrants embraced the democratic American values of their new country, while a discernible "ethnic persistence" remained, which preserved their old-world customs.   At the time, Nebraska had more first- and second-generation Czechs per capita than any other U.S. state.   It is no wonder that in Plattsmouth's Bohemian Town, Czech was the lingua franca.

I told the gentlemen a story that my mother, Veronica Janda, told us children. She was the youngest of six, born in Plattsmouth to Marie Toman and Charles Janda. By the time she started kindergarten in 1925, the family had moved to Omaha. After the first week of school, the principal walked young Veronica home to upbraid her parents for speaking only Czech at home. They were told to expose their daughter to the English language or she'd fall behind academically. Unfortunately, that was the end of the fluency of the Czech language in the Janda household and for future generations.

Dr. Fišer asked about my great-grandaunt Františka, who'd chosen to stay in Plešice. He knew that I was setting out the next day to try to find one of her descendants. From my documents, Františka Jandová married Petr Čaněk in 1863 and they had ten children. Dr. Fišer and I speculated that Petr may have been a landowner with a secure situation and therefore had no reason to emigrate, or perhaps the couple couldn't bear to leave the land they loved and uproot their children. He wished me luck on my excursion.

Our conversation in the charming café flowed so effortlessly that almost two hours had passed. It was nearly five o'clock, and dusk was falling. I thanked the learned man profusely for sharing his knowledge. As I beckoned the waitress over to collect the bill, Dr. Fišer chivalrously said I was to be his guest, and I accepted.

I walked up the hill to Hotel Joseph 1699 and went straight to my room to curl up under my comforter. So much to process. For dinner, I nibbled on tangerines and freshly cracked walnuts as I devoured the novel *I Served the King of England* (*Obsluhoval jsem anglického krále*) by Bohumil Hrabal, in a delectably translated version by Paul Wilson.

The next morning, my cousins and I drove from Třebíč to Plešice, hoping to meet someone from Františka's family, if anyone still remained. Michael came along as our interpreter. It was my second go-round on these dirt roads, the first had been with John years before. But this time, Michael knew the terrain, and there was no getting lost.

We approached the picturesque hamlet of thirty-some dwellings—no shops, eateries, or public square. Not a soul in sight as snow began to fall. We parked our car in a cul-de-sac at the top of a hill and roamed around on foot. Gusts of wind whipped our scarves and chafed our cheeks, but we were protected by winter coats, hats, and solid shoes. A placard on one of the houses with the name "Čankovi" was a promising clue. We knocked on the front door and waited. Knocked again. Waited. A second-floor window creaked open, out of which a rugged face with weathered lines appeared, silhouetted between the large framed shutters.

"*Ano . . . co je?*" a man we later learned was Pan Čaněk inquired, as a woman more diminutive than him peeked around his shoulder, appearing to scrutinize our motley troupe shivering in the wind.

I smiled broadly, beginning with, "*Dobrý den, pane!*"

Pointing to Joey and me, I began my prepared spiel: *Naše matka je Jandová. Její prateta bydlela tady. Provdala se za pana Čaňka. Možná jsme bratranci!* "Our mother is a Janda. Her grandaunt lived in this town and married a Mr. Čaněk. Perhaps we are cousins!"

I suspected the couple at the window, and probably our interpreter, too, didn't know what to make of me.

The couple looked stunned, as if extraterrestrials had landed in their quiet hamlet. After an awkward interchange shouted politely from the driveway to the window, and vice versa, the hesitant couple invited us in. Their house was a large country spread made of concrete. In the airy entranceway, we removed our shoes and walked up a few stairs to a small kitchen where we sat squeezed together at a benched table. Pan and Paní Čaněk remained standing. Beyond them, a pot of soup simmered on the stove. The interchange was not easy. Michael was helpful in translation, and because he was from the region, gave us credibility. I carefully asked Pan Čaněk questions about his family lineage—but it felt like dancing a back-and-forth shuffle, afraid to step on toes, afraid to sound like an interrogator.

Pan Čaněk was unsure about the names of his ancestors, except for his parents, and was vague about his grandparents. He said that, ever since he could remember, their family had farmed a tract of land with other relatives right there in Plešice. Of late, he and his wife were easing into retirement, relieved that one of their adult children would take over the farm. *The generational thread continues,* I quietly observed, *but was the thread from my family's cloth?* After an hourlong chat over coffee and *slivovice* plum brandy for those who imbibed, Joey, Jeannie and I sincerely thanked the generous couple, and left them in peace.

On our drive back to Prague, my cousins and I considered the encounter. Life seemed awfully slow in the wintry rural village we'd visited. Our hosts seemed old-worldly, respectful, with not a smidgen of curiosity about us; but then, they'd been born into communist Czechoslovakia when curiosity was a dangerous diversion. The whole experience felt as if we'd attempted a soft landing that never quite touched down. Had we just visited one of our relatives? We were uncertain; in fact, doubtful.

That night, back in Prague at the Grand Hotel Bohemia, I sat in bed, leaned against a plethora of pillows, closed my eyes, and wept. Retracing my steps, returning to the past, reconnecting with people—some alive, some dead—had overwhelmed me. My tears fell on the suffering this country has endured, and the wisdom it has given me.

I began to think deeply about memory, personal and collective, animate and inanimate (if there is such a thing). We can return to a place, but not so easily to a time. To do that, we must walk the land and let it awaken our intuition and reveal its ancient lore. Attune ourselves to the memory imbued in the soil, as we are the progeny of its deep and vibrant roots.

My thoughts turned to the first time my husband and I visited Moravia to explore my ancestral lineage, when John and I were content to stroll the ground my forebears walked, worked, and loved. It made no difference that we were lost. I was cradled with certainty. The land touched my soul. The wind whispered a song of belonging to the homeland—*rodina mojí maminky*—the family of my mother.

I am a child of Ireland. I am a child of the Bohemian lands.

18

A NEW FREEDOM

M_y *Prague venture was two years old* in the spring of 1994, and like an unbridled toddler, it traversed every nook and cranny of the expanding marketplace. The Czech Republic was a four-year-old democratic society which had flung open its doors to the world. As more and more foreign investors entered the fresh market, we early birds who'd taken more risk were ahead of the game. My office buzzed with calls from new kids on the block—the likes of Bouygues, Searle Monsanto, and Microsoft Consulting—seeking our assistance in finding staff, conducting training, and explaining the labor code. I enjoyed showing the lay of the land, and my competent staff was eager to help others succeed. As our clients' businesses grew, so did ours.

Although the post-totalitarian years were marked by tremendous effort and uncertainty, they were extremely exciting. Optimism and exuberance were as stentorian as the trumpet fanfare of Dvořák's *Symphony No. 8 in G major*. The masterpiece was written in 1889, one hundred years before the Velvet Revolution, perhaps as a prophetic homage to its centennial events. In this symphony, Dvořák's originality and Czech spirit are exposed through spontaneity and freshness. The first movement opens to a tranquil mood tempered in minor melancholy until, out of the blue, a single birdlike flute whistles lightheartedly. With one promising call, the world transforms from bleakness to hope. In the fourth movement, the trumpets must peal in faultless unison with a collective precision that requires the musicians to let go of individual ego, open eyes and ears, and hear each other's breathing, intonation, and timbre.

After the revolution, the Czechs sharpened these same attunements to compose together a new society, a structured but flexible system that would stimulate innovation and originality. They then coursed on to something great. With a playwright as president, creativity was practically decreed. Insofar as Dvořák's *Eighth* melded moments of mournfulness and gentility, when the trumpets blew, they blared with joy. This kind of euphonic roar struck an energetic chord during Prague's early nineties for those of us, foreigners and Czechs, bounding together headlong in the business world. During a rehearsal of the *Eighth*, conductor Rafael Kubelík aptly nailed the Czech spirit when, at the opening peal of trumpets, the maestro faced his orchestra and said, "Gentlemen, in Bohemia the trumpets never call to battle—they always call to the dance!"

I can attest that as the fifth year of the new democracy began, people were moving in synchronicity, lending hands, boosting one another. The initial fear that freedom could be a temporary phenomenon was dissipating. Liberty and independence seemed assured. The Czechs in my professional life kept an upbeat pace as they worked hard. These included my employees who helped build my company and candidates seeking our help to find solid career jobs. Most were women—bright, bilingual, and skilled. But their enthusiasm reflected only part of the story.

I knew then, and realize even more now, that they'd faced hardships. Today, my longtime Czech friends tell me what they couldn't at the time, that they were trying to make sense of it all. In varying degrees, they struggled to adjust, were afraid to speak openly, felt resentful toward foreigners, bore guilt about complicity in the communist system, and had apprehensions about their country's future. The shifting political and social landscape coalesced into conflicted private thoughts they couldn't articulate, even with each other.

Martin Palouš pinpointed some of these misgivings in an essay "On Political Ideas in the Period of Transition":

> The developments which followed the collapse of Communism have simply shown that the sharp distinction "between serfdom and freedom" . . . proved also to be an ideological simplification. Interpreting the post-Communist transitions merely as the re-openings of temporarily closed societies, and seeing the principal problem of the societies of East Central Europe in transition as a "stark choice" between just two options, with no "third way," missed what was, and still is, at stake . . . It has never been just a question of how to get rid of an already very rusty and entirely unattractive version of European Communism. It was not only the matter of the homecoming of post-totalitarians, their sometimes relatively easy, sometimes toilsome march from the "Babylonian captivity" in the Soviet Empire to the European "paradise of plenty," but the beginning of a new era in the history of mankind.

Captivity. Freedom. Stark choices. Themes not foreign to my own inner world. I knew captivity from the inside, tied and blindfolded by addiction. I understood little about captivity imposed by an outside force, a tyrannical hammer that pounded entire nations into submission. I was clueless about where the Czechs' scars were hidden or the psychological toll they paid as subjects of the former regime. As Havel wrote, "One pays dearly for this low-rent home: the price is abdication of one's own reason, conscience, and responsibility, for an essential aspect of this ideology is the consignment of reason and conscience to a higher authority."

I, too, had paid the price of abdication—thrown myself into the clutches of alcoholism, which I couldn't admit or face, yet was gripped by nonetheless. I wish I had known this was a disease and not a decision. Only now can I see its cockeyed kind of purpose. The progressive illness had weakened me, roped me into secret desperation. Secret, because it crouched beneath my impressive success. When I first met the Czechoslovak people, my buried pain viscerally recognized their hidden suffering. I connected with their frailty as well as their triumph. An inner voice whispered so softly that only my soul heard: *perhaps here I can be healed.*

Engaging my strength and vulnerability, I reached out to the Czech people and was wholeheartedly embraced. With their help, I found a new start, and my company rolled expeditiously along an often bumpy terrain.

One significant jolt came without warning in March 1994 when my bank went bust, cutting my company off from its business funds.

To back up a bit, when I first established AYS in 1992, I set up an account at Citibank, one of the first foreign banks in Czechoslovakia that provided commercial services to the newly emerging private sector. I'd met the general director at an American Chamber function and he had encouraged me to become a customer. A few months after doing so, Citibank sent a letter stating its intention to drop its small and medium accounts. I arranged an appointment with the director, hoping he'd make an exception for an American-owned company that was training his frontline workers. When I arrived, he had appointed an underling to meet with me.

"No exceptions," the courteous junior associate said with resignation. "Headquarters made the decision, and it's out of our hands." I recognized a losing battle and begrudgingly left.

Then, an American business friend recommended Banka Bohemia. The recently established Czech bank was attracting customers with its unusually high interest rates on savings accounts. But high yields weren't a drawing card for me, as funds flowed out of my account as quickly as they streamed in. I chose it for its close proximity to the office and my desire to support a local, independent bank. For over a year, I was a happy customer until I woke up one morning to the news headline: "Regulators force four newly established Czech banks to close their doors."

Czech citizens who had taken their life savings from the old state bank or from under their mattress to deposit into Banka Bohemia were devastated. They'd been lured by a 14-percent interest rate, compared to the single-digit rate offered by the former bank monopoly *Česká spořitelna*. In a television interview, an elderly retiree whimpered that all the money to her name, twenty thousand crowns (nearly 700 dollars), was frozen. She feared it was gone forever. The bank told her nothing. Its doors were locked. Like the rest of us, she only knew what she read in the papers and saw on television. Media sources confirmed that *Česká národní banka*, the country's central bank and financial market supervisor, had taken over Banka Bohemia and other banks on the verge of collapse.

I feared ruination from this crisis. With no access to my hard-earned revenue which just barely exceeded costs, and with bills and salaries imminently due, I needed help. Fortuitously, all the Big Six accounting firms were my clients. Usually, they solicited my services, but this circumstance turned the tables. I phoned Price Waterhouse and Coopers & Lybrand and spoke with the country managers at length. Both experts gave me similar (and free) advice, urging me to begin a three-step process straightaway.

First, they told me to look through our accounts receivable, call all customers with outstanding invoices, and request they hold payment until further notice. And most certainly, no further deposits should be made into the defunct bank. Second, I must quickly establish a new account at a reputable international bank. Third, I should call the customers back with our new bank routing number and urge them to pay our invoices in advance of their due dates. My grounds were compelling: through no fault of our own, my company had lost access to its money. Hundreds of thousands of crowns were frozen, maybe lost for good.

There were additional steps I took on my own. One was to bring my staff together and explain the reality.

"Because we're a small, privately owned company, the advantages are great," I said stoically. "We are nimble and can mold our services quickly to the ever-changing marketplace. We are independent and don't answer to an out-of-touch headquarters somewhere across the Atlantic. On the flip side, though, we have no headquarters to bail us out."

The half-dozen or so employees, having formed a circle with their chairs around where I leaned against a desk, sat in silence. A look of expectation was on their faces as they waited for me to continue and offer a solution.

I portrayed confidence as I sought their help in getting through the immediate hurdle. "You have no obligation, but if anyone is in a position to postpone receiving your salary next week, please see me privately." I offered them my reasoning. "Fresh funds will soon be deposited into our new bank account. I can't promise an exact timeline, but you know better than I that new orders are coming in steadily. As we fill these orders, invoices will be sent to clients who've agreed to pay them upon receipt."

Then I asked Mr. Jiruš to report on the current status of our accounts receivable and state the total amount owed to us. It was a healthy sum.

That afternoon, I was touched when, one by one, individuals knocked on my door.

"I live with my mother and contribute to household expenses, but I called her, and she said to skip this month so I can help you," said one.

"I can wait to be paid, because I have some savings to draw from," said another.

"Please forgive me because I would like to help," one young mother softly expressed, "but my family depends on my timely income."

Our newest employee explained, rather dispassionately, "I'm sorry, but it's all too uncertain. I need my salary on time, and then I would like to quit."

"You mustn't concern yourself about me," Mr. Jiruš assured. "I can live sparingly off my pensioner's income for as long as you need."

Tallying the salaries and other expenses that couldn't be delayed, I withdrew money from an account John and I had in the States—a thin cushion of funds—and dug out the tin can of emergency cash buried in our backyard.

The next step was to go to Banka Bohemia and raise hell as diplomatically as possible. My efforts to call Pan Válek, my personal banker, had failed. The line was dead. Approaching the bank on foot, I spotted a flock of people haphazardly forming a winding queue, mostly old folks in worn winter coats and hand-knitted woolen caps, desperate to enter the doors and learn the fate of their savings. I'm ashamed to say that I bypassed them all. Employing my "privilege tactic" (well-heeled and lofty air), I headed straight to the security guard, and in commanding Czech, lied through my teeth: *"Jmenuji se Anne Marie Kenny a mám schůzku s Panem Válkem."* In other words, I announced myself and said that I had an appointment with Mr. Válek. Embedded in the lie was a half-truth. Early on, he'd given me an open invitation to visit anytime I needed anything.

The bewildered guard cracked open the door, and I slipped in. It was a madhouse inside the building, with bank clerks scrambling around. I saw few, if any, customers. Not pressing my luck, I spoke to no one and walked around like I knew where I was going, until I spotted Pan Valek. The young professional caught my eye. With a gulp of defeat, he escorted me into a small office.

"Please tell me what's going on," I pled in earnest. "My company's survival depends on having ready access to our funds."

Valek spoke in a chastened, straightforward manner, and seemed genuine in relating what he knew, some of which I'd already read. Regulators had shut down the bank and suspended its foreign-exchange license. Besides the bank making bad loans, the real chaos revolved around a crooked securities scheme involving "prime bank guarantees." Worthless investment instruments—nothing more than paper certificates with an amount to be paid to the bearer on a given day—had been sold under the bank's name. In their defense, bank officials claimed the scheme had been run through foreign brokers without their authorization. When regulators got wind of the bank's nefarious activities, the national bank stepped in. Then came a run on the bank by its depositors, prompting regulators to freeze all accounts.

"Paní Kenny, if you can stay solvent through this crisis," Valek conveyed with a paternal tone, "I believe our national system is solid enough to eventually restore people's money."

He said nothing about when that might happen. As I made my way out of the bank and back through the crowds which hadn't budged since I entered, I thought the worst, and not just about my own interests. Could this situation become a catastrophe like the Great Depression of the 1930s when thousands of American banks failed? When bankruptcies, suicides, and total financial ruin ensued?

In hindsight, the Czech banking train wreck was bound to happen. The sudden shift from communism to capitalism caused thousands of new enterprises to appear, prompting new banks to spring up to provide them capital. Since the end of communism in 1989, the banking sector mushroomed from four state-controlled banks to more than fifty privately held ones. First-time Czech entrepreneurs had no track record to prove credit worthiness. New banks lacked trained loan officers to analyze business plans. They tossed loans at pie-in-the-sky ideas that underperformed or didn't materialize at all.

The banking problem continued at least until the end of 1996, when we saw a headline in the *International Herald Tribune*: "How does a bank lose nearly half a billion dollars? If the bank is Kreditní Banka Plzeň, the eleventh Czech bank to fail in three years, then the answer is a cocktail of craft, guile, and greed, according to prosecutors."

By virtue of my employees' and clients' loyalty, AYS became stronger for the crisis. I didn't have to borrow money then, or ever. My clients cooperated by paying their bills early, which poured funds into our new account at ING Bank. In several weeks, we were solvent and current with salaries and bills, albeit down one staff member.

About six months later, my frozen funds were released. Most former Banka Bohemia customers also had their money returned, but the unwitting souls who had purchased phony securities weren't necessarily repaid. Some bank officials were arrested, and Interpol led a search for the scoundrels who fled the country with swindled money.   I venture to guess that after this major scam, plenty of Czechs slept peacefully again with their *koruny* tucked back under their mattresses.

That summer, John and I traveled to Alexandria, Virginia, to attend the wedding of his oldest daughter, Eugenia, to Steve Ryner. The couple had met in Uganda where Eugenia was on a Fulbright Scholarship and Steve was with the U.S. State Department. They then settled in the suburbs of Washington, DC. John glowed as father of the bride amid his daughters and grandchildren. Afterwards, we spent a week in Omaha seeing family and friends.

I was able to leave the company in the hands of competent staff. The placement system was now streamlined like a rotating conveyor belt that operated with a personal touch. With no software or computer network, our system involved three large candidate binders marked A, B, and C, containing application forms and résumés. It was rare for job seekers to arrive for their first interview with a Western-style curriculum vitae. With permission, we rewrote everyone's résumé in the standardized format our client companies had come to expect. To build goodwill, we gave candidates a copy, knowing they could use it to apply for jobs elsewhere.

Blank job order forms and pens sat on every desk, ready to be filled out when clients called needing a "temp" or "perm" worker. Our goal at this juncture was to act with lightning speed, so the client had no reason to call another agency. We'd flip through binders, pull relevant résumés, type up a cover letter, and fax the pages to the client. The client would then call us to review the options together, ask to meet some candidates, and we'd set up interviews.

Our training courses had grown in variety and frequency. We began to run public workshops on a consistent basis, offering the "AYS Diploma" to those who completed any twelve of our fifteen courses. We never searched for relevant topics; they came to us. When managers lamented the lack of specific skills in their employees, we created a course.

"My assistants are too passive; they do only what they're told and nothing more . . ." inspired our course "Taking the Initiative."

When office workers shared their concerns, we acted on it.

"It's hard to keep up with the demands in my new job; the pace is so different in an international company . . ." resulted in the popular "Working with Stress."

Our approach to bringing Czechs up to speed on the demands of foreign companies stemmed from an egalitarian "information sharing" attitude rather than a top-down indoctrination. I placed a high value on my staff's insights regarding the cultural norms and mentality of our training participants. We couldn't ramrod Western practices and attitudes down their throats, but it was our job to help Czechs adjust to the international business environment.

In this area, PhDr. Erika Gerlová's background in psychology and training was the perfect fit for our needs. Her part-time, steady work for my company helped us immeasurably in creating and delivering educational programs with respect to cultural differences.

There were times when I heard expatriates refer to their Czech workers as "backward," or say that nothing good had come from the last forty years. Because I was in a position to educate, and was irked by their negativity, I'd speak up. The Czechs had gained resilience, courage, creativity, and resourcefulness under the former system. Czechoslovakia's culture of intellectualism, literature, music, and art had actually saved the nation from the bland and homogenous mire of communism. In addition, the Czechoslovak educational system was held to a high standard, the transportation system was remarkably efficient, and in my opinion, there was more high-culture appreciation and aesthetic mindedness in one Czech person than in any ten of us foreigners combined.

Whether my praise of Czech qualities fell on attentive or deaf ears, I'll never know. No question, most Western managers expected their staff to conform to Western ways. They liked that AYS candidates were offered our free "Mini-Workshop," a two-hour crash course that explained the expectations of international companies, and taught customer service, telephone etiquette, correspondence skills, and professional dress and demeanor.

To our list of public workshops, we added "English Composition for the Czech Businessperson." My coauthors, Canadian Karen Reppin and American Brian Rosenblum, had postgraduate degrees in English.

Brian was our newest full-time employee, a soft-spoken, intelligent computer whiz from Colorado who possessed the talent, versatility, and willingness to work in all areas. Brian designed training courses, booklets, proposals, and marketing materials. One day, I asked him to pinch-hit in our placement department. He was so effective that I persuaded him to continue as an employment consultant. As fate would have it, it was then that he met his future wife Eva, one of our candidates. Today, Brian is the co-director of the Institute for Digital Research in the Humanities at the University of Kansas.

Our English Comp course was cutting-edge. We thought that Czechs would enjoy an artistic approach to English letter writing—that composition begins by identifying a *theme*, then establishing *tone*, which is the *voice* of communication. We conducted research by asking fifteen top-level, bilingual Czech secretaries and businesspeople to write us letters in English. After analyzing the letters for style, format, tone, and grammar, we identified the five most common mistakes Czechs make when writing in English—1) word order, 2) subject and verb agreement, 3) articles, 4) tenses, and 5) punctuation.

Our team created a practical and stylish textbook. The light sienna cover displayed nine small-framed illustrations from my husband's portfolio which were fluid, abstract, and evocative.

I enlisted Zdeněk Merta's help to create a video we could use and reuse. Participants were surprised and delighted as the workshop began. Lights were dimmed. On the projector screen, the heartthrob composer with tousled hair was sitting in a comfortable chair, looking natural and friendly, and warmly greeted the audience. Zdeněk invited us to view our work as an art form, and to carefully craft our letters. He described the common elements in both literary and symphonic composition with flourish—idea, preparation, tone, flow, and form.

"Both expressions are intended to communicate," the composer said. "They have the capacity to deliver a meaningful, sometimes powerful, message."

After Zdeněk's persuasive slant, either Brian or Karen taught the fine points of grammar, specifically "The 5 Common Mistakes" and how to avoid them. Whenever possible, I wanted to teach the topics of form and format. Admittedly, I gushed about the distinctive beauty of the standard Czech letter, but I was sincere. Its varied indentations, respectful capitalization of *Vám* (you), and the flowery salutations, openers, and complimentary closes were elegant touches. While a different style was expected for international correspondence, I encouraged retaining the Czech standard for letters in the Czech language addressed to Czech individuals and businesses. I didn't want its graceful form to be lost. But alas, I had to endorse the international standard, the boring block letter format. All parts left-justified. No indentations. No fluidity. No flower.

The course received high praise. Former participants told us their "English Composition" textbook stayed on their desks as a reference guide alongside their bilingual dictionary.

The exposure from our public workshops led to requests for customized, in-house training. One interesting project came from a global accounting firm wanting AYS to improve the customer relation skills of their approximately twenty-five bookkeepers. The manager had received complaints about the accountants' lack of sensitivity toward clients.

Around that time, I met a fellow named Bill at a bar. We got to chatting and he said he did a little writing and designed board games. I asked if we could brainstorm ways to teach communication skills through role-play. The next day, he came to my office and within a few hours, we produced an interesting, yet complex, role-play game in which the participants had to interact while moving through a series of experiences. Winners were those who respected the rules but listened carefully, communicated clearly, and adapted quickly. The game generated lively discussion among the bookkeepers and revealed eye-opening lessons.

I later found out that Bill was *the* William King, author of dozens of novels and the award-winning creator of *Gotrek & Felix* and the *Warhammer* series. He kindly helped me on a few other projects, yet never wanted credit or money.

In a poetic sense, because I was composing, orchestrating, and working with talented players, I rarely missed my singing career. Maybe I was too busy to think about it. Praise from grateful customers felt as rewarding as a standing ovation. Furthermore, my music profession never came close to bringing the steady and robust income that my new enterprise engendered.

Everywhere, Prague's business scene drummed like a spirited tarantella, complete with kicks and tambourines. It had us all dancing on our toes. The whirl of nine-to-five activity held me together. It was at night that I unraveled. The adage that alcoholism is a progressive disease was true in my case. I know that now. Once or twice a week, I'd stop at a bar for a quick drink. The first sweet and sour tang of red wine on my tongue started a chain reaction that took control. It set me on a track with no end. My brakes were failing, and I couldn't stop. I'd finally go home, too sloshed to cook or eat. I felt John's exasperation and worry, but I couldn't deal with that. Sometimes I crawled up the hallway stairs because when I stood, the paintings on the walls spun round and threw me off balance. Once upstairs, I'd plop into bed and wake in the morning to a new day, new clients, new candidates, new legislation, and new ideas to streamline our services.

One morning, I dreaded opening my eyes. Barely lifting a lid, I caught the morning light through the shadow of lashes. *I'm in my own bed, but how did I get here? Who took me home?* Memories from the previous night blinked by like a damaged film reel with overexposed frames flashing against blank ones. I caught a momentary glimpse of me angrily exiting Jo's Bar, but no picture appeared after that. *Did I get into my car?* No memory. *Did someone come to my rescue?* No memory. As I lay with the covers over my chin, I told myself that forgetting didn't matter, nothing mattered. But I knew better.

I recalled going to the expat hangout with my new friend JM. My gentle former lover had flown amicably away. His explanation had been, and I remember his exact words: "This relationship just isn't fun anymore." He was right. I'd become cranky and argumentative. Soon after we split, I went with a girlfriend to Radost, a music club and vegetarian restaurant that was a hit among expats and Czechs alike. It was there I met JM, an engineer from Scotland who traveled to Prague about twice a month. I never broke my rule that men I knew professionally, whether clients or employees, were strictly off-limits as lovers. JM fit neither category. He was nice enough and good-looking in a former-rugby-player sort of way, although not particularly intelligent or interesting.

Motionless in bed, trying to rewind the previous night's events, a scene came into focus. JM and I were sitting at one of the small wooden tables by the front window at Jo's Bar. The place was crowded and noisy. He was a big drinker himself, so his criticism felt ludicrous and offensive.

"Are you aware that you've just had three glasses of wine to my one?" he informed, as his bushy black hair and dark eyes suddenly looked frightfully unattractive.

"Why are you counting?" I snapped back.

"Because I'm worried about you."

I lit into him. "Worry about yourself. I'm fine. You're the lush."

Looking back, I should have given him credit for his honest concern, but I had no use for moral correctness then.

He didn't let up. "You change when you drink like this. You become difficult to be with."

That did it. It was the second time in only a few weeks that I'd been hurt by cruel finger-pointing. I shot up from the table and stormed out with the inelegant stride of a soused, scowling woman. And that was my last memory before waking up to uninvited sunlight. I forced myself out of bed and into the bathtub. I dressed for the day and went downstairs to discover my car was sitting in the garage. I had driven myself home. In a blackout. I could have killed someone.

After that, I tried to avoid the bars.

Around the same time, John had an alarming incident. I came home in the late afternoon, a while after his nurse had left, and found him on the kitchen floor unable to get up. Without thinking, I reached under his armpits with my forearms and hoisted him to his feet. He was dejected. He'd been sitting there for over an hour with a distraught Miss Two cuddled at his side. Heartbroken, I tried to console him. We called Dr. Stejskal who came to the house the next day. Nothing broken, he assured, but arteriosclerosis and other complications were taking their toll on John. As he left, the doctor quietly told me that John shouldn't be alone for long stretches. I started to leave the office earlier, until I found someone to keep John company between the nurse's shift ending and my arrival home. After trying several temporary helpers, including my nephews, my new assistant from Zambia recommended her lovely friend with fluent English. Her name was Beauty, which suited her perfectly.

John's frailty and my fears spoke to my innermost self. I wanted so badly to be a good wife, but there was no blueprint for managing our starkly different physical stages. As the days went along, our compassion for one another intensified as we tenderly responded to each other's debilitating weaknesses.

One late afternoon, I went straight home from work, except for a quick stop at Fruits of France on Jindrišská ulice to purchase some items for dinner. This new shop in Prague sold a variety of wines, mustards, honey, olives, cheeses, fresh fruits, and vegetables imported from France. The offerings were quite different from the staple vegetables found in local grocery stores. I bought some fresh basil, tomatoes, and lettuce to make spaghetti marinara and a green salad for John and me. I also picked up a fine bottle of Bordeaux. After jumping out of my work clothes and into comfortable slacks and a sweatshirt, I began to prepare a nice meal. I sipped Moravian red, saving the French bottle for dinner. John joined me in the kitchen. He sat nearby with his beer and cigarette to watch me cook and asked about my day. All felt so well and right.

After dinner, during which I drank more than I ate, John helped me with the dishes. We stood side by side at the sink. I looked into his gleaming eyes set in his handsome, lined face, and with no warning—or perhaps it was something he said, I don't know the trigger—I broke down. I cried and then sobbed. I wasn't completely inebriated, but the wine had untied my knotted emotions and set them loose. Fear of the future and how to care for John pressed so hard on my heart, it burst open. Guilt for my sexual escapades ran in streams from my eyes. Confusion about why I drank so much begged for an answer. My laden heart emptied into fragmented phrases.

"Oh, John, I have to talk to you. I . . . I . . . I love you . . . more than anyone in the world," my voice stuttered in fits and starts, "but . . . I'm dishonest and unfaithful."

John tried to quiet me, arrest the woe he saw coming, but my words spilled over his hushing sounds.

"I have other men . . . lovers . . . but it was never love. It's you who've always been so good to me . . . but you need to know who I really am, what I've done . . . what I'm doing. You can hate me now, but it won't be as much as I hate myself. I'm so sorry. I am so sorry."

I had never planned to breathe a word to John about my affairs; consequently, I hadn't imagined his reaction.

As I bawled in his arms and begged for forgiveness, he held me tighter and tighter.

"Anne Marie, stop crying. Please. Listen to me."

I looked at him, tried to listen, wiping my wet face as fresh tears flowed.

John spoke soft and low. I felt his soothing voice vibrate from his chest to mine as he held me inseparably close. Nothing could have prepared me for what he would say.

"You are my love, my wife, my life. I know you love me. I know how hard you are working, for us. In everything you do, my love goes with you."

I couldn't grasp the significance of his words. I remained silent, still catching my breath. Calming my rate of inhalation and exhalation, I slowly uttered, "But I know I've hurt you."

"Anne Marie, listen to me . . . in all you do, you have my blessing."

That time it sank in.

Into a suspended moment of silence.

A moment that lasted. That lasts even now.

John backed away ever so slightly, keeping his hands on my arms. He looked straight at me in all seriousness and said, "I only ask two things of you."

"Yes, anything. Whatever you say." My voice broken, my heart broken.

"I ask that we never talk about this again. And that no matter what happens, you'll always come home to me."

I looked again into his eyes, now welled with tears.

"Yes, my love. I promise." My voice stabilized. I understood the request and knew that my response was a solemn oath. There was nothing more I could say.

The conversation could not be, nor was it ever, rehashed.

John helped me upstairs. The man who had trouble climbing steps became my pillar to lean against. I felt tears dry on my face, their saltiness crinkling my skin. I went into the bathroom, shed my clothes, and wrapped myself in a thick chenille robe. When I walked across the narrow hall into the bedroom, I saw John had turned down the covers. I felt his steady hand on my back as I slid my limp frame onto our bed. The bed that supported the weight of our bodies through sleep, prayers, and lovemaking all our married days in Omaha, Paris, Nice, and Prague. John placed the sheet and comforter over me, quietly walked to the other side, and laid himself down beside me. He gently took my hand. I had known love before, but at this moment, we entered into a whole new realm. Pure love radiated from the human being next to me. I could do nothing but accept it, undeservingly, and feel its warmth.

On the surface, my work continued, my drinking, my trysts. I cannot say exactly how, but something intangible was changing in me. The sacred sphere into which John and I had slipped held open a door for me.

Around Thanksgiving, I went to the U.S. alone. I lined up extra home help for John. On the whole, he was managing well. My nephew Dave was still in Prague living independently, and by now was joined by his brother Mike. The boys promised to look in on their uncle. I'd found Mike an apprenticeship with a local electrician. Dave was working for our entrepreneur friend Grady Lloyd from Mobile, Alabama. Grady had come to Prague in 1991 to teach English and wound up starting the popular Laundry Kings, the first self-serve laundromat in the country.

Our friends Phyllis and James assured me that John would be welcome at the Thanksgiving dinner they had planned for about fifty guests ranging from diplomats to medical personnel to businesspeople. To accommodate everyone at a sit-down dinner in their large flat, James took the hinges off several interior doors to extend their dining table for the festive occasion. The hosts seated John at the head of the table and asked him to lead the group in prayer. Phyllis and James considered John the patriarch that day, as they had for their wedding less than a year before. At Phyllis's request, John had proudly walked her down the aisle, as a father would for a daughter.

In the meantime, I was in my hometown receiving my own dose of parental love. As always, my mother prepared a memorable Thanksgiving dinner, paying as much attention to setting a pretty table as she did to making her famous homemade rolls, pumpkin pies, and turkey with all the trimmings.

The next night, I went out to dinner with an old friend. I got so drunk that, when it was time to leave, I fell back in my chair as I tried to stand up. Aware of my incapacitation, I pressed against the tabletop and unsteadily rose, then commanded my feet to step—left, right, left, right—toward the door, concentrating on putting one foot in front of the other without stumbling. My friend drove me back to my childhood home. I slept it off and woke to a binge's all-too-familiar aftereffects.

That morning, I received an international call on my mother's landline. It was Grady. He said Dave had gone missing and everyone was worried. I called John. He was worried, too. I knew that drugs were cheap and ubiquitous in Prague and that Dave was dabbling in the hard stuff. My heart sank. I would go home to confront yet another problem in the already rickety mix. I took Dave's situation personally. How could I, a poor role model, convince him to sober up? I felt ill, mentally and physically. My body ached. My mind couldn't string thoughts together. That feeling of insanity, above all, scared me the most.

I made a snap decision to stop drinking *temporarily* and give myself time to clear my head, figure things out. It was 25 November 1994. I had no intention to quit for good, yet the very thought released a whiff of freedom.

19

MOVERS, SHAKERS,
AND DREAMERS

O*n Christmas Eve, John and I went* to the Zlatá Praha restaurant
on the ninth floor of the Hotel Intercontinental for a traditional Czech
holiday dinner. After serving us cabbage soup, the waiter brought plates
of fried carp and potato salad. For dessert, we chose from a smorgasbord
of beautifully decorated *vánoční cukroví* which were no match for the
delicious Christmas cookies my staff had brought to the office.

Despite having already experienced this culinary pinnacle of Czech
baked goods, John and I were regaled by the hotel's fine fare. We were
in no hurry as we sipped coffee inside the warm dining room and gazed
out from our window table. The clear, cold night offered a sharp view of
the Týn Cathedral's gothic spires rising among medieval structures and
steeples. I remarked to John about my new discovery—how distinctly
flavorful each course tasted when slowly savored instead of flushed down
with gulps of wine.

I was sober. One month already.

John and I reminisced, as people do at the end of a year, taking stock. We had no doubts that we'd made the right decision to move to Prague nearly three years ago. Our financial situation was now solid. John had his own nurse and caregivers whom he loved. I knew he missed the weather and seascape of Nice, but we were both wise enough to know nothing lasts forever. This winter, unlike the previous year, my consuming professional life and feeble attempt to stay the abstinence course prevented us from making it back to the South of France.

The Czech Republic was approaching its second anniversary of the Velvet Divorce with Slovakia. January 1995 would mark two years since the separation. The marriage of the two countries had been consummated at the end of World War I when the Austro-Hungarian Empire dissolved. But I supposed the relationship hardly stood a chance of permanence, because Slovakia had eloped with fascism during World War II, only to have the two neighbors return to their union and live in a tyrannical house of communism. Now, since the 1993 breakup, the Czech Republic was much better off than its *ex*. Compared to Slovakia, its economy was growing at a faster clip, its inflation levels were lower, its privatization process further ahead, and its unemployment rate was lower than most other former Eastern Bloc countries. Some even said, lightheartedly, that the Czechs should teach the West how to run a market economy.

My company prospered, but continued success was never a given. Every day we heard about new businesses starting and others failing. It was sink or swim. There was no floating in Prague's tempestuous commercial environment. But even so, I never felt more up for the challenge, more sure-footed. The once wobbly ground under my feet was steadying.

After returning to Prague from my Thanksgiving vacation, I found my missing nephew Dave. He didn't explain why he'd quit his job or what he was doing, nor did he want a lecture. When I saw his sallow face and thin body, I sensed his life was going off the track, and I wanted to help. Dave had done so much for John and me. Prague was an exciting and cultured city, but I prayed that its underbelly, replete with cheap drugs and other undesirable elements, hadn't yet swallowed him. Although I wanted to intervene, I expected he'd point the finger at me and say, "Look who's talking!" I needed to defer any heart-to-heart talk until I had earned some moral authority by being sober longer.

I'd seen announcements in the *Prague Post* classified ads for "Alcoholics Anonymous in English" and always wondered what poor saps frequented such meetings. But now, I thought this group might be an answer to Dave's situation—either I'd try to get him to join or learn how to effectively confront him.

When I mentioned my intention to attend an AA meeting to my friend Phyllis, she unhesitatingly said, "I'm going with you." Too blind to see that Phyllis wanted to support me, I assumed she needed to learn about the organization as a resource for her healthcare patients.

"Not necessary," I reasoned. "This is research, to get ideas on counseling someone with addiction issues."

Phyllis wouldn't let go. "I'd like to come with you. I'll pick you up."

The following Sunday evening at 5:25, we walked into a small meeting room in the four-hundred-year-old Kostel Nejsvětějšího Salvátora and saw eight or nine people sitting around a wide, timeworn table. No one looked as scruffy and dolorous as I'd imagined. Phyllis and I found two empty chairs opposite each other. Right on time, a British-accented man started the proceedings by welcoming everyone. During the reading of a preamble, the twelve steps and twelve traditions, I thought, *What the hell am I doing here?* Everyone was asked to introduce themselves "however you see fit." Around the circle, after individuals gave their first names, they added "and I'm an alcoholic."

I felt so sorry for them.

When our turns came, Phyllis and I said our first names, followed by "and I'm here to listen."

And listen and learn I did. I was serious about my mission to help someone else. I told myself that certainly I drank to excess sometimes, but I had every reason to believe that I wasn't an alcoholic. I limited my intake to evenings, with some exceptions. Sure, I overindulged at times, but that was due to stress. Furthermore, I hadn't had a drink since the night after Thanksgiving, and that had been more than a month already.

An hour later, the meeting closed with everyone standing in a circle, holding hands, and saying the Serenity Prayer. It felt rather odd, but the words of the prayer, which I'd not heard before, were brilliant:

> God, grant me the serenity
> to accept the things I cannot change,
> the courage to change the things I can,
> and the wisdom to know the difference.

Individuals from the motley group thanked me for coming, but no one questioned or bothered me. Later in the week, I went to another meeting to gather further information in my quest to help Dave. Seated next to me in a business suit was a woman about my age named Susan. When she spoke to the group, I related to what she said. Indeed, the pictures others painted about their relationship to alcohol—the way they drank, how much they drank, how one drink led to another, and descriptions of binges and blackouts—struck me as uncomfortably familiar. Nevertheless, I held steadfast to my mission.

After another meeting, Susan invited me for coffee. We went to a hole-in-the-wall *kavárna* and nestled around a tiny table, perfect for deep conversation. I freely shared about my nephew's problem. She let me talk. Then she asked about my drinking, which I dismissed as unimportant. Susan didn't press, but I felt exposed, as if she saw right through me.

And for the first time, so did I. A long-shuttered window had opened just a crack.

Between meetings, snippets of people's stories wouldn't leave me, almost possessed me. I tried to shrug off the unsettling feeling but it was too late. My hibernation in the throes of denial had been roused. Now that I was somewhat clearheaded, my behavioral patterns came to light.

The old lever switch that regulated my ability to jump on and off the wagon—binge one day and abstain the next—had irreparably fractured. Whether or not I was drinking, my inability to face my addiction gave rise to convoluted rationale. When my hands shook as I sipped coffee or picked up a pen, I knew that a glass of wine would calm the tremors. But rather than correlate the shakes with alcohol, I feared the onset of a motor disease, and saw booze as a temporary cure. When I woke up in the morning not knowing how I'd gotten home, I pretended it was a one-off situation which I'd never let happen again. Yet now, when I heard people in those AA rooms admit to all of this and more, I could no longer fool myself.

At the next meeting, with no forecast or fanfare, I succumbed with a sigh, "I'm Anne Marie, and I'm an alcoholic."

I doubted my ability to stay sober for any length of time. But no one thought that far ahead. It was one day at a time for them. I asked Susan if she'd be my sponsor. She agreed.

I learned that we can't change anyone but ourselves, which meant Dave was no longer mine to fix. My own mental health had to be the focus. I stopped going to bars. I dropped my paramour. From a clear-headed angle, he was no longer attractive. Downright disgusting, I'm sorry to say. My aim each day was simply to not pick up the first drink. From that rudimentary baseline, I was more attentive to my marriage and ran my business with greater alacrity.

By then, my business needed me on top of my game. Our offices on Spálená ulice had become crowded with our growing staff and the number of job seekers breezing in and out each day. The additional desks and chairs left little elbow room. For candidate interviews, we tucked a small chair alongside the consultant's desk. For our weekly Mini-Workshop, we cleared my office by shoving furniture against the walls and bringing in chairs. For our public workshops, we rented external venues, usually at the Hotel Intercontinental. It was time to expand and upgrade, and we could afford it. For quite some time, accounts receivable had well outpaced accounts payable, and our bank balance trended up, up, up. My staff and I began looking for new quarters.

I called James Woolf, a property developer whom I'd met months before at a business function. He was eager to show me his newly refurbished office building on Žitná 8. It was only a five-minute walk from my current offices and a stone's throw from Karlovo náměstí, the city's largest square. The urban green space with benches, a baroque fountain, and sculptures was also a transport hub with a metro station, tram lines, and bus routes.

Workshop coordinator Vlasta Kalousková and placement consultant Gabriela Hejmová went with me to see the office space. The facade of the five-story nineteenth-century art nouveau building drew us into its stateliness. We walked under a large stone entryway into a courtyard where I spotted James talking with the construction crew. The hotshot investor was a square-jawed, blue-eyed man in his early thirties who stood at the ready like a high-strung thoroughbred. Noticing our arrival, James swiftly wrapped up his conversation and greeted us with an extended hand. We climbed two levels up a stone staircase with ornate iron railings. James held open the office doors that led into a long, wide hallway. I mentally recast the barren space into a hospitable reception area with a desk and a small table flanked by two chairs for visitors. The same transformation occurred as we moved into four other ample rooms, and a cubbyhole that beckoned to hold our one-on-one candidate interviews. The large, freshly painted window frames and high-ceilinged walls were crowned with decorative cornices. Two more additional features were sure to win over my employees: a kitchenette with sink, stovetop, and mini-fridge, and a restroom with all new fixtures.

I tried to hide my enthusiasm, but James could see that we loved it. Still, I demurred and said it lacked an open area to hold training programs, a feature I'd counted on. James hesitated for a moment, then resolutely asked us to follow him up another floor. On the third level, he opened the doors to a spacious room with three huge windows that showered light into every corner. Vlasta, Gabriela, and I locked eyes with a "wow" look. It was the ideal atmosphere and size for our training sessions. We estimated the room could comfortably seat twenty to thirty participants around tables. James showed his poker hand by admitting that the stand-alone space didn't adjoin any other office and might be tough to rent. Then, off the cuff, he handed me a pro forma agreement and, with a no-nonsense tone, offered to throw the extra room into the deal if I'd immediately accept his offer. I thanked him and asked for forty-eight hours.

On the short walk back to our offices, we dreamed out loud. Vlasta described the logistical convenience of offering our public workshops onsite rather than renting space elsewhere. She started calculating the savings in rental fees.

Vlasta was one of my more senior staff members who'd had relevant work experience before the revolution. She'd graduated in 1985 from the Vršovice Business Academy in Prague 10 and gone straight to work for Československý film, where she organized international travel for movie stars and executives. The 1989 revolution put the state enterprise in flux, and her position was eliminated. After a brief interim job, Vlasta ventured abroad, to work in London as an *au pair*. Two years later, armed with cultural awareness and proficient English to augment her previous work experience, she came to AYS as a candidate, and I persuaded her to work for us.

That afternoon, I faxed the lease agreement over to attorney Dr. Zima for his review and pored over the financials with accountant Mr. Jiruš. That evening at home, I discussed all angles with John. Compared to our offices at the neglected Knižní velkoobchod building, the new site was triple the square footage, fivefold the rental price, and a thousand times classier. We'd be able to interview more job seekers daily, expand our candidate pool, give more options to clients, make more placements, and save money on external training venues. Workshop participants would now come to our attractive offices, meet our staff, and become familiar with our company.

The husband, accountant, and attorney were all *yes* votes. I signed the papers the next day. We moved the first weekend of April 1995.

In May, our training room was inaugurated with our first weeklong Public Workshops Series. I had purchased inexpensive but sleek folding tables and chairs at the newish IKEA store and had them delivered. From Monday through Friday that week, the bright upstairs training room was full. After the courses, participants returned to their offices with polished skills and an enthusiasm to grow professionally. Their managers took notice. Our phone started ringing with more and more requests for customized in-house training at the clients' workplaces.

In that same month, my calendar showed appointments for training needs assessments at four different companies in diverse industries—McKinsey & Company, the American global management consulting firm; Ernst & Young, the London-based accounting and professional services group; Asea Brown Boveri Ltd., the Swedish-Swiss multinational engineering and electrical giant known as ABB; and Dupont-Conoco, the American company that had recently teamed up with two other international oil companies to buy a 49 percent stake in the Czech Republic's oil refineries.

I had known little to nothing about the multinationals before they became my clients. There were no Google searches at that time. When they called, I plainly asked them about their company's history, mission, and specific operations in Central Europe. They were eager to oblige, inform, and ask for my help in accomplishing their goals. We were all neophytes in one way or another, whirling in the velocious winds of transformation.

A case in point was when the head of ABB's European operation began shifting some of the company's operations eastward soon after the fall of communism. Quoted in the newspaper, the executive declared, "It's like a shot of adrenaline to sit in Berlin and realize that one hour away by car, in a country where you no longer need a visa to travel, labor costs are only 5 to 10 percent of what they are in Germany." He went on to say, "The emergence of a low-cost, highly trained labor market in Central Europe is one reason why, despite the economic recovery, unemployment in the western part of the continent remains high: 10 percent in Germany, 12.6 percent in France, and more than 20 percent in Spain."

That shift toward cheap, skilled labor spurred my company and other employment agencies to play a dynamic intermediary role between foreign companies and local workers. It was also my duty to remind smug managers, like the aforementioned one, that wage scales were relative. Given the region's difficult past history and current cost of living, the "low wages" that gave him an adrenaline rush were hard-won and respectable by Central European standards.

Another new client was Radio Free Europe/Radio Liberty (RFE/RL). At the invitation of President Havel, the U.S. media organization had recently moved its broadcasting center from Munich to the former Parliament building in Prague. Havel offered the space practically rent-free, which President Bill Clinton was grateful to accept, given that the U.S. Congress had cut back financial support for it. Many of the station's nearly one thousand employees in Munich opposed the move. Their workforce had already shrunk by 50 percent since the Berlin Wall collapsed. Relocating to Prague diminished their ranks even further, to about four hundred employees, the majority of whom were hired locally. That's where my company came in.

When Radio Free Europe (commonly named such, even after it merged with Radio Liberty in 1976) contacted AYS, it awakened memories in my staff. My ears perked up on the rare occasions I heard the Czechs talk about the "old days." Since 1950, at the beginning of the Cold War, the people of the Eastern Bloc countries had relied on programs and news reports aired by RFE. My employees said they used to huddle with their families around receivers—the volume turned very low so neighbors couldn't hear—to obtain uncensored news; that is, when officials weren't jamming the signal.

Although some critics diminished Radio Free Liberty's importance, Václav Havel said that its significance was "great and profound and not propaganda publicity nor black or white ideological broadcasts," and that its impartiality, independence, and objectivity was vital to their closed society. Even stronger were the words of Polish labor leader and soon-to-be-president Lech Wałęsa, who told an audience in 1989 that the role played by RFE in Poland's struggle for freedom "cannot even be described. Would there be Earth without the sun?"

I found it gratifying to assist with the personnel needs of epoch-making institutions like RFE, the Peace Corps, the United States Embassy, and the European Bank for Reconstruction and Development. Their presence in this former communist country was affirmation that change was real.

Those of us living in Prague in the 1990s operated in a shared environment where the building blocks of democracy were being erected layer by layer. We heard Havel's voice encouraging citizens to take an active part in the construction of a civil society through personal accountability and responsibility. I took his message to heart and was motivated to do more.

With two like-minded Americans, Ann Baker and Norbert Auerbach, I started a Prague chapter of the Association of Americans Resident Overseas (AARO). Although we met for the first time in Prague, each of us had been AARO members in France. We believed in the work of this nonpartisan association founded in Paris in 1973. Its aim was (and still is) to research issues that affected the lives of overseas Americans and keep members informed about their rights and responsibilities as expatriates. For John and me, AARO helped us find health insurance, stay abreast of tax issues, and cast absentee ballots in U.S. elections. Since I'd already organized the 1992 Voter Registration Rally in Prague under the AARO umbrella, the leaders in Paris were glad to endorse and support our Prague chapter idea.

Ann, Norbert, and I contacted U.S. citizens in Prague through the American Embassy and Chamber of Commerce to introduce them to

AARO and its benefits, including some fun social activities we had planned.

We started an annual tradition of holding our AARO holiday party at the U.S. ambassador's residence in Prague. I became acquainted with three generous ambassadors and their spouses who opened the palatial residence to us—Adrian A. Basora, Jenonne R. Walker, and John Shattuck. For the dressy holiday affair, we hired a pianist to play the grand piano in the Wintergarden, a rotunda with a floor-to-ceiling, retractable glass wall that looked out onto manicured formal gardens. Sometimes I'd sing and lead carols with my opera diva friend, Janice Edwards.

The sumptuous one-hundred-room mansion with a curving facade was built in the early thirties by industrialist Otto Petschek. The house's enthralling story was told by Norman Eisen in his book, *The Last Palace: Europe's Turbulent Century in Five Lives and One Legendary House.* Eisen's mother Frieda was a Czechoslovak Holocaust survivor who'd been banished to Auschwitz, then returned to her country, and later fled. Years later, she would see her son move into this mansion when he became the U.S. ambassador to her homeland.

Bon vivant Norbert was on a first-name basis with all the ambassadors and livened up our parties and functions. He was diminutive in height, balding at the crown, and sported a paunch under his tweed jackets. His deep voice, colored with ringing overtones, articulated English, French, German, and Czech with fluency.

Born in Vienna in 1924, Norbert had grown up in a luxurious Prague villa on the grounds of the Barrandov Studios. His father was a Czech film producer who worked with Miloš Havel, uncle of the future president, to help finance the film studio, still one of the largest in Europe. Life was good for Norbert's bourgeois Jewish family during the First Republic. Then came war.

When Nazi Germany was about to invade, fourteen-year-old Norbert and his family escaped to Paris, then Brazil, and finally, the United States. After college, he joined the U.S. Army, serving in France during the

Second World War, and later returned to the States to finish his education and begin a film career. From errand boy to executive trainee, Norbert ultimately became president and CEO of United Artists. In 1989, when Czechoslovakia threw off the yoke of communism, the semi-retired movie mogul returned for a visit. The magnificent city of his childhood enticed him to stay.

When I first met Norbert, he was a consultant for Lucerna Film and Barrandov Studios, as well as a philanthropist supporting new Czech nonprofits. Ann was the president of AARO and I was the vice president at the time. Norbert wanted to be involved. His connections and ideas were invaluable, so we asked him to become secretary-treasurer. I admired Norbert for his altruistic desire to help others and the tangible ways he made that happen, but it was Ann and I who did the grunt work, wrote the letters, licked the stamps, and kept the records.

Ann and I were too busy to socialize, but we enjoyed working together. I held Ann, who was several years younger than me, in esteem. Her demeanor was modest, but she spoke with a warm tone that carried a voice of authority. Her style, more French than American, had a modern flair, but was never flashy. Focused and analytical, she expressed ideas and concepts clearly. Besides being a lawyer, wife, and mother of two young children, she was an artist. In her spare time, she painted on canvas and sculpted decorative puppets from papier-mâché. Ann's mother was a painter who'd been a math and physics teacher. Her father was a partner at Baker McKenzie, the global law firm founded by his father. Born in Chicago, Ann was only three when her family moved to Brussels and just five when they settled in Paris. She attended primary and secondary school in France, and Wellesley College and Tulane School of Law in the U.S.

Embarking on a law career in New York City, the polished, cosmo-politan attorney met a dashing, inspired photographer with a Manhattan studio and a charming accent. As a Czechoslovak emigré, Karel Steiner had lived in the United States since the age of sixteen. The couple's immediate attraction sparked friendship and romance. Within two years, they were married and living in France, where Ann had been transferred to her firm's Paris office. Karel's artistry thrived in Europe; he scored major commercial clients and exhibited his photography in renowned galleries. Although moving to France brought him closer to Czechoslovakia where his parents lived, it was complicated and risky for a Czech-Jewish emigré to cross Eastern borders.

I've known Karel and Ann for more than twenty-five years, but until I started to write my memoir, we hadn't spoken about Karel's growing-up years. Now I realize how little we know about our friends, until we ask. Express interest. Are willing to listen . . . with an implicit promise to hold their delicate stories of loss and love with a trusting hand and heart.

Not so long ago, Karel, Ann, and I sat around a small table at the Kavárna Obecní dům drinking tea. Our chairs were close together, but I had to lean in as Karel's naturally low and sonorous voice went deeper still, like the soft humming of a spiritual hymn.

His parents, Walter Steiner and Věra Waldeková, had grown up during the First Republic, when the Jewish population made up less than 3 percent of the country's citizenry, yet comprised 10 percent of university students and 33 percent of capital investment. Concurrent with their prosperity was the deepening of anti-Semitic attitudes and activities throughout Europe.

Věra and Walter's plans to marry were dashed by the 1939 Nazi invasion of Czechoslovakia. They were sent away to Terezín, the concentration camp that, despite horrific living conditions and the constant threat of deportation to the death camps, boasted a cultural life. But this "show camp" propaganda was a damnable insult for the tens of thousands who died there of disease, starvation, and torture, or were transported to Treblinka and Auschwitz extermination camps in occupied Poland.

Věra and Walter were married inside Terezín in a ceremony officiated by a rabbi, a fellow prisoner. Shortly afterwards, Walter was transported to Auschwitz and later taken to Bergen-Belsen, before being sent as slave labor for a munitions factory in a subcamp of Buchenwald concentration camp. Věra remained at Terezín.

Miraculously, both Věra and Walter were alive in May 1945 when Buchenwald was liberated by the United States Army, and Terezín was taken over by the Red Cross and, a week later, liberated by Soviet forces.

Věra made her way back to Prague. After a long search, she found Walter in Bulovka Hospital recovering from having a bullet removed from his skull. During the death march out of the camp, a German soldier had shot Walter when he bent over to pick potatoes growing near the road. Wounded and still starving, he kept walking.

After the most horrendous adversity, they forged a life together, and dreamed of giving their children the life they'd never had. Karel was born in 1953 and would be their only child.

Karel grew up when Prague's lively, pre-war Jewish community had disappeared. He was the only Jewish student in his class. Occasionally, his parents took him to the Jerusalem Synagogue, which the young artist loved for its confluence of art nouveau and Moorish architectural styles.

When Karel turned thirteen, Věra arranged a meeting with the rabbi to see about his bar mitzvah. She had been preparing her son at home. On the day she presented him, the rabbi questioned the young man, after which he said, "No, paní Steinerová, he is not ready."

When Karel told me this story, his voice intoned resignation and forgiveness. He noted, "There was no more discussion about it. I'm not sure whether the possibility existed so soon after the war for a Jewish child to receive formal bar mitzvah instruction."

But it seems that Karel was not the exception. A 1975 *New York Times* article, "Czech Jews, A Vanishing Group," stated:

> Judaism suffered its heaviest blow here during World War II with the extermination of at least 77,000 Jews by the Nazis. Of 360,000 Jews in the country before the war, 5,000 practicing Jews remain. Little is left of Judaism in Prague but two functioning synagogues,

a kosher restaurant catering mainly to aging pensioners, social get-togethers during the High Holy Days, and memories. The last rabbi, Dr. Richard Feder, died five years ago at the age of 95 . . . Two cantors do what they can to keep organized religious life alive.

In early 1989, one of those cantors wrote: "When we think that in recent years, there have been few ritual marriages, not a single circumcision, *not a single bar mitzvah* [emphasis mine], and we have had 50 funerals every year, we cannot but ask how long will we last."

From what I have learned from Jewish friends, the rabbi who met with Karel and his mother should have told them that a Jewish boy on his thirteenth birthday automatically becomes a bar mitzvah—a son of the commandment—with or without a formal ritual.

To be sure, Karel's coming-of-age was put to the test. He was soon forced to make a mature and personal decision, prompted by the aftermath of the 1968 Prague Spring.

When the reform movement was met with tanks and troops, Věra and Walter saw black clouds darken an already bleak situation. *This cannot be the future for our child. He must live in freedom.* They stealthily contacted relatives in the United States who agreed to take Karel under their wing. Under the pretense of a temporary visit, the teenager left for New York City.

Karel was exiled for nineteen years. For the first eight, he never saw his parents. After that, he made a few visits that rendered equal measures of joy at the greeting and heartache at the parting. Then the revolution of 1989 changed everything. He could come and go freely.

One year later, Karel and Ann moved from Paris to Prague with Věra and Walter's two grandchildren in tow. Providentially, Ann's law firm Debevoise Plimpton had asked her to open an office in Czechoslovakia. The firm had been selected to represent Česká správa letišť (Czech Airport Authority) in the privatization of the Prague airport and construction of a new terminal. Ann's role was to help her client negotiate with the various foreign companies, one of which was Bouygues, the French construction giant.

As it turned out, Ann and I were both working with the same company. That's how things were in Prague's business scene, everyone connected tangentially in some way. I'd been given a high-level introduction to Bouygues by my friend Jacques Surugue, the international human resources director at Bouygues, who had called me from Paris.

"Anne Marie, you may be getting a call. After two years of dragging negotiations, Bouygues just sealed the deal to construct a terminal at the Prague airport," Jacques said in his direct manner. "I had lunch last week with the guy in charge. He's on his way to Prague and I've recommended you. He'll need to hire a lot of people, from construction to clerical types."

"*Merci mille fois, mon ami!* I will be delighted to work with him," I replied, elated.

"No you won't," he laughed. "He's a real hard-ass. Tough negotiator. He'll try to talk you down on any proposal you make. Expect a call from Axel Faivre, and be on your toes."

When Monsieur Faivre contacted me, I went to his makeshift office on the old airport grounds. He was all business in some regards, but took pleasure in trying to throw me off guard with personal comments that bordered on condescension or flirtation, or both. I had been forewarned, and held my ground. I smiled and let the comments sail over my head or I snapped back with a one-liner. Luckily, I'd lived in France and could speak, argue, and schmooze in his language. Axel was slightly taller than most Frenchmen, with a meticulously combed, full head of dark hair. He typically wore a tailored suit accented by a silk pocket handkerchief that coordinated with a necktie clipped onto his monogrammed shirt. Even in my wilder days, and had he not been a client, I would not have wanted a romance with someone so tidy.

Just as Jacques had predicted, Axel could ruffle my feathers. He was notorious for being late in paying invoices. I made futile phone calls and gratuitous visits to his office; no doubt, his intention was to reduce me to beggar status. His arguments were clever, with a new reason each time for why he was late. Sometimes he'd speak to me like a vulnerable friend, confiding that his cash flow was *embouteillé* (backed up) for one reason or another, and he was in a tough spot. I always allowed more time. It was a lot of money, and I knew he was good for it.

In the end, Axel turned out to be a likable straight shooter. We placed hundreds of temporary and permanent office workers at Bouygues while the new world-class terminal was being erected and the dingy Ruzyně Airport was remodeled, creating what was later named the Václav Havel International Airport. Each time I fly in or out of Prague, I take quiet pleasure in knowing I was part of the project.

My days were filled with fascinating work and encounters with the movers and shakers on the scene. My employees and I helped them succeed. Each morning provided me with a renewed bargain—a daily reprieve from alcohol. My evenings were relaxed at home. After dinner, John and I would read, listen to the radio, or just talk. John was as alert and conversant as ever, but his body was weakening at a precipitous rate.

The first days of 1996 rolled out a foreboding carpet, a short swath of brocaded tapestry with a visibly finite edge.

20

SONG OF YOUR ABSENCE

A *filtered light is cast* on the living room of our home. Chronological time has lost all meaning. John lies in our bed that days earlier had been toted down to the main floor of our Prague residence because he could no longer manage the stairs to our second-story bedroom. Above the bed's wicker headboard are five of his colorful acrylic paintings. When we first moved into our concrete Bauhaus-style house in Suchdol—our quiet neighborhood on the northern edge of the city's sixth district—John chose those particular tableaux among stacks of artwork from his prolific ten-year French period and carefully arranged them on the north wall to complement the designer crimson couch placed boldly at their base. Now, the vivid canvases are the backdrop of their artist's deathbed. It is February 1996.

I reflected on how that same bed, in company with our Chickering grand piano, a Widdicomb writing desk, Eames chairs, mid-century dining set, several Chagall, Matisse, Dufy, and Picasso drawings and lithographs, and all of our other precious heirlooms and ordinary house-hold goods had a sojourner story of their own. Thirteen years earlier, they had been transplanted from Omaha to Paris, where they nestled happily inside a spacious apartment on the Île Saint-Louis overlooking the River Seine and the buttresses of the Notre Dame Cathedral, before trailing us to Nice into a smaller apartment directly across from the Mediterranean Sea, until they found their ultimate destination—not for them but for their patron—of Prague. Their patron was an artist, a refined gentleman, and the love of my life.

John exited the world in a time of great transition, much like the world he entered in the late September chill of 1917, when young American men were being drafted to fight overseas in the "war to end all wars." His father, Glen Chappell Bull, not only exceeded the draft age by one year, but was excluded from serving because he had three dependents. The postwar years of the Roaring Twenties were prosperous for the Bull family and other Americans. Glen and his wife Ruth owned a large home across from the Village Green in Winnetka, a peaceful town on the North Shore of Chicago, which was, and still is, one of the wealthiest communities in the nation. The family had a full-time cook, nanny, and gardener. Summers were spent at their property on Miller Bay in Canada, inherited from Ruth Loop Bull's side of the family.

Life was good until the crash of 1929. The family lost their fortune, forcing them out of their home and into a lifestyle of lesser standing. John worked nights through high school to supplement the family income. He would go on to fight in World War II, marry Natalie Carr from Indiana, raise four daughters, become a successful advertising executive, be widowed, marry again, and move to Europe with his new bride. And there he would die.

As I sat by his bedside, my years with John, whether in Omaha, Paris, Nice, or Prague, were vividly lit in the foreground of my mind. To the world, John and I were an incongruous pair all the way around, starting with our generational age difference. To us, it was love. We were committed to our marriage and the pursuit of each other's dreams.

We approached life with compatible imagination and artistic sensibility. Music and language and performance were the gateway to my aesthetic universe. Beauty and color and line were his. Having already lived through an extraordinary history, read voraciously, and worked as a top executive in the advertising and media industries, John possessed what I regarded as an encyclopedic store of knowledge. Although never pedantic, he could share deeply about world affairs and wide-ranging historical and cultural subjects. His outlook sprang from a place of awe and wonder, and it seldom soured. John called himself a "Rooseveltian Democrat," referring to his belief that government had a duty to level the playing field so everyone had a fair chance. I married someone with experience and wisdom far beyond my years, and I knew I could never catch up.

But I didn't have to; it was there for the taking.

And what did I bring to John? I smiled, recollecting what he always told me when in my lighthearted moods I'd playfully ask, "Honey, why do you love me?"

He'd answer, "Because you're beautiful."

How that irked me! I'd admonish him with half pleasure, "But what about my mind, my personality, my talents?"

"Sure, Darlin', that, too," he'd appease.

Sweet memories like these waltzed through my mind as John journeyed to his eternal home. While I kept vigil, the medley of our lives together played in my heart. Those few years as newlyweds in Omaha ran past like an allegretto love song. Memories of France glided in like an unrehearsed ballet flowing from one act to the next. We were now at the finale, at the death scene on a Bohemian stage, with a rich and melodious aria singing the life of a great man.

The room was palpably steeped in his spirit. My focus was not on us as a couple; it was on him, his whole person and entire life. His presence seemed to float from the here and now to the beyond. In moments of partial consciousness, he murmured a word or two that seemed to be short descriptors of his visions. A castle. His parents. His first wife Natalie.

When our priest came to the house to perform the last rites, I knelt at the bedside in prayer as Father greeted John with soothing assurance.

He absolved him of all sins through the sacrament of reconciliation, then placed his hands on John's head and anointed him with holy oil. John could not speak, but he was fully aware with eyes wide open. His face reflected glory in a way I'd never seen before, a heavenly kind.

The day before he died, he was surrounded by loved ones—our best friends, Phyllis and James, Mari and Steve; his devoted doctor, Richard Stejskal; the youngest of his four daughters, Carole; and his loyal Scottish terrier near the foot of his bed, who never left her master's side.

According to his wishes, John experienced the end of his life without sedatives or pain medicine. As his body shut down, his spiritual faculties appeared to heighten, but I couldn't know for sure. We who look on will never know what happens at death's door until it's our turn to walk across that threshold. To this day, I still hope that John's suffering was eased by the decline of his physical senses. Though there were periods of wrenching and writhing, there were longer intervals of peace and calm. It was only on that last afternoon, when we saw John's agitation heighten, that Dr. Stejskal injected a small dose of Valium. Within seconds, John was calm, his facial furrows smoothed in relief.

As evening turned to night, our friends whispered to John their final farewells and went home. Carole retired to the upstairs guest room. John and I were alone. I vowed to stay awake until the end. Lying on the couch near his bed, I listened to his breathing. It grew increasingly labored. Further and further apart was the rattling of inhales and exhales. Hours passed. I thought each breath was the last. I'd wait . . . wait . . . wait . . . and I'd hear another prolonged inhalation. Over and over again. My mind finally surrendered to exhaustion, and I fell asleep.

I awoke to total silence.

His body lay still. His soul had been released.

I sat up . . . absorbing John's spirit still permeating the room. I sat in awe for the longest time, in the presence of life after death.

Seven days later, after the cremation at Krematorium Motol and a religious service at the Church of St. Joseph attended by our good personal friends and some professional colleagues, I was en route to Washington, DC. Waiting for my flight to be called, I sat with a carry-on at my feet, a large brown leather satchel containing a pottery urn with John's ashes. A white-haired gentleman took a seat next to mine, and we recognized each other from the American expat community. He was the writer Alan Levy, editor-in chief of the *Prague Post*. Alan's attempt to engage me in casual conversation fell flat. Within minutes, I told him that I was on my way to Arlington for my husband's burial. With wry satisfaction, I added that his remains sat between us on the floor.

Alan expressed his sympathy and began asking pointed questions about John's life. He whipped out a pen and paper from his lapel pocket and asked permission to write an obituary, which I granted. The following week, a tightly worded notice appeared in the *Prague Post* with the title line: "Artist who spent the last years in Prague to be buried in Arlington as war hero."

American artist and advertising executive John Howard Bull who died of heart failure at 78 in his home in Prague on Feb. 9 will be buried with full military honors in Arlington National Cemetery near Washington, D.C., on February 23rd. Wounded in Italy during World War II, Bull received the Silver Star, Bronze Star and Purple Heart for gallantry in action. After 35 years as an advertising account executive in Chicago and Omaha, Nebraska, Bull retired in 1983 to France, where he resumed an earlier painting career, and later had shows in Paris, Nice, Monaco and London. He came to Prague in 1992 with his wife, Anne-Marie Kenny.

I boarded, buckled in, and sat quietly while my tired mind went over the sequence of plans that lay ahead. After landing at Washington Dulles, John's eldest daughter Eugenia and her husband would meet me and drive us to their home in Woodbridge, Virginia. Eugenia was the director of the FBI Academy Library, and Steve was a senior foreign service officer with the U.S. State Department. I would spend six days and nights at their house surrounded by forest near the Occoquan River. Conversation was always easy with them, and time in their company would be soothing. After this respite, I would rent a car to pick up my mother and sister Susan at the Baltimore airport and drive the three of us to the Hilton Hotel in Old Town Alexandria. The next morning, we'd arrive early at the administrative offices of Arlington National Cemetery to be briefed by the chaplain and other military personnel on the protocols of the service and burial that would take place in the late morning. A few hours later we'd greet family and friends who were instructed to gather at the Old Post Chapel, also known as Memorial Chapel.

On 23 February 1996, wearing my tailored black wool Emmanuelle Khanh skirt suit, sensible black pumps, and the pillbox black wool hat with veil that I'd purchased in Prague a few days before, I set out early for the briefing and paperwork. The administrative staff at Arlington displayed the utmost professionalism, efficiency, and care. We then moved to the chapel, where loved ones had gathered. It was the first time I saw everyone together—all four of John's daughters, their spouses and children, John's brother and sister, other family and friends—since my husband's death. It was an emotional reunion, but stoicism and humility overrode my grief. Surrounded by the souls of war heroes on those hallowed grounds, and knowing that John's wishes to rest in peace with his fellow soldiers had been granted, I was never prouder to be his wife, and to be an American.

Present among our friends living near the nation's capital was my first voice teacher, Diana Morrison, who provided music for the service. Diana's dramatic soprano voice rang out in the historic chapel, as she sang Dvořák's "Goin' Home" and the spiritual "Shall We Gather at the River." At the conclusion of the memorial service, a uniformed army soldier marched over to my side and bent his elbow into a perfect 90-degree angle. I tucked my hand under his arm as he escorted me out the main door where a horse-drawn caisson bearing the casket awaited.

Tradition, custom, and symbolism are revered in this sacred resting place. Six horses in three teams of two stood at attention, waiting to pull the caisson through the lanes of the peaceful cemetery. All six were saddled, but only those on the left had riders, to honor a tradition from the days of horse-drawn artillery, when one horse of each team was mounted while the other carried provisions. Military personnel held rifles vertically in their left hands as their right hands saluted the casket. A military band played a reverent, but spirited march as the chaplain led the way to the gravesite followed by the horses and caisson. Our vehicle, with Steve as chauffeur, carried Mom, Susan, Eugenia, and me, and rolled closely behind the caisson. The other cars trailed in procession until we arrived at the designated gravesite where a tent was erected to cover two rows of chairs and standing room. There was little waiting, yet nothing was rushed.

I had no idea what a military funeral with full honors would be like, and now I was living it. The gravesite ceremony moved along like a symphonic poem in a single, continuous movement, with every gesture and word holding symbolism, elegance, and profundity. The soldiers stretched a flag over the urn of ashes that was placed atop the graveliner. The chaplain recited lines from scripture and asked all to rise. The honors leader commanded his squad to "present arms," and forthwith the soldiers fired their weapons in unison for three volleys.

As the band played "America the Beautiful," six soldiers ceremoniously folded the flag thirteen times with gentle drape-and-crease movements. Every single fold holds a specific significance, beginning with life, then eternal life, and ending with trusting in God. The flag was presented to me, as next of kin, with words of gratitude on behalf of the U.S. president and the entire nation for John's service to his country. At one point, a stranger approached with a handwritten sympathy card. She was one of the Arlington Ladies, a society established after World War II, which sends a representative to every funeral at Arlington National Cemetery to make sure that no soldier is ever buried alone.

The component that brought, for me at least, a profound sense of closure and peace was when the bugler stepped out of the band formation and rendered "Taps."

> Day is done, gone the sun,
> From the lake, from the hills, from the sky;
> All is well, safely rest, God is nigh.

At the sound of the first singular tone, I felt John's spirit, saw him smile, and knew he was free.

Although John had rarely spoken of the atrocities he experienced on the front lines in Italy and Morocco, or about his battle wounds—and never spoke of his own heroic acts—there were times he'd tell me stories about military life, particularly when the memories were fond or touching. One memory was when the soldiers' day was done at 2100 hours and a bugle called into the night with its mellow tone and familiar melody to calm and comfort the troops. Today, his beloved "Taps" was being played, and this time, for him.

I returned to Prague as a forty-four-year-old widow with a business to run, grief to bear, and memories to cherish.

And though I've never told anyone about this before, I want to tell it now.

A couple of days before John died, during a lucid stretch, we had our last intimate talk as husband and wife, as best friends, and faithful companions.

"I love you," I whispered, snuggled close to him.

"I know, Darlin', I love you, too." His voice was soft and clear.

I wanted him to share his feelings with me. "Tell me . . . are you afraid?"

"No," he quietly assured.

After a moment, he added, "Well . . . only that you might start drinking again."

This unexpected admission threw me. If I respond, I thought, it has to be with honesty.

"Oh, my love . . . I can't promise such a thing. I can only do my best, day by day."

He looked at me with eyes more radiant than ever.

"You know how proud I am of you. I only want you to be happy."

I understood. He'd seen me at peace in the last fourteen months. He must have wondered if his death would send me reeling.

John slept. I lay there with him for quite a while, feeling his warm body and beating heart. What had just transpired slowly sank in—that John, who was at death's door, and about to step into eternity, was concerned for me, not himself. I asked God to see to his safe passage. My mind slowed way down. Stopped thinking at all.

There is nothing more to say except through the poetry of Viktor Kripner and the melodic contours of Vítězslava Kaprálová, the sublime woman composer who epitomizes the musicality of the Bohemian lands. If only somehow here I could sing her "Píseň Tvé nepřítomnosti" (Song of Your Absence), and play the undulating piano arpeggios that echo the waves of the sea and tremolo of the rain. At the very least, I can offer the words—to you, and to John.

"Song of Your Absence"

The sea for me is not the sea,
without you, my love.
You are for me, however, always you,
near or far.
You are above me like a cloud,
like an eternal seagull above the water,
while in the tremolo of the rain
shadows swirl in the fawn-color sand.
You are above me like radiance.

21

MODULATION

A*s I suffered the profound loss of John*, the president and the citizenry of the Czech Republic were also in mourning. During my husband's final days, Havel's wife of thirty-two years, Olga Havlová, passed away at home on 27 January 1996. She had been terminally ill with cancer for more than a year. Olga had devoted her life to helping others, always shunning the limelight. I so admired her as a human rights activist and for the charity she founded, Committee of Good Will, which helped foster social inclusion for disadvantaged groups. Olga was beloved by the entire nation. Like a soothing pall, the massive outpouring of public grief for her settled over my sorrow as well.

While I was away for John's burial, my company spun like a top with our office manager, Midia Katema, in charge. She faxed a one-page report every Friday on the week's activities—number of candidate interviews, job orders, placements made, workshop participants, and revenue generated. My employees had a vested interest in how well we did. On top of a solid base salary, everyone received a percentage of the week's revenues on the following payday.

Consequently, there was little slacking off since extra effort led to extra earnings. But money wasn't the primary incentive. I hired individuals who had a natural desire to help others. One example was Zuzana Jokešová, whose bright smile and innate confidence shone at our first meeting. She was fresh out of secondary school, but her willingness to learn reminded me of myself when I wanted someone to give me a chance. Zuzana became a top-producing consultant, placing job seekers into good positions and building relationships with clients.

Now the owner of her own employment agency, I recently visited Zuzana at her office, and she reminded me of something I'd forgotten. "Anne Marie, I'll always remember my first day on the job," she reminisced. "You took me to lunch. I was so surprised when on the way back to the office, we stopped at a fancy boutique, and you bought me my first business suit and a pretty blouse."

I then recalled her delight in trying on fashionable clothing at the shop. I had started purchasing outfits for new employees entering the professional world for several reasons, not the least of which was that recent high school graduates had no money. Besides that, during the communist era, clothing was utilitarian with drab colors and virtually no decorative or frilly features. Access to Paris, London, and New York fashion was restricted to the Tuzek shops (a chain with Western products unaffordable for most Czechs) or found only on the black market.   In Prague's post-revolutionary years, boutiques began selling quality clothes, but nothing compared to the couture I'd seen on the streets of Paris.

My employees and I had an added responsibility to model the standards taught in our training courses: professional conduct and dress, eloquent speech, and a focus on the customer. My mother's maxim to "look the part" was never truer than at my company.

Being home in Prague and on my own, I took refuge in keeping busy. The workplace atmosphere lifted my spirits. I also saw friends, volunteered for AARO, and hit AA meetings.

One of my first tasks was to see Dr. Richard Stejskal and thank him for the exceptional care he'd given John. I made an appointment to drop by his office. During our conversation, our eyes welled with tears. Richard had gotten to know John over the last three years and said that, for him, John was an example of America's "Greatest Generation," exuding qualities of integrity, humility, and intelligence. I listened as Richard related a few conversations he'd had with John to which I hadn't been privy. For Richard, those man-to-man talks, rooted in mutual respect, left an indelible mark.

Not wanting to keep the doctor from his patients, I stood to take my leave. As I gathered my coat and purse, I asked if he had an invoice prepared which I could pay right then.

"Nothing doing, Anne Marie. There will be no bill," was his unequivocal answer.

"But, Richard, you looked in on John at least a dozen times during his final weeks. You were there the night he died. You came when I called early the next morning to issue the death certificate, and you—"

"I wasn't only checking on my patient," Richard cut in. "I was caring for my friend. In all the time I've been John's and your doctor, I've billed you. But, please allow me to offer my last few visits as a gift."

He was resolute, and I was awestruck. We shook hands and I parted.

Richard remained my doctor. In addition to his education in general medicine, he was an endocrinologist who had studied the Chinese practice of acupuncture while his father worked in Asia. Although I had no major ailments, I made several appointments for acupuncture treatments to alleviate stress.

There are slogans in AA that make sense only to an alcoholic. One of them is: "The good news about sobriety is you get your feelings back, and the bad news is you get your feelings back." No longer drowning painful or uncomfortable emotions with booze, I had to sit with those sensations, face them, feel them. I was learning to experience both my heavy grief and lighter tensions while stone-cold sober. This was a whole new trip for which I needed to pack healthy new habits. I don't know whether the positive effects of acupuncture were the result of the thin needles penetrating strategic meridians of my body or those thirty minutes of quiet stillness while resting comfortably on the table. Either way, the treatments gave me a feeling of well-being.

Aware that Richard had traveled abroad as a youngster due to his father's position during the Soviet era, I wondered—yet never asked—how those traveling privileges were earned. Many years later, I found out.

One evening not long ago, Richard and I had dinner at Restaurace Století, a short walk from my hotel on Karolíny Světlé. I asked him if he'd be my guest and also grant me an interview for the memoir I was writing. Století had the perfect ambiance for a good talk. The cozy dining room is tucked behind an entrance bar with a large stone fireplace that warms patrons the moment they step in from a chilly night. Earth tones surround old-fashioned drapery, heavy furniture, ceiling beams, and paintings reminiscent of the Rudolphine period.

We enjoyed our gastronomic quandary in selecting from the menu of typical Czech dishes. Neither of us could resist the roasted duck leg with red cabbage and potato dumplings as our main course and the soup of the day as a starter. Richard's expressive face sparkled with news and ideas while we chatted about our lives and enjoyed the meal. I waited for the opportune moment to delve into a subject we'd never before broached. Nearing the end of our meal, as we soaked up gravy with the last morsels of our dumplings, I asked Richard if he'd tell me about growing up in Prague in the seventies and eighties. With his permission, I switched on my audio recorder while he began to speak with a warm affect about his childhood.

"My father was a bright guy who was recognized for his managerial and leadership qualities," Richard said with a satisfaction bent toward pride. "He had a choice to work in a small office as a mid-level clerk for the rest of his life, or join the Party and rise through the ranks within the transportation industry. He chose the latter option and was eventually offered the international directorship of Czechoslovak Airlines, first assigned to Cambodia, then Morocco, Singapore, and Amsterdam."

Richard affirmed unapologetically that his father's trade-off in joining the Communist Party made good sense. He did what was necessary in order to use his talents fully.

"My father didn't consider his choice as a major compromise, and he told me that I should eventually do the same," Richard stated matter-of-factly.

So taken by what I heard, I didn't notice our plates had been cleared and replaced with a dessert menu. Normally, I'm self-conscious conducting an interview, wanting to ask the right questions in the right way, but my concerns were allayed. As Richard sat near the edge of his chair diagonal to mine, he poured out unprompted words, spilling sensitivities that I could only guess had long been submerged. At one point, he slid back in his seat with a sigh—as if he were about to turn a page toward a shadowy chapter.

"I had always wanted to be a doctor and was happy to be accepted at the First Medical Faculty in Prague," he began. "In my second year of med school, two professors took me aside and rather collegially offered me membership in the Communist Party. I'd already been asked to join the Party in secondary school by a teacher we all admired. Back then, I had the distinct impression the instructor was obliged to ask us. I remember replying, 'Thank you for the offer, but I don't feel that I'm ready,' and he backed off with an air of relief."

"Yet when I was a few years older and confronted again, it was different," he continued. "One can refuse or defer such a precarious offer once, but probably not twice, and certainly not three times. For that reason, I vacillated between two responses: 'This is an honor, I would like to join,' or my former stalling tactic, 'Thank you, but I don't feel I am ready.' When I tried the latter response, they spouted back, 'Yes, you are.'"

With eyes that had mostly been downcast, Richard looked up, perhaps to see my reaction. At that point, something happened that I can best describe in musical notation terms. When a fermata, or hold, is placed over a rest, all instruments lift to create an absence of sound. The suspension gives the music just played some time to settle and germinate what is to come. Richard's story reached a fermata over a rest. We hung together in suspension. His expressive facial lines became as smooth as a cherub's on a still-life painting. I bided the moments, protectively, respectfully.

When Richard resumed in a lower-pitched *sotto voce* and a tempo modulation from vivace to adagio, I was open to whatever might come.

"I will tell you, Anne Marie, that I agreed with the gentlemen who told me I was ready, and I was ashamed from that day forward. I knew that most of my colleagues would regard my decision with contempt. As students, we'd had discussions about communist ideology, and we were against it. Prior to my crossing the line that should not be crossed, I stood on their side. But in fact, most of my fellow students would not have been in my situation. The communists only asked people they'd already vetted who weren't likely to refuse. I was a sitting duck. Declining their offer would make problems for my dad, who would be reprimanded, even demoted, for poorly raising his son."

My dinner companion continued to speak with a visage as placid as a still lagoon, but I intuited a rumbling in his soul. The lights in the Století, already dim, grew dimmer. Our little table candle cast a flickering glow on one side of my friend's face and a mottled shadow on the other.

"It's true, I joined the Party and was ashamed," Richard admitted. "Those of us who did so found ways to reconcile our decision by focusing on the positives. My red book was like a certificate that guaranteed a good position in my field. Had the communist regime gone on forever, I would have been chief doctor or some other high position. But the truth is, I wasn't overly ambitious; I just wanted the chance to do my job and do it well."

Richard said that he attended Party meetings for three years before becoming an official member in 1987, the same year he became a doctor. "I was twenty-four and saw no other possibility than the evolution of socialism, even though I didn't believe in its principles. By the 1980s, very few did. And absolutely no one expected the decade to end with such a total change."

Finally an unrestrained grin brightened his pallor. "Two years into my medical practice and new party affiliation, I found myself among the cheering crowds on Wenceslas Square celebrating the revolution. Days later, I officially turned in my red book."

At this point, there were only a few other guests in Století's dining room. We ordered a dessert. Richard's demeanor lightened, maybe because he felt his disclosure had fallen on sympathetic ears.

"Today, when I see people voting for the Communist Party and hear young people brandish around unrealistic ideas, I wish they had lived through the 1980s when we were forced to choose between professional success and low-level work. I made a choice. I've learned to live with it."

My emotions were stirred by Richard's honest admission, and I told him so. It was rare to hear firsthand someone speak about life inside the communist regime. I said that he'd obviously given considerable thought to this hugely consequential part of his life.

But I didn't do or say what I wanted to do and say. I wanted to place my hand over Richard's at the table and whisper reassuringly, "I cast no stone, my friend! I, too, have caved to pressure. I, too, know what it means to compromise values, morals—to feel shame." But I held back, fearing my own examples would appear as tactless false equivalents; and besides, it just wasn't appropriate to shift the focus to me and my regrets.

Then, and still today, I think of the adage, "There but for the grace of God go I," and I wonder how I'd have survived, trapped under the anvil of repression.

In a 1987 interview, Václav Havel offered his view on the matter: "Everybody has some basic certainty that gives them life support—it may be a job, a home, a car—and they don't want to lose it. That's why they'll remain quiet and obedient. Dissidents are actually those lunatics who decide, one fine day, that they don't care if they lose everything."

None of what Richard revealed lessened my respect for him. I knew his intrinsic goodness. Had it not been for him, another doctor would have hospitalized my husband. Instead, Richard admired our desire for John to die quietly at home, surrounded by friends. "This wasn't usual in our country," he explained. "It seems people are afraid to encounter death, although it's the natural conclusion to the cycles of birth, living, growing, and declining."

What Richard shared with me that night at the restaurant—a painful part of his past—only made him more human and lovable. I wished I could repay the gifts of assurance and solace he brought to John and me. Maybe rare benevolences like that can only be paid forward.

Back in 1996, when I went to thank Richard at his office, we wouldn't have shared such personal admissions as we did much later after years of friendship. Exiting his medical center that day, the fresh air hit me like an exhilarating reveille, an awakening call. I noticed how alert I was compared to the grogginess of yesteryear's hangovers. As I headed home, I thought about how much I'd changed since leaving France for Czechoslovakia. I'd already felt more grounded nearly six years before, when I first walked on Bohemian lands. Now, as if a tiny tectonic shift had occurred, the road of recovery and widowhood modulated my step. This new path was on elevated terrain that I'm sure John would have wanted for me, away from booze, bars, and indecorous behavior. I prayed to stay the course, not for his sake, but in his honor. The farther I was from my last drink, the better I slept, the clearer my mind, the stronger my vivacity, and the greater my hope that this could actually last.

With free weekends, I had time to volunteer at St. Thomas Church, the parish for Prague's English-speaking Catholic community. The church is part of a centuries-old Augustinian monastery complex at the end of the Charles Bridge on the Malá Strana side. It was hard to refuse Pastor William Faix when he asked me to lead the choir. He was a friar in the Order of Saint Augustine, a native New Yorker of Polish descent, and a historian. He'd first moved to Poland in 1979 to re-establish an

Augustinian presence that had dismally diminished during the Hitler and Stalin eras.

The friar mingled and prayed with Polish citizens before, during, and after the fall of communism. In 1995, he was transferred to Prague where he's ministered ever since. His work was cut out for him in his new country. Unlike Poland's large Catholic majority, Czechoslovakia's Catholic population was at 90 percent in 1910, down to 39 percent in 1991, and at 7 percent in 2021.

I enjoyed helping out at the parish, and at the risk of sounding opportunistic, it was also fertile ground for networking. One Sunday, I sang a solo from the choir loft at a small neighboring church where Mass was being held while St. Thomas underwent renovations. After the service, I ambled down the creaky narrow staircase. At the bottom of the steps stood James Horstkamp, co-owner of the only other independent, American-owned staffing firm in Prague. While my employees saw all other agencies as minacious competitors, I didn't. I often reminded them that AYS was the only personnel agency specializing in support staff, that no one had our expertise and market niche, and that the only contest was to be the best we could be.

I was surprised to see James, as I hadn't known he was a member of the parish. He was all smiles and compliments about my singing. "Anne Marie, you sang my favorite song 'Amazing Grace' beautifully. Would you please sing it and the 'Ave Maria' at my wedding here at the church in a few weeks?"

"Of course, James. I'd be happy to."

The sharp, clean-cut, and handsome fellow looked and acted older than his twenty-something years. A one-week college trip had brought James to Prague in 1990. He returned in 1991 to teach international finance at Prague University of Economics and Business. He helped establish the Central and East European Studies Program, which still exists today.

"While the teaching position sounded glamorous, and truly was exciting," James chuckled, "I was earning 8,000 crowns (less than 300 dollars) a month, and lived in a one-bedroom efficiency." But bigger money was in store when he and business partner Ellen Hayes grew their staffing agency.

When James later returned from his honeymoon, he came to my office bearing a bountiful bouquet of flowers. My staff was shocked, and I had to give them the noncompetitive-mindset speech again. James and I became trusted colleagues thereafter and contacted each other about staffing trends or new legislation affecting the industry.

Other interesting people came together through the church's social committee, which an Irish nun and I formed to create a sense of community for the diverse, international churchgoers. Most of the Sunday worshippers lived in Prague, but a good number were vacationers passing through.

Sr. Patricia O'Kane, my committee cochair, was a Belfast-born registered nurse and Sister of the Medical Missionaries of Mary (MMM). She had moved to Prague in 1996 after living for twenty-five years in rural Nigeria caring for people with leprosy. She confided in me that compared to Nigeria—a country and people she grew to love—her assignment in Prague was unfulfilling and uncomfortably plush. She had been sent here to assist Sr. M. Adalbert (Bibi) Šimáková, the only MMM Sister of Czech descent, who managed Cardinal Miroslav Vlk's private residence located in the Archbishop's Palace on Hradčanské náměstí. The building, with four wings and four courtyards, was built in sixteenth-century Renaissance style and renovated over the centuries in a rococo baroque fashion.

On a few occasions, I was invited by the sisters to dine with them and the cardinal. During dinner conversations, he seemed most interested in gleaning our ideas about the world, whether in business or society, or the role of the laity in the church. He'd speak about himself only when asked, which I did.

The young Miloslav Vlk had grown up on a farm in Southern Bohemia and had always felt akin to plain, rural folks. He was ordained a priest during the Prague Spring of 1968, after which the communist authorities gave him a parish in the remote regions of the Bohemian forests. He became so loved by his parishioners that the authorities considered him a threat. In 1978, government officials revoked his ability to perform pastoral activities. The priest became a factory worker, then moved to Prague and worked as a window washer. Prague residents who yearned for spiritual counsel knew they could find Fr. Vlk at his worksite. He often talked with people and heard their confessions while standing on scaffolding.

In an interview years later, Fr. Vlk said that he'd never felt freer than in those days:

> I was washing windows, and I thought, *so what more can they do to me?* They could have thrown me in jail, but that was politically unacceptable at the time, so it was clear they had robbed me of what they could, and I felt liberated to such an extent that I would take risks and play a cat and mouse game with the secret police, lead them on a wild goose chase and so on.

In 1991, Pope John Paul II nominated Miloslav Vlk as the archbishop of Prague. In 1994, he became Cardinal Vlk.

I was keenly aware that sharing a meal with the sisters and cardinal was extraordinary, almost sacred. We'd sit at a large, modestly laid table in a spacious living-dining area, Sr. Bibi's classic Czech cuisine on our plates. Through the dim lights, my eyes spanned the features of the gracious living quarters, replete with quality old furnishings and ancient bookcases holding volumes of literature and scripture which perfumed the room with the woody scent of old tomes.

Pat, as she wanted me to call her, was my friend and confidant. She was about fifteen years my senior, with white hair and a slender frame. Her blue eyes and toothy smile could light up a room. Pat's faith was refreshingly down-to-earth. She affirmed my nonconformist perspective that God is Mystery, a source of all being, and not some overlord with a beard. Pat sympathized with my grave concerns about the institutional church's discrimination against women and gays and its child abuse and cover-ups. But despite it all, Pat modeled a church I could belong to.

We were on social-hour duty one Sunday when a stranger entered the coffee area, a worn-out anteroom located along an arcaded pathway that surrounded the monastery's cloister garden. Since our job was to greet newcomers, we closed in.

"Welcome to St. Thomas," I said cheerfully and gave my name.

The tall, wholesome-looking gentleman was quick to smile and offer his hand. "I'm Alan Wernke from Minnesota. Just got to town a few days ago."

"And just what brings yourself to Prague?" Pat practically sang in her lilting brogue.

"I've been sent by Microsoft Consulting to establish operations in four Central and Eastern European countries. When they asked where I'd like to headquarter, my wife Dorene and I did a little research and Prague was hard to beat." He pivoted the conversation to us, "And what are you both doing in Prague?"

After Pat described her assignment with the cardinal, I piped up.

"I own and operate a personnel agency that specializes in support staff. We also offer training." Lest I appeared to be client-hunting, I switched to small talk and told him how I was also from the Midwest and that my husband and I had lived in France before moving to Prague.

But Alan had picked up on "personnel agency" and said he needed an office assistant. "Can you help?"

"Sure, we could send someone as early as tomorrow on a temporary basis," I replied as I handed him my card. "Feel free to call."

He phoned the next day. We sent a "Temp-to-Perm," a person willing to work short-term assignments but open to long-term employment. The person was a hit, and we became Microsoft's staffing partner. Alan, Dorene, Pat, and I became friends, and Dorene joined our social committee. Alan continued to add workers to his Prague headquarters as he set up networks in Poland, Hungary, Russia, and the Czech Republic.

I called on Alan in March 1997 for cultural adjustment tips as I prepared for a business trip to Russia. I'd been contacted by a consortium of international law and consulting firms in Moscow—among them were Allen & Overy, Deloitte & Touche, and KPMG—who'd heard about AYS training through their branches in Prague. They said there was nothing existing in Moscow like the professional development we offered for administrative assistants and secretaries. The consortium asked for three consecutive days of training for about thirty executive assistants. They proposed a favorable training fee, business-class air travel, and hotel accommodations.

My top trainer, Zdeňka Ledecká, helped design and present the program. Neither of us had been to Russia. I was excited, that is, until Alan rattled off his survival travel tips: (1) carry cash in case you get held up, but don't worry, they don't want you, they just need money; (2) hire a private driver for your entire stay, avoid cabs and public transportation; (3) arrange for your own translator-interpreter, never rely on the other guy's; (4) stay in the right hotel, a.k.a. an American chain; and (5) have a detailed itinerary and share it with the office and those you love. The list went on. Other people who'd done business in Russia also cautioned me.

While undeterred by the dire warnings, we still followed Alan's advice. However, I had no control over hotel choice. Our hosts booked us into a staunchly Russian four-star (at best) hotel. In the small, gloomy lobby, a group of big Russian thugs continually stood around conversing under their breaths and making what we imagined to be sordid deals. Zdeňka and I made sure to walk swiftly past them, either toward the front door or into the large restaurant. The blockish, middle-aged waitresses were gruff and glacial. No amount of charm made them crack a smile, but we got fed.

We had flown into Moscow four days early to soak in the culture of the grand capital of the former Soviet Union, now the Russian Federation.

Alan had arranged for me to hire his driver, Leonid, a polite and professional English-speaking guide with a black Mercedes. The chauffeur service was at our disposal morning until night.

On our first evening, Zdeňka and I went to a hangout for foreign businesspeople recommended by someone, I don't remember who. We dined in the restaurant adjacent to what looked like a trendy singles bar. The international menu and food were excellent. We ate slowly, observed others, talked minimally, and left, rather tired after our travels. The next morning, I couldn't find my credit card. Worried sick, I retraced my steps and remembered having used it to pay the dinner bill. Rummaging inside my purse, I found the receipt with a phone number at the top. I called from the phone in my hotel room, and as I dialed and listened to the ringing, all the warnings about corruption circled over and over in my head like rounds of a song.

A pleasant male voice answered. I gave my name and asked if someone had found a bank card.

"Yes," he assured me, "it is here, securely in our safe until you can retrieve it."

I called Zdeňka, then Leonid. We were on our way within the hour. The courteous restaurant manager said the card had been under lock and key since I'd left it at my table. I believed him, a refreshing debunker to Alan's foreboding and a fine start to a fascinating week.

From there, we asked Leonid to drive us to the Metropol Hotel. I'd heard of this historic art nouveau landmark near the Bolshoi Theater. We ate lunch in the grand dining room under four immense candelabra and a leaded-glass skylit dome. The Metropol seemed fancier than the Paris Ritz, partially because the colorful opulence starkly contrasted with the drab gray metropolis outside.

Leonid trailed us in his car as Zdeňka and I strolled on foot along Theater Square to the Bolshoi. I desperately wanted to see a Russian opera at the iconic theater. To my delight, as we approached, we saw posters advertising *Iolanta*, the last of Pyotr Tchaikovsky's eleven operas. The box office clerk waved his hand before I could get any words out and said in clear English, "Sold out, all remaining performances." Dragging ourselves out the heavy door, between the limestone columns, across the esplanade, and into our car, Leonid saw our disappointment and said, "Let me see what I can do."

Later that day, our chauffeur produced two tickets for that night's performance with seats near the center aisle in the coveted belle-étage section. Zdeňka suspected he got them on the black market, but we didn't mind a bit.

I wore a black dress with a gorgeous new, forest-green and gold shawl that I had purchased at Moscow's legendary Levsha flea market. Zdeňka had on an elegant midcalf-length gown with gold pumps. I'd heard that the Bolshoi theater was in rapid decline, having been ravaged by economic and artistic deprivation during the communist years. True, we did notice the wear, tear, and neglect, yet the grandeur of Russia's most famous and influential cultural institution was on full display—visually, aurally, and spiritually. *Iolanta*'s theme of light over darkness was uplifting. The soaring voices of the singers swirling amid the voluptuous choir and magnificent orchestra formed a sonic impression on me. This was exactly what I needed to connect with the Russian executive assistants I'd soon be meeting and teaching.

Zdeňka was indispensable on the Moscow trip. Prior to working for AYS, this Dušní Academy graduate had been a retail secretary for two years at Shell (Oil) Czech. While there, she had completed all of the AYS workshops, earning her our Professional Secretary Diploma. One day in late 1995, the impressive young woman made an appointment to see me. As we sat down in my office, she asked for career advice, explaining that she was planning to leave Shell. I offered her a job on the spot.

The first thing one noticed about Zdeňka—besides her bright eyes, coiffed pageboy hairdo, and tailor-made business suits—was her stately posture. When she accompanied me on client visits or training programs, I, too, stood taller and prouder. People also rose to attention at the sound of her clear and commanding voice, which could also ease into a soft, intimate sound or break into hearty laughter.

I discovered the secret of Zdeňka's uncanny mix of formality, friendliness, and grace when I was invited to her home. Entering the small flat where she and her parents lived in the city center, I encountered a feast for the senses. My nose captured a delectable aroma, and my eyes took in oil paintings against flowered wallpaper, handcrafted furniture from generations back, and the rich textile of window drapery. With a kind smile, her mother, paní Ledecká, poured tea into delicate porcelain cups while Zdeňka brought from the kitchen a platter of *koláče* as exquisitely decorated as they were scrumptious. In our pleasant conversation, I learned that her *babička* had been the family's bedrock. She was a grande dame, born in 1921 and raised during the First Republic. She passed down elegance and appreciation for the arts and the finer things of life to her daughter and granddaughter. Each one of the three women was an only child and educated in the social graces at home, even when communism threatened anyone scented with "bourgeois" attitudes. But Zdeňka's *babička* cared little about class distinction; her focus was on modeling a refined and respectful manner of living.

Zdeňka's reaction to Moscow was similar to mine, although our training experience was quite different. The city was such a contrast to Prague—that small, mystical, beautiful jewel. Moscow was huge in scope, a city of contradictions, with dilapidated buildings juxtaposed against remnants of a spectacular imperial past. We saw astonishing extremes of breathtaking opulence and staggering poverty. Bands of thuggery seemed ubiquitous, whereas in Prague, one had to search out seedy places to find mob hangouts and edgy lowlife. I learned that hundreds of rich Russians were killed and kidnapped in Moscow each year. Bodyguards with walkie-talkies were a necessity and a status symbol for the up-and-coming. Three-quarters of the small businesses and 60 percent of the banks in Moscow admitted to needing protection from the Russian mob, and those numbers were probably underestimated.

During our initial four days, my former client, Axel Faivre, hinted at how Moscow's underworld operated. After building the Prague airport, his company Bouygues had transferred him to Moscow to manage another construction project. I met Axel at his office in a newer business section of the city, and we walked to a nearby restaurant. Axel and I jabbered away like we'd known each other forever. He said the Czech project had been a piece of cake compared to the "bureaucracy" in Russia. I understood this euphemism for "corruption" and dared to ask Axel how the system worked.

He explained that with top international companies like his, the mafia might be less demanding. But at minimum, businesses have to pay for protection.

"How does one know who, how, and when to deal with them? Does one slip an envelope of cash under the table to sleazy handlers?" I naively questioned.

He said it was more sophisticated than that. Areas of town are controlled by certain mafia bosses who own "security" companies. They knock on your door soon after you establish a business and offer to protect your operation. They pretend it's an insurance policy, with no option to refuse.

I didn't pursue the subject with my formerly difficult client who suddenly seemed like a close friend. Over a good lunch, we chatted mostly about the cities we both knew well—Paris and Prague.

On the first day of our training, Zdeňka and I were well rested. Zdeňka's reaction to the chicly styled, sophisticated participants was different from mine. Apparently, under Gorbachev's *perestroika* in the eighties, fashionable dress was acceptable in Russia, and fashion magazines from Western Europe were allowed, and included the patterns for sewing the latest styles, which women tried to do at home in all communist countries.

For Zdeňka, a top-notch dresser, albeit traditional rather than avant-garde, the problem wasn't the Russian women's attempt at haute couture.

It was that some, but not all, wore haughty attitudes as well. When a few of the training participants fawned over me and spoke condescendingly to her, Zdeňka felt the pangs of inferiority and powerlessness that Czechs had experienced during their Soviet occupation years. I, too, noticed the historical top-down relationship on display.

At the end of our first training day, Zdeňka and I talked over dinner at our hotel's restaurant. I thought her analysis was spot-on, that the participants had felt captive, not understanding why they needed training. Most likely, some had attended at their bosses' requests. The majority were university graduates, several with doctorate degrees, who worked as secretaries in international companies because the salary and opportunities were multiple times greater than at state agencies.

Zdeňka placed her fork and knife on her dinner plate, lowered her head to look over her glasses, and peered straight into my eyes. "Anne Marie, the proud Russian soul cannot figure out what more there is to learn—certainly not from an American, or, heaven forbid, a Czech."

She nailed it. We changed strategy. The next day, I did most of the training and Zdeňka provided support. I modulated my teaching style from amiable mentor to knowledgable pedant. I rapidly delivered information followed by quick verbal quizzes, keeping everyone on their toes. The participants agreeably rose to the challenge. The atmosphere clicked like a metronome ticking at bright presto.

Slowing the beat by midafternoon, we discussed the value of cultural enrichment when working in a multinational, cross-cultural environment. As Zdeňka and I shared our sublime experience seeing *Iolanta* at the Bolshoi, a Russian participant raised her hand, and spoke glowingly of Janáček's opera *Příhody lišky Bystroušky* that she'd recently seen. The conversation blossomed. Everyone concurred that experiencing another country's art, music, and literature was the most effective and enjoyable path toward cultural competency. By then, we'd gained their trust and moved into sincere discussions about topics like business ethics, best practices, and professional networking. At the close of the program, we were wholeheartedly applauded.

Zdeňka and I flew home, tired and happy.

Back in Prague, my mind spanned the dramatic transformation I'd seen in Central and Eastern Europe. I saw myself riding its wave of change. My singing career had been swept into a new profession that provided services I was proud of, good at, and rewarded by. I was surrounded by fascinating people; many were my friends and colleagues. All was well on the outside, yet nothing felt the same with my husband gone. My home with all its accoutrements felt hollow. I knew deep down that a change in rhythm and key, a musical modulation in the purest sense, had begun its progression.

22

RESOLUTION

The *euphoric post-revolutionary balloon* popped in the late nineties. What had been seen as an economic miracle in the first half of the decade looked different in the second half. There was little else to celebrate during this downturn, other than on 18 February 1998, when seventy thousand Czechs in Old Town Square, where three giant television screens had been installed, erupted in joy to see their ice hockey team beat Russia at the XVIII Winter Olympics in Nagano.

As get-rich-quick fantasies floated away, reality sank in for the average Czech. They now faced rising inflation, high unemployment, and currency depreciation. Cynicism set in when the privatization process was exposed as little more than a transfer of wealth from the state to a small group of nouveau riche. It was a time when Czech businesses were beleaguered by mismanagement, parliamentarians bickered for power, and state-owned banks were nearing collapse. Particularly tough for the Czechs during this "velvet malaise" was that neighboring Hungary and Poland were thriving, having made harder economic sacrifices early on.

Also thriving were most foreign-owned businesses, mine among them.

My company had grown exponentially every year. The *Prague Post* published a list of the "Largest Personnel Firms in Prague," ranked by the total number of workers placed in 1998. AYS Placements and Workshops was in second place, surpassed only by Manpower. Had the rank been based on revenue, we'd have been further down the line. We were all about volume, and had to be. Compared to executive search firms that charged a hefty commission for filling a single top executive position, we had to place multiple secretaries to earn the equivalent. No other agency wanted such a narrow focus, fools that they were. I loved our niche. More people served, more people happy. We were not the jack-of-all-trades, but rather, master of one.

Yet our steady success presented problems in need of resolution. The greater the demand, the more our processes and infrastructure needed updating. My job became that of managing growth, taking me further away from our core services like interviewing candidates, matching job orders, and training in our workshops. I missed talking one-on-one with job seekers, hearing their hopes and dreams, or having international country directors call, wanting to talk *only* to me. Now, layers of infrastructure had been added to our clients' organizations and their executives had human resources departments that communicated with my consultants. My friend Steve Kelly would half-kiddingly say, "My people will call your people."

Soon after we moved offices to Žitná, I hired Steve to help me outline a strategic plan. He and partner Mari Novak were consultants in the field of performance improvement and organizational capacity building. I explained our three services—permanent placements, temporary placements, and training. We had a core staff of twelve, yet up to one hundred temporary workers were on our payroll roster in any given month, whether on active assignment or not, as required by Czech labor law.

In addition to analyzing our processes and financial data, Steve spoke with my employees and a number of clients. His final report recommended ways to improve and monitor operations as we continued

AYS Placements and Workshops
CLIENT LIST

3M
Asea Brown Boveri
ACE Media
Affordable Luxuries
AGIP
AIG
AIG/Lincoln
AKIT
Alianz
Aliatel
Allen & Overy
Alliance
Altheimer & Gray
American Chamber of
    Commerce
AMCICO
American Embassy
American Express
Apotex
Aral
Arthur Andersen
Arthur D. Little
AT Kearney
Balírny Douwe Egberts
Bank Austria
Baker & McKenzie
Bates Saatchi & Saatchi
Benckiser
Benson Oak
B. I. G.
Black & Veatch
BNP Dresdner Bank
Bohemian Flowers
Bouygues
Brasserie Mozart
British Chamber of
    Commerce
Brooks Travel
Brown-Forman Worldwide
Business Leaders Forum
Business Office Services
Cameron McKenna
Canadian Embassy
Capital Solutions Group
Carrefour
CBR
Central European Foods
Cisco Systems
Citigroup
Citygrove Europe
Chase Manhattan Bank
Clifford Chance
Coca Cola Amatil
Coca Cola Company
Colgate Palmolive
Colliers International
Commercial Union
Compaq Computers
COTY
CPC Foods
CPC McDowell
Credis
CS Mott Foundation
Czech Management Center

Český Pioneer Beton
ČEZ
Čokoládovny
Deloitte & Touche
Delvita
Dewey Ballantine
DHL
Digital
Dun & Bradstreet
Dupont Conoco
East Port
EBRD
ECK Generating
Egon Zehnder International
Eli Lilly
EPD
Ernst & Young
Equity Search Prague
Estée Lauder
Eternity
Euro RSCG
Eurotel
FE Reality
Ferrero
FTI Finance
Galena
Glatzová & Co.
Glaxo Wellcome
Gleeds
HBO/TV Max
Healey & Baker
Heidrick & Struggles
Hewlett Packard
Hines Real Estate
Hogan & Hartson
Horizon Energy Development
HSBC Investment Services
Human Accord Group
IBM
ICL
ING Barings
Irish Trade Board
Internet Securities
Investment Strategies
Jan Becher
Jenewein Management
Johnson & Johnson
JWA
King & Co.
Klein, Holec, Došková
KNO Worldwide
Kocián, Šolc, Balaštík
KPMG
Kraft Jacobs Suchard
Laboratoires Fournier
Larive Holland
Lintas
Leo Burnett
Levi Strauss
Lexxus
Lovell White Durrant
Lufthansa Airlines
Lucent Technologies
McCann Erickson

Mary Kay
Margaret Astor
Master Foods
McCain Foods
McDonalds
McDowell CPA PC
McKinsey & Co.
Merck, Sharp & Dohme
Microsoft
Motorola
NBEA
Nicholson International
Novo Nordisk
Obchodně finanční spol.
Oesterreicher a spol.
Opel Leasing
Orco Group
PA Consulting
Panasonic
Pegasus
Pepsi Cola
Prague International
    Securities
Prague Investments
Pražské Pivovary
PricewaterhouseCoopers
Procter & Gamble
Radiomobil
Raytheon
Regus
RJ Reynolds
Rothmans of Pall Mall
Searle European Monsanto
Skanska Property
Skanska Stav
SmithKline Beecham
SPT Telecom
Squire, Sanders & Dempsey
Tabák Philip Morris
Tamoil
Tarmac HBMO
Tesco
Tetra Pak
The Fleet Sheet
Toyota
TNT Express Worldwide
Unilever
Unisys
United Distillers
US Embassy
Váňa, Pergl & Partners
Volvo Auto Czech
Wegener Direct Marketing
Weil, Gotshal & Manges
White & Case
Whitehall
Wood & Co.
WPI Ringier
Wrigley

8 December 1998

AYS Client List for 1998 brochure

to grow. It pointed to our strengths, which were the envy of any business—volume, client diversity, and steady revenue stream. Cash flowed in from the continual orders we filled for a client base of nearly two hundred major Czech and foreign enterprises.

The plan called for me to delegate more responsibility to my staff. A boost in salary and duties for the office manager would lessen my load. Further, when openings occurred, I should employ higher-level professionals with international experience or education. In the first years of post-communism, this would have been nearly impossible. But much had changed in six years.

I found such leaders.

One was Martina Pátková, who worked as an AYS Temp while finishing her master's degree from the Faculty of Arts at Charles University. As soon as she graduated, I asked her to join our team. Martina led our temporary placement division with efficiency and innovation. Her sharp analytic mind was striking, along with her regal bearing and sculpted facial features framed by a dark-haired asymmetrical bob. Martina's four years at AYS helped grow our reputation and revenue as she became immersed in the staffing business. She's now HR Director for a global consulting firm.

A young woman from Zambia came through our doors at the beginning of 1995. It was very rare to see a Black person at the office, or on the street, for that matter. Midia Katema was one of the few candidates completely fluent in English. She'd grown up in Lusaka, and English was the only language spoken at her private boarding school run by German nuns. Back then, she dreamed of becoming a lawyer, but her mother pushed Midia, one of eight children, to study abroad. She won a scholarship for a student exchange program in Czechoslovakia.

In 1988, she and five other Zambian high school graduates boarded a plane heading toward a whole new adventure. Midia and one other were assigned to the University of Agriculture in Brno where they began a six-year undergraduate and master's program. The first nine months involved immersion in the Czech language. The African students found the Czech language challenging, the winters cold, and the culture very different from home, but they stuck it out. After Midia earned her engineering degree in economics from Mendel University (renamed after the revolution), she wanted to remain in Prague and continue her education.

When I saw Midia's résumé, I set up an interview to discuss a temporary position at AYS while our assistant-receptionist was on an extended leave. She arrived early to the appointment. She carried herself with sophisticated aplomb. Not a hair of her jet-black chignon was out of place, framing her rounded, sable-colored features. She was overeducated for the position I had to offer, but she was beginning her career and said she was willing to start at any level to get her foot in the door and prove herself. It sounded like something my mother told us kids to say when job hunting, and she was so right.

In short order, Midia's business and financial abilities advanced her from assistant to office manager. She was a big-picture thinker and a whiz at math. She took direction well and could respectfully communicate her opinion even when contrary to mine. Midia and I worked side by side on many projects, like crunching payroll and bonus numbers. No matter how tired we became, her robust sense of humor kept us going. I can still hear her rippling laughter.

In August 1996, I offered Midia a promotion package that I hoped she couldn't refuse: additional responsibilities and compensation, plus enrollment in an Executive MBA program fully paid by AYS. She had expressed interest in a new program at the Czech Management Center, an affiliate of the University of Pittsburgh's Katz Graduate School of Business located on the outskirts of Prague. My goal was for her to become AYS Managing Director before the two-year program ended. She was thrilled to accept.

A couple of years later, a seasoned administrator, Jaroslava Tyllerová, came onboard. I had already met Jaroslava—or Jarka, as we called her—at my office on Spálena during my company's early days when I conducted all the interviews. Her résumé of high-level experience, skills, and references presented someone who'd be an asset to any company. Equally impressive was Jarka's genuine smile, professional dress and demeanor, and refined manner. From one of the first interviews I had arranged, she received an enviable job offer as executive assistant to a director of a top consulting firm.

Instead of immediately accepting the position, Jarka asked to see me. She was torn between the higher-paying position and another offer she found on her own with more flexible hours. She then disclosed to me her family situation. Jarka's daughters were still in school and she wanted to be available to them while staying professionally active. After an open discussion, I recommended she take the job that best suited her family responsibilities, knowing I'd forfeit a sizable commission. A trusting relationship blossomed from that day between the two of us, which would forever solidify our respect for each other. She knew I had her best interests at heart, and I admired her honesty and conscientiousness.

Soon, Jarka became a client. Her new position included hiring staff, and she called on us for help. She began taking our courses. Finally, in 1997, Jarka made an appointment to meet with me. She was looking for a career change. I all but begged her to come and work for AYS, and she did. She headed our permanent placement division and versatilely pivoted to the training arena when the need arose. What was uncanny, and unpredictable, was that Jarka's eventual rise through my company's ranks would ultimately outlast me. She would become the future conduit and keeper of my mission and vision, and take the company to new heights.

With this solid leadership team, dedicated assistants, and back-office personnel, I could step back for a clearer view of my enterprise, and my life.

As for whether my staff could run the company without me, I was given a chance to find out in early 1998. My sister called to say that our mother, who still lived in the three-story house where we'd grown up,

AYS Weekend Retreat 1998. Left to right: Jaroslava Tyllerová, me, Václav Jiruš, Věra Loudová, Michaela Topinková, Pavlína Špičková, Martina Pátková, Midia Katema, Zuzana Jokešová

Vlasta Kalousková, Erika Gerlová, and Brian Rosenblum in the early days, at our offices on Spálená

Erika Gerlová, Zdeňka Ledecká, and me with my new haircut, at an American Chamber conference in 1996

had fallen, broken an arm, and sprained an ankle. My siblings had done their fair share over the years to assist Mom, who was otherwise in good health, but nearing eighty. This accident prompted me to take my turn at helping out. I left the company in Midia's hands for over a month, promising to return early if she needed me.

Those five weeks in Omaha rolled out so slowly and quietly, compared to the treadmill I'd been on, that my recollections are only opaque snippets.

Mom humming ballads. Me playing her spinet. The breeze on her front porch.

I remember wondering on the flight to Omaha whether Mom really needed me or if I needed her more. Since John was gone, I was lonely, especially in the evenings. Once I arrived at her place, the answer was obvious. Mom's predicament was bad. She used her unbroken arm to hold a cane that took pressure off her sprained ankle. As for the broken arm, the plaster cast had rubbed the skin and created a sore that caused a wound infection, a diabetic's nightmare. She needed help getting around, cleaning and cooking, bathing, and running errands.

But Mom was tough. Our favorite spot was her screened-in front porch. With her on the rocker and me on the glider, we talked, laughed, and gossiped while watching neighbors walk by and kids ride past on bikes. My sisters and brother would stop over, as did several of Mom's many friends. One morning, we peeled at least five pounds of apples on the porch, then ambled to the kitchen where Mom taught me how to make apple strudel. It was a full-day's project. She sat and gave directions while I followed commands. The trickiest part was rolling and stretching the homemade dough thinner and thinner. As I smoothly stretched the third one, Mom smiled with pride, and I knew I'd mastered the art of Bohemian strudel making.

During this time away, I thought about my bustling office and the beauty of Prague, compared to the familiarity of my hometown and the mother-daughter bond, rejuvenated after my years abroad. At night alone in my old room, feelings from childhood returned, a time warp back to the days of my dolls, night terrors, playing my guitar, doing homework, and dreaming of Paris. And now I was a sober, widowed, and successful international business owner, sleeping in that same room.

There were no surprises when I returned to the office. Productivity and spirits were high. The demands of caring for my mother were a tiny fraction of the demands in my business world. But each one, family and work, provided what the other couldn't offer, and I was certain that my well-being depended on both.

After this respite in Omaha, I felt a new equilibrium back in the Czech lands and could take the current political and economic situation more in stride. President Havel had been reelected for a second five-year term starting in January 1998. He was weakened, yet provided a sense of continuity. His health had been sapped by two major surgeries that had removed part of his lung and part of his intestine. It bothered me that he faced scolding from his fellow citizens who frowned upon his marrying actress Dagmar Veškrnová not quite a year after Olga died. On this issue, there was no criticism coming from my office. I knew firsthand the loneliness of losing a spouse and was happy for the president. My staff was excited because Dagmar's daughter, Nina, had been one of our Temps who worked in our clients' offices, and provided clerical help in our training department.

Despite physical setbacks, Havel had decided to run for reelection out of public duty. In a radio address on 13 July 1997, he explained that he wanted to be of service to his fellow citizens and to bring the country into a new world of collective responsibility. He added, "I hope to be President when the Czech Republic becomes a fully fledged member of NATO and the European Union."

Havel openly blamed himself for some of the current malaise in his country—for trying to remain above the political fray, for having allowed political power struggles to further entrench party cronyism, and for not enacting stricter reform measures. He regretted that he had acquiesced to the lustration laws that barred thousands of people from government jobs based on unchecked secret police files.

But Havel didn't take all the blame. His innate politeness that had formerly prevented him from attacking political opponents began to change. An article on 22 January 1998 in the *International Herald Tribune* read:

> In an extraordinary speech to Parliament in early December, just after the government fell, Mr. Havel said society had fallen into a "post-Communist morass," which he blamed largely on Mr. Klaus's "cloak of liberalism without adjectives" that allowed "the most immoral people" to achieve the greatest success.

In fact, Václav Klaus had been forced to resign as prime minister in November 1997 over a political financing scandal. He didn't go quietly. He was outraged that leaders of his own party, the Civic Democrats, had forced him out after—among other scandals—a secret Swiss bank account was found to have millions of dollars in party funds, apparently from contributors who'd been given favorable treatment in the privatization process.

But Klaus's career was far from over. He would take the stage again and again.

For many of us living there, the rumors surrounding Klaus were believable. Of course, Havel had his share of wrongdoings, but his were of a personal nature that made him more human. Besides, I'd rather be labeled a naive moralist than a brash opportunist. Havel was, for many, a moral beacon; and for me, a fellow artist without whom I'd not have been there.

I was merely a musician at heart and businessperson by chance—definitely not an economist or politician. While I acknowledged that Klaus might have done some good during the economic transition, I found his ideas troubling—Euroscepticism, denial of climate change, criticism of homosexuality, and his let-the-market-decide-everything economic plan. Moreover, I could not abide his crass comments about Havel.

With the economic downturn in the late 1990s, I noticed consequential changes in the staffing industry. International companies doing business in the Czech Republic started to limit their number of foreign executives. Already by 1995, the human resources director of Procter and Gamble said in an interview, "We have downsized our international people considerably. Our objective is to build a local Czech organization." This new course direction in staffing affected headhunters and executive search firms, but not AYS, which supplied bilingual administrative workers, indispensable to every business.

I was accustomed to adapting to the ever-changing trends and laws. But when Dr. Zima informed me about a new amendment to the *Živnostenský zákon* (Trade Licensing Act) concerning a company's *jednatel* (representative), it was a game-changer. The amendment allowed trade to be conducted by a foreign individual only if that person "proves before the appropriate trade licensing office his ability to communicate in Czech." Otherwise the individual must appoint a responsible representative.

The new law created a stir among my American entrepreneur friends. The American Chamber of Commerce jumped on the situation by holding seminars, which I attended, on how to appoint and register a *jednatel*.

Dr. Zima and I devised two courses of action. Plan A was for me to attempt the Czech language test. If I failed, which was more of a probability than a possibility, we'd move to Plan B and appoint Midia as *jednatel*. I was grateful for her willingness to assume legal responsibility without a financial stake in the company. Her maturity belied her twenty-some years.

Midia and I went together to the trade licensing office on Podskalská ulice early one morning. Under my arm was a file of documents that Dr. Zima had prepared for me. We took the fifteen-minute walk along the verdant length of Karlovo náměstí before turning right toward the river. We didn't converse much, as I was repeating my memorized lines over and over:

> *Dobré ráno. Jsem Američanka a majitelka firmy v Praze. Jsem v České republice velmi šťastná. Moje společnost zprostředkovává práci Čechům a zajišťuje odborná školení. Jsem tu, abych absolvovala test z českého jazyka, abych tak mohla být jednatelkou své firmy. Zde jsou požadované právní dokumenty.*

In essence, I explained that I was an American business owner in Prague, that I was very happy living in the Czech Republic, that my company helped Czechs find jobs and offered training, that I was there to take the Czech language test so I could be my own legal representative, and here are my legal documents.

We arrived at the five-story office building and stood before the thick carved-wood doors to review the plan. I would go in alone while Midia waited outside, poised to present herself for the test after I'd inevitably come out with a failing grade. We were almost sure of that outcome, but we knew I had to try.

I'd taken formal Czech lessons on and off. What came easily was the diction and accent, and reading the phonetic language. Most difficult was finding opportunities to practice, except with shopkeepers and waiters. With bilingualism a requisite to work in the global marketplace, Czechs in my business and social circles were keen to speak English with me. I didn't blame anyone but myself for not mastering Czech as I had with French. But I must say that French people had forced me to suffer through conversations in their language until I got very good at it. Quite the opposite in my new country. The Czechs would gently dismiss my efforts with, "It's a very difficult language," then switch the conversation back to English.

The Czechs were subtle but firm about what they held most dear. They protected their language like a precious treasure. It was an intrinsic part of their cultural identity that had been threatened throughout history. Even as recent as the Nazi and Soviet occupations, the German and Russian languages had been forced on the Czechoslovaks, as well as censorship of their literature. I took it to heart, but without offense, that the Czechs coveted their beautiful language so much that it made them cringe when someone like me riddled it with mistakes. Conversely, I was doubly happy when I did manage to communicate well and my Czech interlocutors responded in Czech with surprised delight.

Inside the entryway of the trade licensing office was a notice that seemed to direct people to the next floor. I dared not ask questions and appear unable to read the signs. Upstairs, I stepped inside a large space that looked like a bank lobby with clerks behind counters on parallel walls. I stood for a moment and looked around, trying to figure out the system, but saw no waiting line or seating area. One of the clerks spotted me and raised her hand for me to come forward. It was my cue to walk on stage with confidence and follow the script no matter how hard my heart was pounding. I took a singer's diaphragmatic breath as one would to nail a high-C, and marched straight to her counter. Before she could ask something I wouldn't understand, I said my lines in one fell swoop with a deferential smile. The clerk beamed with delight, a broad grin appeared over her face, as she said in Czech, "You speak so well! You will have no trouble with the test!"

She laid the morning edition of *Mladá Fronta Dnes* on the counter and pointed to an article. She asked me to read it silently and then summarize the story aloud. The Fates were truly with me that day. It was a brief article about the record-cold winter the country had just experienced and how warmer weather and springtime were on the way. I recognized all of the nouns and most of the adjectives: *jaro* is spring, *zima* can mean winter or cold, *teplý* is warm, *počasí* is weather, *špatný* is bad, and *předpověď* is forecast. As I began to paraphrase, the middle-aged clerk wearing an old-fashioned frock—who was so friendly that I'd have wanted her for my next-door neighbor—was already stamping my papers.

I thanked her sincerely, walked gingerly out of the room, then tore down the staircase and bolted out the door, yelling, "I passed!" Midia grabbed me with a huge hug. We skipped back to the office, stopping for lunch along the way.

Yes, I was proud of this accomplishment, but I had advantage over other foreign businesspeople: I was a classically trained singer. Our skills include memorization of long lyrics, mastery of foreign language diction, and performance composure even when shaking in our shoes.

In 1995, I started attending an annual staffing industry convention in the United States. It was held in a different city every year, and I brought a staff member each time. During the conferences, we soaked up as many training sessions and discussions on employment topics as possible. Surrounded by huge global firms and some smaller ones, I was perhaps the only independent owner of an overseas staffing agency.

The October 1998 convention in Palm Springs, California, proved to be a major turning point. I was with Martina Pátková, who headed up temporary placements, our fastest-growing division. My goal at this conference was to get ideas for steering a growing company galloping beyond its infrastructure. I also wanted to research staffing software—a new phenomenon, along with the internet. Our placement process, the binder and paper system, was becoming inefficient.

My burgeoning business caused a tension between wanting to serve people and companies in the new democratic free market and becoming an impersonal factory, churning out numbers. My unease was like discordant harmonies needing resolution, or at best, trying to sustain a tenuous equilibrium. Finding resolution in music means bringing dissonant (yet interesting) chord changes "home" to where the progression began. The home is the tonic, the tonal center. In my symbolic case, it was my initial mission—to stay true to my desire to make a small contribution to this country I loved.

I had already sought the advice of Dr. Zima about our growth dilemma. I explained that my company had the reputation, longevity, and trust among our clients. And we had never advertised! But international staffing firms were entering the market with their slick marketing campaigns and big bucks. I knew we could hold our own, if—and it was a big "if"—we could elevate to the next level. It would mean investing in automation, hiring information technology experts, and moving yet again to even larger offices.

We discussed four options: (1) continue on my own and control growth; (2) take on a business partner; (3) merge with a similar-size human resources firm; and (4) sell to a larger staffing company. Dr. Zima laid out the legal process and ramifications for each scenario.

I gave it a lot of thought. A merger or sale seemed most practical, if I could pull it off.

On the first morning at the Palm Springs convention, hundreds of people gathered in the ballroom of a swanky hotel for the welcome ceremony and keynote presentation. I sat at a round table with strangers, except for Martina sitting opposite me and out of earshot. I conversed with the person on my left, who looked surprised when I told him my company was in the Czech Republic. He pointed clear across the crowded room to someone who "knows everything about industry trends in

Europe." I could hardly see the person, except the man had a bald head and wore a light blue sport coat. The keynote speaker began to talk, and I forgot all about the impromptu chat.

Martina and I read over the list of break-out sessions for the next three days. We agreed to each choose our own topics and separately attend the seminars. We'd reconnect for lunch and at day's end to share what we'd learned. One program title jumped out at me: "Staffing Industry Mergers and Acquisitions." I planned to go, but kept it to myself.

The session was held that afternoon in a room with about thirty folding chairs on each side of an aisle. I arrived early and sat in the second row. Someone plopped down next to me. I courteously said "hello" and continued reading the convention booklet when I abruptly realized it was the bald man in the light blue sport coat. Before I could process this, he turned to me and said with a distinctively Brooklyn accent, "Ya buyin' er sellin'?"

"Uh . . . well . . ." my tongue tied as I tried to think fast, "I'm here to learn . . . but, well, not about buying."

"Whad'ya got?" asked the man of few words.

"A staffing and training company in Prague, second largest in the Czech Republic in terms of placements, just behind Manpower," I answered, suddenly getting my guts and voice back.

He stared in my eyes, then gave me a split-second glance up and down as if sizing me up, not in a lascivious way, more like critical analysis.

"There are two international staffing firms wanting to enter the Central European market. Here are their names." He scribbled on the back of a piece of paper and handed it to me.

That was that. The program started, and we didn't speak again, although I knew how to find him.

The talk was fascinating. Peter Collins, a Brit living in New York, was the speaker. He presented to the audience a point-by-point process for positioning a company for sale. He clearly explained the valuation formula, the due diligence process, finding the right buyer, the role of a broker, and everything else I didn't realize I didn't know, but now did.

At the end of the session, I approached Mr. Collins and asked if I could take him to dinner to discuss potential collaboration. He was as brief as the bald man. "I only broker large deals. What's the annual revenue?"

I didn't disclose my financials, in case they wouldn't meet his minimum, but I highlighted other information—no debt, niche market, great reputation, big client list, devoted employees. When I stated the location, his ears perked up. When I said I already had two reliable leads, I had his attention. There was no dinner; he was flying out of town that afternoon, but he gave me his card, and we set up a phone meeting.

When the synchronicity of life rolls out a carpet in front of us, it is what Joseph Campbell calls the invisible helping hands. Something miraculous comes if you find your passion and let it lead you. You begin to meet people in your field of bliss and they open doors for you. Whoever that bald man in the light blue sport coat placed next to me by invisible hands was, I thank you.

The sale of my company began exactly like that. Peter Collins became my broker. One of the companies written on the back of that scratch paper, Select Appointments, became my buyer. Looking back, it all happened quickly, yet felt insufferably slow at the time. During the seven-month negotiation and due diligence process, I had two other unsolicited offers. One was from the owner of a recruitment firm in Vienna, but he was wishy-washy, and I bowed out. Another was from James Horstkamp, who visited me at my office in early 1999. He and his partner were in talks to sell their business to what became Monster.com. James offered me a place at the table, but it sounded complicated, and I declined. Fortuitously, these offers became leveraging tools used by my broker to raise the EBIT (earnings before interest and taxes) multiple from five to six, increasing the sale price significantly.

One of Collins's precepts in positioning a company for sale was to prove that the enterprise could run smoothly without the owner's constant presence. So I traveled more—to Paris for a week to visit friends and study voice with Janine Reiss; to Ireland to sing at the wedding of a friend's daughter; to Copenhagen to visit my opera singer friend Janice Edwards who'd moved there from Prague; to Maryland on a ten-day spiritual retreat with one of my favorite cousins.

When the deal with the intended buyer looked promising, I gathered my staff around our big round conference table and explained the situation. They knew our company was on the cusp of something and ready to move to a new level. I assured them of their job security and that I'd stay on as part-owner for a minimum of two years. I might have sounded syrupy when I said how proud I was to watch them counsel, train, and inspire others, just as I had done for them. We should all be proud, I told them, of the successful careers and business climate we've helped build. Up until then, we had placed thousands of people in jobs and trained even more, considering that our free mini-workshop was offered to all job seekers who came through our doors, whether or not we placed them. We had earned a golden reputation through goodwill, high standards, and hard work. The ensuing discussion left a mixture of excitement and uncertainty in the air. My job was to stay positive and upbeat for their sake as well as mine.

Looking back on that time of negotiation and due diligence minutia, a combustion of anticipation and angst sparks inside me again. Having given up alcohol, I had nothing to take the edge off, to dull the senses. In all my adult life, I had subdued my feelings with booze, half-facing them through a sotted veil. In sobriety, I still teetered between feeling perfectly fine and scared to death. I feared the emotional toll of this major life change would overwhelm me. I considered getting drunk like in the old days and pouring my guts out to someone I picked up in a bar, or having a fast and furious fling and being fully released of all tension.

But I didn't do any of that.

Instead, I sat with the discomfort, or went to the piano and sang a melancholy Roberta Flack song, or called my sponsor, or hit an AA meeting. I went to bed each night, grateful I hadn't picked up a drink that day. My nightly prayer reverted to what John and I always prayed at the outset of big decisions, like when we moved from Omaha to Paris in 1983, and from Nice to Prague in 1992. "Dear Source of All Being, I'm about to take a big step. If it's not meant to be, just shut the doors as I move forward. I trust you'll open another."

Although the word "I" replaced "we," I felt John by my side and a calm settled over me. As I lay in bed whispering the words, my arm instinctively slid over to take his hand. And there it was, touching mine.

The deal went through in August 1999. The daunting paperwork was comprehensible thanks to my attorney and broker. Dr. Zima—so sharp—had taken me through every clause in the contract and caught several mistakes. Collins played hardball and made sure I got everything I wanted—80 percent of the valuation price upfront and 20 percent continued ownership for a minimum of two years, during which time I would be involved on a consultancy basis.

To illustrate the fast-moving acquisition of staffing companies at the time, before the ink was dry, Select Appointments was acquired by the Vedior Group. In a handful of years, Vedior was purchased by Randstad, the world's largest staffing firm.

23

MÁ VLAST

The 1990s were nearing an end, giving way to a new millennium. In the final year, much happened. The Czech Republic, Poland, and Hungary marked their spiritual homecoming to the West, as all three countries became NATO members. And my company joined forces with a global staffing group that guaranteed its continuity into the future.

I would remain part owner and have a presence on two continents for at least two years. My lease on the Suchdol house ended, and I rented a furnished pied-à-terre in town. In Omaha, I found a brick ranch house nestled in a woodsy area, ten minutes by car to my mom's place.

While I prepared the new management team and answered questions about the history of AYS, the past decade swept before my eyes. The thrill of freedom had been replaced by the hard work of democracy. Cynicism, the vice that Havel warned against, had set in for some, while others stayed hopeful, even during the economic downturn.

Among these were many of my Czech friends, especially the artists—musicians, painters, poets, and writers—who were born innovators. Equally hopeful were my American entrepreneur friends who'd woven their own creative threads into the new country's tapestry.

I thought about my friend Zdeněk Merta who told me that, even during the communist regime, an artist's life held meaning. Living in "totality," as he called the tightly controlled period, produced a survivalist kind of creativity. The artist's struggle went underground and tunneled deep until it churned into a creative form. If the work of art didn't extol the virtues of communism, the endeavor either remained a secret or was revealed with great risk. "Anne Marie, especially back then, creative freedom was a mosaic of contradictions. It was as much an internal conflict as an external one."

Although I grew up in a free society, somehow I understood him. Creativity does not come without struggle. Its first impulse is a kind of tension that is healed by the art form itself. My hardships caused me to give up making music to create a new venture in a new democracy. Art blooms from the world we experience, imagine, and hope for.

When I first visited Prague, the artwork of Jiří Votruba was all over town in souvenir shops and galleries. The images made me smile; they were clever, playful, and intrinsically Czech. A few years later, while browsing along the cobblestoned streets of *Staré Město*, I passed a Votruba painting in a gallery window. There, in a square wooden frame on a vivid orange background, stood a figure with hands raised over a stemmed flower, as if growing it, praising it, offering it to the world. I went inside and walked out with my purchase.

It hung behind my desk, greeting me and everyone who entered my office. Sometimes, I'd shut the office door and lean back in my chair with my feet on the desk. I'd think about author Herman Wouk's notion that "true symbol is reality distilled." The flower on the canvas enfleshed my internal freedom. The hands became a wand of faith, trusting that beauty grows from sincere effort. I knew this to be true. Just as the Czechs had escaped the chokehold of communism, I'd wrenched myself from the vise of addiction. Yet, whether freedom is given to a collective or individual, it's a delicate reprieve, a tentative condition that must be nourished and protected.

At my new, spacious office on Žitná, with Votruba's painting behind my desk, and a Jobul painting on the right.

I learned long ago that artists view the world in unique ways, from a realm of endless possibilities. They're connected by a mutual affinity and a responsibility to make good on their gifts. I humbly belong to this group.

As did Havel.

Although the playwright, essayist, and philosopher had abandoned his artistic profession for the love of country, he was, above all else, an artist. Through his writings and speeches, he portrayed his vision for democratic values and civility in society. Havel shared his mind and spirit through artistry and deed. He was the ultimate humanist who believed that our salvation lies in the human heart.

To be sure, the naysayers pointed to his weaknesses. They charged him with elitism, intellectualism, and idealism. They gossiped about his extramarital affairs, reproached him for remarrying too soon, and frowned at his overindulgence of cigarettes and alcohol. But to me, his human frailties were endearing.

"Hope is not the conviction that something will turn out well but the certainty that something makes sense, regardless of how it turns out," Havel wrote, and added that hope is not optimism, not even something of this world. It is an orientation of the spirit and heart.

Havel was the reason I came to the country, drawn not by his notoriety, but by his ideals.

Madeleine Albright expressed my sentiments perfectly in her memoir *Prague Winter*: "If this complicated book has a single message, it is to heed the wisdom of this matchless man."

The Prague Nineties. It was a transformative decade for the world, and a personal turning point for me. I had accomplished my two missions—to provide John comfort in his old age, and contribute to a country I fell in love with the moment I witnessed, via satellite, its peaceful revolution. My affection was not unrequited. This place and time healed me with its wand of faith. From my first glimpse of Hradčany castle back in 1990, the prophetess Libuše drew me into the ongoing legend with her soundless whisper. She cast me forever under her spell.

As I boarded my flight across the Atlantic, my worldly possessions had already set sail. The piano, furniture, paintings, and household goods were on a steamship rocking once again on ocean waves, heading back to where they'd come from before traveling to Paris, Nice, and Prague. It was their "Farewell to Bohemia" journey, but not mine. I'd be going back and forth from my birth home to my heart's home.

I snuggled into the blue-cushioned seat of the Czech Airlines craft poised to take off from the brand-new Ruzyně Airport terminal. Had I been flying into Prague instead of out, the second of six symphonic poems from Bedřich Smetana's masterpiece *Má vlast* would have played when the plane started its descent into the city. There was no such custom for outbound flights.

But no matter. My soul had recorded it. As our wheels lifted off the ground, the tone poem "Vltava" began to fill my heart, starting with a flute singing the gentle ripple of the river, accompanied by pizzicato strings. Then came the grand theme, a Bohemian folk song like no other. It rose to a peak, then subsided, rose again, and subsided. I hummed to the swirl of Smetana's symphonic cycle. I imagined the composer writing it, totally deaf, feeling the tones deep within. Never should it be said that Czech music is merely lovely in local color and dulcet in national charm. It is all that, and more. Its flowing humanity transcends limits and boundaries.

This is what my ancestral homeland and its people did for me. I was lifted beyond limits and boundaries. And in their pursuit of freedom, I found mine.

ACKNOWLEDGMENTS

To *the awe-inspiring characters* in this book who influenced my life, I am deeply grateful. Many granted me interviews, and I was humbled by their honesty. When my fellow companions from the Prague Nineties shared their memories, a common theme emerged: something mystical about that transformative place and time had changed us forever.

I wish I could personally thank each person who worked for my company, AYS Placements and Workshops. I owe my business success to them. Together, we helped thousands of people find jobs and prepare for the new, international marketplace. Our company clients relied on our high standards, and my staff didn't let them down.

During my research and writing over the past five years, a handful of former employees offered me immeasurable assistance—Jana Křivánková, Zuzana Jokešová, Erika Gerlová, Amira Shehatová, and Zdeňka Ledecká. These women contributed creatively and practically to my project and exuded enthusiasm and encouragement. In particular, Amira carefully read my entire manuscript at two different stages, providing valuable feedback, and she became the official editor of the Czech-language version. And Zdeňka has helped me over the years in a public relations capacity, as an eloquent speechwriter, letter writer, and spokesperson.

My Czech publisher Martin Vopěnka made my dream a reality: to offer this book first in the Czech language to the people of my ancestral homeland. All along, they were my inspiration. Because Martin is both a publisher and an award-winning novelist, he understands the mind of readers as well as the heart of writers.

I consider myself quite lucky that Kateřina Klabanová, a gifted translator in high demand, agreed to translate this book. She read my manuscript with sensitivity, absorbed the essence of its meaning, and placed my words into the lyrically rich voice of the Czech language.

The firm 1106 Design, with its high quality publishing services, helped bring my original, English-language book to the international market. The 1106 owner, project manager, proofreader, and design team were a dream to work with.

This book may not have seen the light of day without my friend and editor Holly Richmond. It all started in November 2019 while Holly and I were in Normandy, France, as part of an Alliance Française and Sister Cities delegation. We were sharing a room together, when late one night as she was tapping out her third novel, I said, "Holly, I think I have a book in me." She closed her laptop, listened attentively, and responded, "Get started. I will help you." That night, I sketched an outline and wrote the first page. Since then, Holly has edited and guided my endeavor all the way through.

My longtime friend, Shelley Bance, meticulously proofread the English version. She enjoyed an illustrious career as a writer and editor in New York City, but I met her well before then, when we lived in Paris in our early twenties, single and fancy-free.

My beta-readers were Michael Kelly, Janice Edwards, Steven Denenberg, and my sister, Susan Kenny Stevens. They took time from their busy schedule to read the manuscript in an "almost there" draft form. Their verbal applause buoyed my confidence, and their concrete ideas for changes were heeded.

My sister Susan has been my rock. She "got it" immediately when I said I was writing a memoir—that my personal story would be a thread in a much larger tapestry. She and her husband Patrick Stevens have lovingly bolstered my efforts with their practical and moral support.

In this short space, I cannot properly thank Martin Palouš for whom I have tremendous admiration. I first contacted Ambassador Palouš to ask if he'd kindly offer historical context to my research. He has become my partner in dialogue and cherished friend. This great philosopher, public servant, and friend of Václav Havel is, for all of us, a touchstone to the ideals of democracy and freedom.

My heartfelt thanks also go to Peter Sís, for gracing the cover of this book with his artwork. My grandchildren and I have read dozens of Peter's beautiful books, which have educated and enriched us in the most delightful manner.

To John, and all my family, living and passed—I am who I am because of you.

Finally, I am beholden to Václav Havel, who first invited me to Prague, and affirmed my artistry by responding to the gift of poetry I had sent to him. Havel's life and message continue to challenge me to be better, do more, bridge divides, and live in truth. This book is my attempt to tell the truth as I remember it, and keep hope and dreams alive.

ABOUT THE AUTHOR

AUTHOR

ANNE MARIE KENNY

is an American singer, writer, and entrepreneur. She lived her early adult years in France where she performed at the Paris Ritz and on television, radio, and film. When the Iron Curtain fell, she moved to Prague and started a staffing and training company that would be ranked #2 in the Czech  market. Anne Marie currently lives in the United States, often returning to Paris and Prague where she feels equally at home.

FOREWORD

MARTIN PALOUŠ

is a diplomat, philosopher, lecturer, and author. One of the first signatories of Charter 77, he was a founding member of the Civic Forum. After the Velvet Revolution he was a Member of Parliament, Deputy Minister for Foreign Affairs, and Ambassador of the Czech Republic to the U.S. and United Nations.

NOTES

xii "**The salvation of this human world**": Václav Havel. Speech by the President of the Czechoslovak Republic to both houses of the U.S. Congress. Washington, February 21, 1990. Available from Václav Havel Library (vaclavhavel-library. org).

2 "**Those who have for many years**": Quote from Václav Havel's speech to demonstrators in Wenceslas Sq., 22 November 1989. In *Works* 4, 1161.

3 "**He warned that 'the enforced mask of apathy'**": Václav Havel, *The Art of the Impossible: Politics as Morality in Practice,* translation by Paul Wilson and others (New York: Alfred A. Knopf, Inc. 1994), 5.

4 "**Janáček . . . dedicated his work to honor contemporary free man**": Phil G. Goulding, *Classical Music: The 50 Greatest Composers and Their 1,000 Greatest Works* (New York: Fawcett Columbine, 1992), 526.

8 "**Aragon wrote: If ever the world changes**": Roslyn Sulcas, "Andy de Groat, 71, Downtown Choreographer, Is Dead": *The New York Times,* Jan. 23, 2019.

14 "**had the United States, Soviet Union, and China**": George C. Herring, "The Cold War and Vietnam," JSTOR: *OAH Magazine of History*, Vol. 18, No. 5, Vietnam (October 2004), 18-21.

19 "**All the time. It is miraculous**": Joseph Campbell, "The Hero's Adventure," PBS Series with Joseph Campbell & Bill Moyers on *The Power of Myth,* Ep. 1, 21 June 1988.

33 "**Substance abuse in Vietnam was rampant on the bases**": Adam Janos, "G.I.s' Drug Use in Vietnam Soared—With Their Commanders' Help," History.com website, 29 August 2018.

33   "the average World War II infantryman in the South Pacific": David Hack, "Vietnam War Facts, Stats and Myths," U.S. Wings website, 2021.

34   "During the 1960s, the city started demolishing": Kelly, Michael, *Uniquely Omaha* (Omaha World Herald Publishing, 2015), 3.

49   "Although colonized Algerians were legally French nationals": Jim House, "The colonial and post-colonial dimensions of Algerian migration to France," University of Leeds, U.K.,The Institute of Historical Research (2006).

50   "Economic growth boosted manufacturing": Matthias Grenon, "Immigration and Integration in France (1945-1974)," Boston University History Research Guides website.

52   "Statistical information is unreliable because French law": Jeremie Gilbert and David Keane, "How French Law Makes Minorities Invisible," *The Independent*, U.S. Edition, 14 November 2016.

52   "in the 1980s, around three million Muslims were living in France": Houssain Kettani, "Muslim Population in Europe: 1950–2020," *International Journal of Environmental Science and Development*, Vol. 1, No. 2., June 2010, ISSN:2010-0264.

57   "When it opened in 1898, it was hailed as the swankiest hotel": Stuart Green, "A History of the Hotel Ritz," Luxury Link website, May 8, 2020.

64   "The nuclear meltdown at Chernobyl": Mikhail Gorbachev, "Turning point at Chernobyl," *Daily Times*, April 17, 2006.

64   "I believe that communism is": Johanna Neuman, "Former President Reagan Dies at 93," *Los Angeles Times,* June 5, 2004.

65   "Europe's demarcation lines still held strong and no one predicted": Timothy Garton Ash, *The Magic Lantern* (New York: Vintage Books, Random House, 1993).

80   "di Stefano reveled in his image as a bon vivant": Jonathan Kandell, "Giuseppe di Stefano, a Tenor Whose Career Flamed Out Too Early, Is Dead at 86," *The New York Times*, March 4, 2008.

87   "Life itself holds such tristesse": Gustave Flaubert, *"La vie est en soi quelque chose de si triste qu'elle n'est pas supportable sans de grands allègements"* from Correspondence to his niece Caroline, 28 octobre 1870.

92   "The passage of time produces its own": Garton Ash, *The Magic Lantern*, 160.

92   "I find people completely prepared for history rather suspect": Václav Havel, *To the Castle and Back,* translated from the Czech *Prosím stručně* by Paul Wilson (New York: Alfred A. Knopf, 2007), 58.

104 **"Libuše was a young prophetess"**: Petr Čornej, *Great Stories in Czech History* (Nakladatelství Práh, Praha 2005), 7-9.

115 **"a revolt of decent people against indecent people"**: Václav Havel interview for Czechoslovak television on 22/12/1989 (Rozhovor Václava Havla pro Československou televizi).

115 **"When I talk about the contaminated moral atmosphere"**: Václav Havel, "New Year's Address to the Nation," speech, Czechoslovakia, January 1, 1990, Czech Republic Presidential Website, Speeches Czech Republic.

117 **"It is comforting and amazing to write about"**: Olga Kittnarová, *A History of Music in Outlines* (vysokoškolská učebnice v anglickém jazyce), UK v Praze (Nakladatelství Karolinum, Praha 2007).

119 **"The Wall"**: Peter Sís, *The Wall: Growing Up Behind The Iron Curtain* (New York: Frances Foster Books. Farrar, Straus and Giroux, 2007) no page numbers, section: "From My Journals."

129 **"East Europe's Sale of the Century"**: Steven Greenhouse, "East Europe's Sale of the Century," *The New York Times,* May 22, 1990.

131 **"in 1991 the minimum monthly wage"**: Kamila Fialová and Martina Mysíková,"The Minimum Wage: Labor Market Consequences in the Czech Republic," *Czech Journal of Economics and Finance,* 59, no. 3, 2009, Table 1, 259. Note: the 1991 exchange rate was 27.15 CZK to 1 USD.

132 **"Czechoslovakia was one of the worst polluters"**: Marlise Simons, "Upheaval in the East: Pollution's Toll in Eastern Europe: Stumps Where Great Trees Once Grew," *The New York Times,* March 19, 1990.

143 **"seventh most industrialized state in the world"**: Tim D. Whipple, *After the Velvet Revolution: Václav Havel and the New Leaders of Czechoslovakia Speak Out* (New York: Freedom House, 1991), 46.

143 **"When they arrested me"**: *Václav Havel Toward a Civil Society, Selected Speeches and Writings 1990-1994* (Nakladateslství Lidové noviny). English translation Paul Wilson & others. A joint session of the U.S. Congress, February 21, 1990.

144 **"President Bush lifted former trade restrictions"**: Thomas Friedman, "Upheaval in the East: Czechoslovakia; Bush Praises Havel and His New Page," *The New York Times,* Feb 21, 1990.

146 **"The wall which for many years divided Berlin"**: quote from Peter Sís on the Czech Center of New York website featuring a 2021 exhibition of Sís's book *The Wall.*

149 **Křížem krážem . . . Anne Marie Kenny"**: Zdeněk Merta, *Křížem krážem: aneb Dobrodružství potulného muzikanta* (Prague: Mladá fronta, 2014), 74.

163 **"When I suddenly found myself in a political office"**: Havel, *To the Castle and Back,* 58.

163 **"The underground economy had been practically non-existent"**: Valeriy M. Rutgaizer, "The Shadow Economy in the USSR," *Nat'l Council for Soviet & East European Research*, Berkeley-Duke Paper #34, Feb 1992.

165 **"I am convinced that we will never build"**: Václav Havel, *Summer Meditations,* translated from the Czech *Letní přemítání* by Paul Wilson (New York: Vintage Books, 1993), 18.

165 **"I have become aware of how immensely difficult"**: Havel, *Summer Meditations,* Foreword.

165 **"[Vilímek] became one of the most famous publishers"**: "Josef R. Vilímek, Nakladatelství a tiskárna (Publishing House and Printer)," website page, https://cs.wikipedia.org/wiki/Nakladatelství_a_tiskárna_Josef_R._Vilímek.

166 **"Peace Corps in Prague. Its volunteers had arrived"**: Francine S. Kiefer, "Peace Corps Burgeons in Europe: The U.S. program grows fast in Czechoslovakia, where volunteerism is almost unknown." *Christian Science Monitor,* March 10, 1992.

169 **"She has red hair after her Irish father"**: Andrea Vernerová, *Ahoj na sobotu.* Edition 24 (1992), č. 14, 12.

175 **"I observed this regressive trend"**: Martin Palouš, *Once Upon a Time of Transition: Fourteen Exercises in Political Thought* (Washington, DC: Academica Press, 2021), 12-13.

176 **"But he was where he wanted to be"**: Palouš, *Once Upon a Time of Transition,* 21.

177 **"the intellectuals in the castle"**: David Remnick. "Havel Takes a Bow" *The New Yorker,* February 9, 2003.

178 **"Klaus argued that civil society did not exist"**: Raj M. Desai, "Václav Havel's Economic Legacy," Brookings Institution, Dec 19, 2011, https://www.brookings.edu/blog/up-front/2011/12/19/vaclav-havels-economic-legacy/.

178 **"I am a liberal economist"**: Whipple, *After the Velvet Revolution,*168.

178 **"enormous human, moral, and spiritual potential"**: Václav Havel, "New Year's Address to the Nation," speech, Czechoslovakia, January 1, 1990, Czech Republic Presidential Website, Speeches Czech Republic.

179 **"We learned that the Bosnian Serbs, vehemently opposed"**: Chuck Sudetic, "Serbs Denounce Breakup of Yugoslavia," *The New York Times,* Jan 17, 1992.

196 **"Across the nation, health services were being decentralized"**: Marshall W. Raffel, PhD, and Norma K. Raffel, PhD., "Czechoslovakia's Changing Health Care System," *National Library of Medicine, Public Health Reports.* Nov-Dec 1992, Vol. 107, 636-643.

204 **"we spent thousands of hours"**: Havel, *To the Castle and Back,* 98.

205 **"someone who had taken an oath to defend"**: Havel, *To the Castle and Back,* 99.

218 **"At this consequential moment, The New York Times headline"**: Stephen Engelberg, "Czechoslovakia Breaks in Two, To Wide Regret," *The New York Times,* Jan 1, 1993.

222 **"The state bureaucracy had absolute control over labor force"**: Jiří Večerník, "The Labor Market in Czechoslovakia: Changing Attitudes of the Population," *Czechoslovak Sociological Review,* Vol. 28 (Aug 1992), pp. 61-78, Institute of Sociology of the Czech Academy of Sciences.

225 **"First, the Czech Republic lies in the very center"**: Václav Havel, "New Democracies for Old Europe," *The New York Times,* Oct 17, 1993.

226 **"The Velvet Revolution left behind"**: James Dean Le Sueur, "The Art of Dissent (2020)" *Los Angeles Review of Books,* July 11, 2020. https://lareviewofbooks. org/article/the-art-of-dissent/.

226 **"In turn, Cibulka published the lists"**: Dita Asiedu, "Czechs wait thirteen years for official names of secret police collaborators," *Prague Radio International* 3/34/2003.

227 **"President Havel had opposed but quietly acquiesced"**: "The Perils of 'Lustration'" *The New York Times Opinion,* Jan. 7, 1992, Section A, 14.

227 **"According to Havel during a 1991 interview"**: *Czechoslovak Radio, Czechoslovak Television and ČSTK,* interview of the President of the Czech and Slovak Federative Republic, Václav Havel, on 17/10/1991. Knihovna Václava Havla (vaclavhavel-library.org).

230 **"Hundreds of labor camps dotting the country"**: Barbora Holá and Thijs Bouwknegt "Jáchymov's Hell: Trekking in the memoryscape of Czechoslovakia's communist forced labour camps," *International Criminal Law Review* 22, Jan 2022, 328-346.

242 **"genealogical research done by my brother"**: Joseph A. Kenny, "Kenny Family Tree" website, www.kennytree.com.

245 **"As one of the most industrialized regions"**: Petr Čornej, *The Fundamentals of Czech History,* (Prague: Prah Publishers, 1992).

246 **"We were here before Austria:"** Richard Georg Plaschka, "The Political Significance of Frantisek Palacky." *Journal of Contemporary History* 8, no. 3 (1973): 35–55. http://www.jstor.org/stable/260279.

248 **"while a discernible 'ethnic persistence' remained"**: Josef Opatrny, "Problems in the History of Czech Immigration to America in the Second Half of the Nineteenth Century," from *The Czech-American Experience,* Lincoln, NE: Vol 74, 1993, 121.

248 **"Nebraska had more first- and second-generation Czechs"**: Bruce Garver, from *The Czech-American Experience.* Nebraska History, Vol. 74, Nos. 3 & 4.

254 **"The developments which followed the collapse of communism"**: Palouš, *Once Upon a Time of Transition,* 63.

254 **"One pays dearly for this low-rent home"**: Václav Havel, *The Power of the Powerless,* Translated from the Czech *Moc bezmocných* by Paul Wilson, (London: Vintage, 1978), 10.

256 **"They'd been lured by a 14-percent interest rate"**: David Rocks, "Czech Bank Failures Keep Savers Wary, Regulators Busy," *Chicago Tribune,* June 7, 1994.

258 **"In their defense, bank officials"**: "Czechs Take Over Bank," *The New York Times (Reuters),* Mar 31, 1994.

259 **"the banking sector mushroomed"**: Rocks, "Czech Bank Failures Keep Savers Wary."

259 **"How does a bank lose nearly half a billion"**: Peter S. Green, "Czech Bank Failure Linked to Securities Deals," *International Herald Tribune,* Sep 21, 1996.

260 **"Some bank officials were arrested"**: "Czech Bank May Return Scam Millions to U.S. Church Group," *Bloomberg Financial Review,* Jun 17, 1994.

278 **"Dupont-Conoco, the American company that had"**: "Czech Republic Signs Refinery Sale Accord," *Bloomberg Business News,* Nov 16, 1995.

278 **"It's like a shot of adrenaline to sit in Berlin"**: Craig R. Whitney, "West European Companies Head East for Labor," *The New York Times,* Feb 9, 1995.

279 **"Many of the station's nearly one thousand employees"**: Craig R. Whitney, "U.S. Packs Up to Move Radio Free Europe and Radio Liberty," *The New York Times,* Aug 21, 1994.

280 **"great and profound and not propaganda publicity"**: "Václav Havel's thoughts on the significance of RFE," video for The *Conference on Cold War Broadcasting Impact,* Hoover Institution, Oct 2004.

280 **"cannot even be described. Would there be earth"**: A. Ross Johnson, "Pressroom: More On The History of RFE/RL," website, https://pressroom.rferl.org/history.

281 **"The Last Palace"**: Norman Eisen, *The Last Palace: Europe's Turbulent Century in Five Lives and One Legendary House* (New York: Crown Publishing, 2018).

283 **"Jewish population made up less than 3 percent"**: Albright, *Prague Winter*, 67.

284 **"Judaism suffered its heaviest blow"**: Malcolm W. Browne, "Czech Jews, A Vanishing Group" Special to *The New York Times*, Aug. 23, 1975.

285 **"When we think that in recent years, there have been few ritual marriages"**: Letter to B. Heller, Chairman, Regional Council of the Jewish Community, Prague, 19 Feb 1989, from "Jewish Life in Czechoslovakia," https://biblicalstudies.org.uk/pdf/rcl/17-4_348.pdf.

298 **"clothing was utilitarian"**: Konstantína Hlaváčková, *Fashion Behind the Iron Curtain* (Prague: Grada Publishing and Prague Museum of Decorative Arts (UPM), 2017), Radio Free Europe interview, 27 Jan 2017.

303 **"Everybody has some basic certainty"**: Marie Winn, interview with Václav Havel, "The Czechs' Defiant Playwright," *The New York Times,* Oct. 25, 1987.

305 **"Czechoslovakia's Catholic population was at"**: Zdeněk R. Nešpor, "Attitudes towards Religion(s) in a 'Non-Believing' Czech Republic," *Anthropological Journal of European Cultures*, vol. 19, no. 1, 2010, pp. 68–84. JSTOR, http://www.jstor.org/stable/43234508.

305 **"and at 7 percent in 2021"**: 2021 Population by religious belief and regions. Czech statistical office, public database. https://www.czso.cz/csu/czso/cso-published-data-on-religious-beliefs-combined-with-age-and-sex.

307 **"I was washing windows and I thought"**: "Cardinal Miloslav Vlk: From window-cleaner to Archbishop of Prague," *Prague Radio International,* Interview by Daniela Lazarová with Cardinal Vlk, March 24, 2017.

310 **"I'd heard that the Bolshoi theater"**: Michael Specter. "A Sleeping Ballet Awakens to the Future: The Bolshoi, After Some Painful Changes, Is Striving to Become Great Again." *The New York Times,* April 10, 1997.

312 **"hundreds of rich Russians were killed and kidnapped in Moscow each year"**: Michael Specter, "Moscow on the Make," *The New York Times,* June 1, 1997.

316 **"the privatization process was exposed as little more"**: Peter S. Green, "As Havel Falters, So Does Czechs' Mood," *International Herald Tribune,* April 24, 1998.

316 **"Particularly tough for the Czechs during this 'velvet malaise' was"**: Peter S. Green, "Forgotten Flames /30 Years Later: A Czech Martyr's Dreams Give Way to Velvet Malaise," *International Herald Tribune,* Jan. 20, 1999.

325 **"Despite physical setbacks, Havel had decided to run for reelection"**: "Havel Will Run Again In 1998 Czech Election," *Agence France-Presse*, published in the *New York Times*, July 13, 1997.

325 **"In an extraordinary speech to parliament"**: Peter S. Green, "Havel Still Czechs' No. 1 Despite Narrow Victory," *International Herald Tribune*, Jan. 22, 1998.

325 **"a secret Swiss bank account"**: Lee Hockstader, "Czech's Downfall Shatters Hope for Economic Miracle: Outgoing Prime Minister's Failed Reforms Viewed as Too Absolute, Arrogant to Succeed," *Washington Post*, Dec. 6, 1997.

326 **"the human resources director of Procter and Gamble said"**: Robert D. Gray, "Employee Recruiters Still Riding Wave of Success in Central and Eastern Europe," *International Herald Tribune*, Sep 4, 1995.

336 **"true symbol is reality distilled"**: Herman Wouk, *This is My God: The Jewish Way of Life* (New York: Back Bay Books; Little, Brown and Company, 1959). 25.

338 **"If this complicated book has a single message"**: Albright, *Prague Winter,* 446.

339 **"Never should it be said that Czech music is merely"**: David Ewen. *The Complete Book of Classical Music* (Englewood Cliffs, N.J.: Prentice-Hall, Inc., 1965), 775.

INDEX OF NAMES